LIBERAL DEMOCRACY BATTLING FOR SURVIVAL:

A PLAN FOR ACTION

TIM MCCORMICK

WOODBRIDGE
PUBLISHERS

Forest House, 3rd Floor 16-20

Clements Road Unit #2048

Ilford, IG1 1BA

ISBN (978-1-918130-55-3) Paperback

ISBN (978-1-918130-56-0) Hardback

ISBN (978-1-918130-54-6) eBook

Cover Design by Woodbridge Publishers.

Find out more about our upcoming releases and authors at www.woodbridgepublishers.co.uk and sign up for our newsletter to stay updated!

DEDICATION

This book is dedicated to the courageous people of Ukraine and Gaza, who are fighting to defend democracy in their countries.

The people of Ukraine suffered terribly when Stalin confiscated their food supplies and imposed mass starvation on them. I admire their courageous resistance in the face of tyranny and revere their spirit of resistance to oppression now, as their Cossack forebears did before them.

About twenty years ago, while I was working in Kiev, over lunch, someone asked me for my advice as to what he should do with the $100 that he had earned. Without any thought, I advised him to deposit it in his local bank. Horrified, he asked me why he should lend his money to a Ukrainian bank. I gathered my wits and explained that I meant an international bank. He then asked if I knew that foreign bank deposits could be subject to a government levy. Neither I nor any of my banking colleagues could envisage that there was a significant risk in making a small retail deposit with a major bank. I only realised the wisdom of the question in the 2008 banking collapse, years later.

Secondly, I dedicate the book to the memory of the heroic Sergei Magnitsky, a Russian lawyer who tried to uphold democratic values in his native land before being imprisoned, refused medical treatment, tortured, and murdered by the Putin regime.

Thirdly, I dedicate this book to Alexei Navalny, a true democrat who voluntarily returned to Russia after an attempted assassination by poisoning to exposé and oppose the Putin regime. He was tortured, imprisoned, and died under mysterious circumstances in a Siberian prison.

Next, I dedicate the book to all journalists around the world who have given their lives to the cause of freedom of speech and the exposure of wrongdoing before sadly dying as a consequence. I am thinking particularly of the Palestinian journalists in Gaza today and Veronica Guerin, who was murdered in Ireland in 1996.

Finally, I dedicate the book to Pope Leo XIV and others who strive for and promote traditional beliefs in peace, equality, and justice around the world.

The entire royalties of this book, due to me as a token, will be donated to Médecins Sans Frontières, which is providing humanitarian aid in their hour of need to the brave and long-suffering citizens of both Ukraine and Palestine as they struggle to create a democratic State. I wish both countries a long-overdue peace after their heroic defence.

ENDORSEMENTS

Mary Robinson

Former President of Ireland, UN Commissioner of Human Rights, and Founder of the Mary Robinson Foundation on Climate Change

"I am happy to endorse this timely book on liberal democracy. The chapters on climate change and inequality are well researched, highly relevant, and a valuable contribution to these critical subjects."

Douglas Webber

Emeritus Professor of Political Science, INSEAD, France

"In this book, Tim McCormick makes an urgent and impassioned plea for democrats and democracies to unite against a rising tide of autocracy spearheaded by Russia, fostered by irresponsible social media, fueled by alienation from democratic processes, and supercharged by Donald Trump's re-election as U.S. president. Democracy faces its greatest threat since the 1930s. This is a timely work that deserves to be widely read."

Shane Ross

Former Irish Government Minister and Journalist

"A well-researched, broad-based, and very readable book. It offers valuable insight into the growing impact of social media and its connection with banking. Essential reading for politicians, students, and anyone concerned with the future of liberal democracy."

Anne Chambers

Irish Biographer and Writer

"In light of the dangers posed by political and technological behemoths, this all-encompassing and timely work is essential reading for every citizen who cares about the future and that of generations to come."

Charles Lysaght

Biographer

"The author clearly identifies the democratic enigma: the decline in the number of democracies despite solid economic performance. He convincingly attributes this to the rise and influence of populist autocrats."

Robert Neill

Former Chairman, Representative Church Body of Ireland Executive

"The book rightly highlights the erosion of fundamental traditional values, particularly in America—an essential perspective for understanding the decline of democracies worldwide."

Aisling Brady

Head of Communications, European Movement Ireland

"McCormick's insights into the role of the EU and transnational institutions such as the UN are especially timely. At a moment of great geopolitical instability, he underscores their potential to serve the common good, while reminding us of the ongoing need for transparency and accountability."

TABLE OF CONTENTS

PROLOGUE

Ireland's Democratic Recor

The Irish Republic has a proud record of democracy, although some citizens regret that it has not achieved the reunification of the island. It has been a democracy for over a century since it obtained its independence from Britain. Ten years after the foundation of the State, Fianna Fáil, the party that had lost the civil war, came into power peacefully after an election. It has remained a democracy ever since, even during the Second World War, when the number of democracies diminished to a mere handful, basically the Allied powers and a small number of neutral countries. The late President de Valera once claimed to know the will of the people by looking into his own heart. This mindset was to prove disastrous. He rejected the treaty negotiated with Britain over a century ago and supported by the majority of the people, thereby starting a civil war. But Irish democracy has matured since then, a century later.

Ireland now has all the hallmarks of a healthy democracy. Freedom House ranks it as one of the freest countries in the world after Scandinavia. It has always upheld the rule of law. The personal freedoms of its citizens remain intact, and it protects the rights of minority groups. The influence of the Catholic Church, which historically has had an important impact on legislation, has been diminished in recent years. Although onerous libel laws exist, television, press, and radio are free from political interference, as is the judiciary, despite the fact that the Government is involved in the appointment of judges. Importantly, political donations are severely restricted and fully disclosed. Donations are limited to €1,000, and those over €800 must be disclosed.

No significant extremist party exists. Unlike many other European countries, there was no swing to the Right in the 2024 general election, and while a number of far-right candidates stood, none were elected. The system of proportional representation favours central parties. The Executive is held to account and normally is part of a coalition government, which necessitates compromise and avoids political extremes. The involvement of the army in politics has always been purely ceremonial.

Although it is a small country, it plays an active and important role internationally, where it has a long history of military neutrality. It contributes significantly to the European Union, where it has experienced strong economic growth.

Mindful of its own history of colonial occupation, it tries to support oppressed people and minorities while upholding international law. Currently, it is led by statements from the Government and the President, Michael Higgins, along with a few other countries, in a search to bring an end to the suffering of the people of Gaza and obtain EU recognition for the State of Palestine, joining two-thirds of the members of the UN who have long since recognised Palestine. Britain later lobbied for recognition, also. In 2024, along with Spain and Norway, Ireland gave formal recognition to the State of Palestine, bringing the number of countries doing so to 142, urging other EU countries to follow suit. It has attempted to introduce trade restrictions on Israel, independently of the EU. Israel responded by closing its Dublin embassy, an extremely hostile act, accusing Ireland of antisemitism. Ireland is, of course, not antisemitic but is opposed to the Israeli policy of territorial expansion.

For many years, it was a Catholic State, but after constitutional changes, it was liberalised by Taoiseach Garret Fitzgerald in the 1980s, when it was transformed into a modern Liberal Democracy. Traditionally, the President was a retired male member of one of the two leading parties. But this mould was broken in 1990, when Mary Robinson from neither party was elected the first female President and went on to develop an international profile. It is unlikely to become a victim of any autocratic takeover. Its Constitution provides the President with the right to refer any legislation to the Supreme Court if there is any doubt over its constitutionality. The Constitution provides an obstacle to any autocrat wishing to control the independence of the Judiciary. If all democracies had equivalent protection, it would better enable them to resist a populist takeover.

Ireland's democracy has its flaws but remains robust, especially in comparison with many European democracies, which face challenges from the far right.

PREFACE

USA: Democracy or Oligarchy?

In a book published in early 2024, Senator Bernie Sanders set out some serious criticisms of the operation of American democracy, claiming that the USA is an oligarchy, not a democracy.[1] The richest three billionaires have more wealth than the total of the poorest half of the population, comprising 165 million people. The top 1% have more wealth than the bottom 92%. The CEOs of major corporations earn 400 times the pay of average employees. He maintains that the oligarchs effectively own America. Both major parties are reliant on them for funding, which gives them a strong influence on legislation. To a significant degree, the oligarchs own the media.

Tens of millions of citizens feel deep anger towards the political, economic, and media establishment. The middle classes are dwindling in number, while many working-class people, especially the young, feel alienated and have no faith in capitalism. They are experiencing a lower standard of living than their parents. Real wages have remained stagnant for almost 50 years despite rising productivity. They do not have a right to a decent job, healthcare, education, food, and shelter.

These are serious charges against democracy, levied by someone who has a long experience of politics in America, and make a mockery of equality as the basis of democracy. But, to quote Oscar Wilde: "Discontent is the first step in the progress of a man or a nation". This book will address and compare democracies with autocracies, both as regards equality and the satisfaction of basic human needs.

INTRODUCTION

Over my life, I have visited more than 50 countries in different parts of the world. With the exceptions of China and Russia, which are centrally controlled, Singapore, a benevolent autocracy, and Myanmar, run by a military junta, probably the remainder would consider themselves to be democracies. Yet they often operate in very different ways with different sets of values and attitudes to democracy. The vast amount of my time over the last three years has been spent understanding, researching, and writing on the subject, building on my undergraduate and postgraduate training with the assistance of experts, colleagues, family, and friends. It ended when the outcome of the 2024 US Presidential Election became known, and its likely consequences were assessed a hundred days later.

I was introduced to American democracy as a volunteer teacher in India in 1963. There, I met two American Methodist missionaries and a Peace Corps worker who imbued and impressed me with their liberal values of freedom of speech, freedom of worship, honesty, unselfishness, generosity, tolerance of dissenting views, and the resolution of differences by peaceful means. These basic values appear to be badly eroded in America today.

Today, the number of these countries that remain democracies has rapidly dwindled. Pakistan, Egypt, and Thailand have been taken over by the military. Syria became a Russian-backed dictatorship for many years, run with massive atrocities. Turkey, Poland, and Hungary have lapsed into illiberal democracies, though Poland only temporarily. Israel's brand of democracy is dubious since Palestinians do not receive equal rights with Jews. India no longer regards Muslims as the equals of Hindus.

Other countries have dabbled with populism. They include two former bastions of democracy, the USA and the UK. In Latin America, Brazil, Argentina, and Peru have all experienced populism. In many cases, the change has been gradual and only discovered after the event. It seems that too many guardians of democracy have been asleep on their watch. As President Kennedy emphasised, the problem is: "The price of freedom is eternal vigilance".

Over Christmas 2022, I received three books. The first was an old classic, *Silent Spring*, written by Rachel Carson in 1962, a seminal work on the then little-studied science of ecology, inveighing against the dangers of insecticides. [1] It was to be many years before democracies addressed these issues. In the meantime, strong vested business interests scoffed at her work and prevented any progress on what was and is now a very serious long-term problem. Democratic decision-making seemed to have been badly flawed.

The second was *Quinn,* the story of a business set up successfully by a local Irish entrepreneur in 1963 in Cavan, a very depressed part of Ireland.[2] Quinn became Ireland's wealthiest man before the business crashed spectacularly some twenty years later. The failure led to costs of more than €1 billion for the Irish taxpayer since he had indirectly pledged insurance company assets to finance a colossal, reckless stock exchange gamble. The underlying reasons seemed to be an autocratic management style and a willingness to accept massive risks. Unfettered one-man capitalism comes at a high cost to democracy.

The third was *What Just Happened* by Marina Hyde, addressing the Johnson scandals in the UK and the fiasco of Brexit.[3] This made me wonder if a referendum was the best method of arriving at complex political decisions, for which reliable information should be required if voters are to make a considered vote. It also highlighted the dangers of populism when the government seeks to bypass Parliament and denigrate the judiciary.

It struck me that all books pointed to a failure of governance, whether in tackling ecological challenges, managing traditional capitalism, or implementing a fundamental political change. The question arises: Can our democratic system, with its diminished popularity, deal effectively with these challenges? Democracy seems to have numerous advantages over other forms of government, but it is seriously in decline internationally. This perplexing and enigmatic conundrum inspired me to write a book to answer these questions.

The book is aimed at those who value the democratic tradition, including students who, with limited time available, want a brief, concise, but wide-ranging examination of the issue involved. For this reason, despite addressing a very wide range of topics, it is kept as short as possible.

In the interest of a fresh and wide-ranging perspective on the topic, the approach covers various disciplines necessary for a rigorous examination of the issue. As well as political science, it contains elements of history, economics, communications (especially social media), psychology, and ethics. The analysis integrates elements of these disciplines to explain the decline in the popularity of liberal democracy and is extensively illustrated with contemporary examples, together with the problems experienced in different countries. It is topical, with over 60% of the 160 works cited in the bibliography dated in the last three years and over half the 300+ references dated from 2023 onwards. It should become one of the earliest books to be published covering the 2024 US Presidential Election, together with its implications for democracy.

Most importantly, it comes up with a plan of action, which, if adopted by democracies, may halt the present drastic decline in the number of democracies. Too often, authors outline the historical trend and explain the reasons for the decline of democracies, but then simply wring their hands in horror.

In trying to identify the reasons initially, it deals with the attractions and benefits of liberal democracy, its history and development, fundamental political divides, different models of democracy, and the link with economic growth.

The next chapters address contemporary democracy, both domestically and across national boundaries, the influences on voters, and the clash with other cultures, autocracy, and populism.

The following chapters compare how liberal democracies and autocracies deal with the major challenges of today: Inequality, satisfying basic human needs, seeking transnational cooperation for tackling climate change, pollution of the oceans, and the maintenance of peace.

I next explain the reasons for the current democratic crisis: How and why democracies fail, different types of autocracy,

autocracy by stealth, the allure of populism, and the role of social media, before reviewing democracy in the USA during the first Trump Presidency, discussing rising polarisation and the perils of complacency.

The book ends with Trump's first hundred days of presidency and my conclusions. It sets out a wish list if democracy is to survive, followed by a plan of action and an examination of the implications of the 2024 American Presidential election.

Readers are encouraged to skip chapters where they are familiar with the underlying issues. Some readers may choose to start with the conclusions set out in Chapter 21.

CHAPTER 1

The Democratic Enigma

In 1989, an academic article was published, later expanded into a book entitled *The End of History.* Francis Fukuyama, writing shortly before the fall of the Berlin Wall, which gave greater credence to his view, argued that there was then a consensus emerging that liberal democracy was superior to all other forms of government, such as hereditary monarchy, fascism, and communism. Unlike other forms of government, it was free from fundamental internal contradictions and would constitute the endpoint of mankind's ideological evolution.[1]

It did not mean that internal problems and injustice could not exist in stable democracies, but these were the result of poor implementation of the twin goals of liberty and justice. While countries might lapse back into more primitive forms of government, the ideal of liberal democracy could not be bettered. There could indeed be grave events and setbacks, but history, as understood by Hegel and Marx, had reached its final state of progress since all the big questions had been settled. The concept of free markets had spread, creating enormous, unprecedented material prosperity. Technological developments should lead to further wealth.

Fukuyama goes on to assert that humans seek equal recognition, and this is not available in alternative systems. Unsurprisingly, military dictatorships of the Right and the communist-totalitarian Left had fallen. Somewhat optimistically, he asserted that following the two world wars, liberal democracies would no longer have any incentive to wage war.

In 2006, he believed that the growth of the middle class, which accompanies liberal democracies, would help reinforce it. The origins of liberal democracy were based on Christian ethics, but were not incompatible with other religions and cultures. The key was a middle class that owned property, a complex civil society, together with a higher level of elite and mass education. He saw that the advances in technology and their abuses could seriously damage liberal democracy. Nevertheless, China had emerged as an alternative model of progress, and Russia re-emerged following the breakup of the USSR.

Following up on his views in 2020, Fukuyama believed that the basic thesis still stood the test of time. Admittedly, there was a threat of Islamic terrorism following the attack on the Twin Towers. However, despite its enforcement of religious beliefs through the adoption of Sharia Law, the core of Muslim beliefs did not threaten liberal democracy. The more serious challenge came from populism, as evidenced by the Brexit referendum in the UK and epitomised by the presidency of Donald Trump. The situation was particularly serious in the USA since, if America were to abandon democracy, it is likely that other countries would follow.

The Evidence from Freedom House [2]

Freedom House, the international democracy watchdog, heavily financed by the USA, which has existed for over eighty years, now examines democracy in about 210 countries. It has vigorously opposed dictatorships in Central America and Chile, apartheid in South Africa, the suppression of the Prague Spring, the Soviet war in Afghanistan, genocide in Bosnia and Rwanda, together with the brutal violation of human rights in Cuba, Burma, the People's Republic of China, and Iraq.

Its annual reports analyse countries on the basis of political rights and civil liberties. Its 2023 report stated that global freedom had declined for the eighteenth successive year. Political rights and civil liberties had declined in 52 countries and only increased in 21 countries. There were now more autocracies in the world than democracies. Pluralism is often under attack.

It blamed problems with distorted elections, including violence and manipulation. Examples included Ecuador, Cambodia, Guatemala, Poland, Turkey, Zimbabwe, and Niger. Most worryingly, the score of America has been declining significantly in recent years. The USA has a strong tradition of guarding liberty through solid democratic institutions, highly respecting the freedom of expression and civil liberties. However, problems with democracy are not restricted to autocracies, as is evidenced by India in Kashmir. Israel and the USA remain classified as democracies, despite their involvement in ethnic cleansing and genocide in Gaza, together with their disregard for international law, while Israel denies civic rights to Palestinian citizens on the West Bank and detains many for long periods without trial.

The downward trend continued in 2024. Four further countries were designated as no longer free: Thailand, Niger, Kuwait, and Tanzania, while Tunisia, El Salvador, and Haiti experienced sharp declines. Civil rights declined in 60 countries and only improved in 34. Attacks on freedom of the press and intimidation of journalists grew worse, especially in Serbia. Attacks on candidates opposing the government were commonplace. Also, anti-corruption legislation was often attacked, particularly in Slovakia.

The same broad conclusion is reached by the Economist Intelligence Unit, which has tracked democracies since 2006. It is estimated that since then, true democracies have diminished from 28 to 24, with the USA described as a 'flawed democracy'.

The Value of Freedom

For many centuries, as liberal democracy developed, freedom became its central value. Its importance has been stressed by all writers tackling the subject of democracy, being both well-understood and appreciated by citizens who live in democracies. People living in any liberal democracy usually take freedom for granted and notice it only when it is diminished or lost. Surprisingly, despite its importance, it has become one of the most elusive values in today's world.

In 1941, President Franklin D. Roosevelt, shortly before the USA joined the Allies in the Second World War, proclaimed that there were four fundamental freedoms for democracy. These are set out below, together with the views of those who gave the Reith lectures in 2022.

The most basic freedom is *Freedom of Speech*. Individual citizens can express their own views, however much they conflict with those of the government, without any fear of reprisal or punishment. The only constraint is the law of libel, which prevents citizens from damaging one another unfairly by making statements that are untrue or inciting hatred. Society allows new ideas to flourish and prosperity to grow.

A famous African author asserts that this freedom is essential for producing literature.[3] It is also the basis of curiosity, creativity, and learning. It is no wonder that a dictator like Hitler insisted that all books that he considered unfriendly be burned. For many years, religions such as Islam have banned blasphemy. Salman Rushdie, the author of *The Satanic Verses,* was subject to a *fatwah* or religious death penalty and was stabbed, while people associated with its publication were murdered. The people of Russia can meet a similar fate if their speeches offend the authorities.

Over the years, *Freedom of Worship* was fought for in opposition to any established religion, often to the point of death. But normally, in democracies today, religious freedom is taken for granted in Western Europe and America. The situation is somewhat different in Muslim countries embracing Sharia Law, based on the teachings of the Koran, where the State limits the freedom of individual citizens.

A former Archbishop of Canterbury argues that this is the most important personal freedom.[4] It is the freedom that allows equal people to believe what they choose, follow their own consciences, and live their spiritual lives accordingly. Whatever the majority may want does not bind the individual, who is free to follow his or her own faith. Questioning what is good and evil, as well as what is sacred, is fundamental in all societies.

Freedom from Want

If citizens do not have adequate food, shelter, warmth, and clothing, they are socially disadvantaged. In recent years, facilities in the British National Health Service have been seriously overstretched, damaged by rising food costs, fuel price increases, and homelessness, together with serious problems of crime and drugs. Charities assist by providing food boxes, clothing, and hostel shelter, but much still remains to be done.

A reformed alcoholic and social activist has campaigned for increased political health, but he emphasises that individuals should personally take responsibility for their own well-being.[5]

Roosevelt's final freedom is the *Freedom from Fear.* This obliges governments to defend the country from external attacks and maintain adequate policing for the protection of its citizens. It was very obviously an essential need during the Second World War. The independence of the military and police is critical if coups are to be prevented. Secret policing is incompatible with democracy.

A prominent Russian expert examined the essential fear generated by Russia's invasion of Ukraine. It may not be possible to eliminate danger, but it is possible to deal with paralysing fear, which is the result of a lack of knowledge. A start must be made by understanding why it happened and what options are open to the Western Powers.[6]

These are not the only important freedoms. Closely related to individual freedom of speech is the *Freedom of the Press* and other media. This is a central way that society can disseminate information to interested parties. It, too, is limited only by libel laws, which vary from country to country. All true democracies should have an independent press and at least one independent television channel. Autocrats and dictators usually aim to control the media so that only the facts as they see them reach citizens and voters.

Another important freedom is the *Freedom of Assembly.* Citizens, especially students, often wish to express their views collectively. It can also be an important release of anger in a peaceful manner when used without violence. This right can also be a valuable way in which governments can gauge the strength of opposition to their policies from the numbers participating in protests. Whether it survives the second Trump presidency remains to be seen.

A further basic right is the *Right to Equality before the Law and to receive a Fair Trial.* Fundamental to this right is the independence of the judiciary. If governments can control the judiciary, they might try to influence any particular case. Traditionally, criminal trials are conducted by way of a jury, which can determine the guilt or innocence of the accused.

Freedom of Movement has grown rapidly in recent years, with the reductions in visa restrictions and the growth of tourism, helped by the availability of low airline fares. Travel, which used to be the prerogative of the rich, who undertook 'grand tours' around Europe in the eighteenth century, is now also freely available to everyone. It has become one of the cornerstones of the Single Market, resulting in the virtual disappearance of the practice of national borders within the EU.

A further freedom is the *Right to Pursue the Livelihood of Choice* for individuals according to their needs and abilities. Forced labour or slavery has largely vanished in the present age. Few societies nowadays reject this freedom, except for short periods of military service.

While these basic freedoms are fundamental to the working of liberal democracy, they do not exist in autocracies or dictatorships. The dangers of opposing Russian autocracy are explained in Chapter 8. Freedom of speech and assembly are not available, as is the right to a fair trial. The media is controlled to support government policy, and dissenters live in a constant culture of fear.

Self-respect and esteem are also important to individuals, as discussed in Chapter 10. This is enhanced in a democracy by the fact that all citizens have an equal voice at the ballot box. This is well understood in autocracies, which do not have free and fair elections. They produce election results that are entirely fictitious in an attempt to persuade both their own voters and overseas commentators that they have the overwhelming backing of the people.

These values, inherent in democracy, are well appreciated by people throughout the world. Many immigrants, just as Irish people did in the past, and refugees seek to gain entrance to democracies, sometimes at considerable risk to their own safety. The fact that they take these risks is a testament to their belief that democracies have many advantages over the illiberal societies that they want to leave.

Economic Growth and Democracy

A key question is whether democracy or autocracy can be expected to produce greater economic growth. An answer has been given by Amartya Sen, the Indian Nobel Prize winner in economics and noted philosopher, who specialises in economic development with a particular focus on the well-being of those at the lower end of society.

Development can be regarded as a democratic and participatory form of political organisation, expanding the freedom that people enjoy. But freedom depends also on other factors, such as social and economic arrangements, including healthcare, industrialisation, social modernisation, and technological progress.[7]

Sen illustrated the advantage of liberal democracy in dealing with famine. Famine is almost always regarded as a serious calamity, often appearing at short notice, though Stalin deliberately imposed famine on the grain-rich Ukraine to bring the inhabitants into line.

Autocrats are usually unaffected and have less incentive to take urgent action to resolve the problem. But no serious famine has occurred in either rich or poor liberal democracies in recent years, except in times of war.

On the other hand, famines occurred in colonial countries, such as India and Ireland; in one-party states, such as Ukraine in the 1930s, China in 1958 to 1961, and Cambodia in the 1970s; in military dictatorships, such as Ethiopia and Somalia, and various Sahel states. More recently, North Korea and Sudan, both autocratic regimes, faced mass starvation. Perhaps if Ireland had had a liberal democracy when its grain was being exported, the devastating potato famine of the 1840s could have been prevented or at least mitigated.

Development requires the removal of major sources of poverty, tyranny, restricted economic opportunities, systematic social deprivation, neglect of public facilities, intolerance, and overcapacity of oppressive states. If this is so, how can autocracies expand at the expense of democracies?

The Enigma

It seems extraordinary that democracy, with all its inherent attractions and benefits, should suddenly be endangered as a system of government. It has a long history of over two thousand years and experienced rapid growth after the fall of the Berlin Wall in 1989. Yet now, the evidence seems to be that its numbers are declining rapidly.

So, the number of democracies, the countries of people governed by democracy, and the perceived quality of democracy itself have all declined.[8] How can this conundrum be explained? The enigma has been brought to the world forcibly by the 2024 US Presidential Election. It is the primary focus of this book, and the solution should interest anyone concerned about the future of democracy.

Liberal Democracy in 2024

Not for a long time has democracy faced such dangers and challenges on so many fronts. For the first time since 1986, there are more autocracies than democracies in the world, 50 autocracies and only 47 democracies.[9] Fewer than half the people in Britain now think that the State is run for the benefit of all the people. A quarter of them claim that they would prefer to be ruled by a strong leader who could ignore parliament.[10] It is difficult to name any country that could not backslide into autocracy. Even the stalwart democracies of the UK and the USA have been targeted by populists. In recent years, the Indian government shut down the internet on 84 occasions, often before or during protests.[11]

Often, opposition to democracy leads to violence. Two British members of Parliament have been assassinated, and a retired Japanese Prime Minister was knifed to death. The latest outbreak was an attempted assassination of Trump in the 2024 election campaign, the first such attempt on a presidential candidate since 1981. The growth of right-wing parties, which have scant respect for democracy, has spread all around Europe as well as further afield.

2024 was forecast to be a critical year for democracy, and so it has proved. More than half the people on the planet held nationwide elections in 2024.[12.] It has been estimated that two billion people from 70 countries headed to the polls. Major countries, from Britain to Bangladesh and India to Indonesia, faced divisive elections. The introduction of illiberal laws in many countries is likely to be enacted, rewarding corrupt politicians. India is turning away from its traditional tolerance of Muslims. Indonesia is trying to entrench a political dynasty. Bangladesh has tried to jail opposition leaders and brooked no dissent. Africa was the continent with the most elections, but discontent with democracy there has resulted in numerous coups. One piece of good news in South America is that Mexico has elected its first female president with an overwhelming majority in a high-turnout election.

The critical event was the election of the President of the United States, which will have major implications for democracy in America and also around the world. [13] One major country, at least, should be added to Freedom House's list of autocracies, while others may follow suit. Liberal Democracy had battled for survival but had been unsuccessful in the home of democracy. It may well be that liberal democracy is the best ideology, but that does not mean that it will always survive. It may need to evolve in a world of resurgent populism, polarisation, changes in digital technology, and the growing influence of social media.

CHAPTER 2

Democracy from Early Days to the Present

Democracy is a system of Government whereby collective decisions are made by the citizens. To understand any democracy today, it is helpful to have some knowledge of its history and to appreciate how it has developed over time in different countries while being aware of its frailties.

The Origins of Democracy in Athens

The democratic systems familiar to us today have very deep roots, though the present model was mainly developed in the twentieth century. It first appeared in Athens, lasting from 508 BC to 322 BC. The historian Herodotus described it in these lines: "In a democracy, there is the most splendid of virtues, equality before the law; its offices are assigned by lot, all officials are subject to investigation, and all policies are debated in public". It reached its zenith in the Golden Era of Pericles, where Pericles, Themistocles, and others epitomised the success of democratic rule. Pericles proclaimed that Athenian democracy did not copy their neighbours but was an example to them.

There were about 40,000 citizens in Athens, comprising all free males, participating in direct democracy. Women, slaves, and those without land were not permitted to vote. The Assembly was the final source of power, meeting 3 or 4 times a month with the right to vote on all major matters of finance, alliances, and wars. It set up an Executive with 500 members elected by lot, permitted to sit for only two years. The functions of the Council included managing the navy, overseeing the supply of corn, supervising markets, repairing roads, organising religious festivals, establishing building regulations, and even collecting dung, all of which were subject to an annual audit. The Court was responsible for upholding the constitution, and its judges were chosen by lot, as were 500 jurors. It has been well described by the first writer on the subject, Plato.

Plato

Plato described democracy and alternative systems of government.[1] 'Timocracy', based on Sparta, a rival city-state, was militarily run with an emphasis on physical exercise rather than academic subjects, later becoming a model for military dictatorships. Oligarchies existed when control was taken over by the wealthiest, who governed in their own interests. Tyranny, the most dictatorial version of autocracy, was the worst form of government, where the interests of the citizens were ignored. These remain the main rivals to democracy today. He warns, however, that democracy or mob rule inevitably degenerates into tyranny and injustice, an unflattering, if understandable, description in today's world.

In one simile, Plato compared Government to steering a ship. The owners are the people who should seek a navigator appointed by the philosopher king to steer the ship and avoid the perils that lie ahead. Some leaders are far from being skilled navigators and try to quell any mutiny with wild promises as the Ship of State enters choppy and dangerous waters. Plato provides appropriate advice to modern populist leaders, who choose to summarily disregard the ideas of experts.

In another simile, he compares men chained in a cave to a fire. Their perception of reality is merely the shadowed reflections on the wall. When released outside into the sunshine, they will see true reality, which he says is 'Reason'. If one person escaped and returned, he would probably be killed since the others do not want their idea of reality upset.

It seems that now some people are happy to live in a world of alternative reality, as seen on their computers or iPhones, together with enhanced reality in the cinema. Many believers strongly oppose any questioning of their alternative reality, which is the information spread on social media. They resent facts which present the view, as seen outside of the cave.

Plato's views were influenced by the death of Socrates, who had been put to death by the democratic vote for allegedly offending the gods and corrupting youth. Nevertheless, he set out a description of democracy in a city-state based on the equality of voters, which was to have a profound impact on those who set out to create democracy for nation-states over two thousand years later. The heyday of Athenian democracy survived for almost two hundred years, with no mean achievement, and was only ended when the city was captured by Sparta. Anyone interested in creating a democratic society based on equality should find it a useful starting point.

After an unsuccessful coup, when the Citadel was captured, the Athenians decided to strengthen their laws to prevent a tyrant from coming to power, based on the drafting of Draco. It centred around ostracism and was introduced by Cleisthenes, the father of Athenian democracy. Each year, the Assembly would vote on whether or not to proceed with ostracism without any names being mentioned. If approved, two months later, the citizens named their targets. The most frequently named person would then be banished for ten years. Donald Trump must be grateful that no similar law exists in the USA today. [2]

The 'res publica' or Roman Republic developed some features of Athenian democracy. The Republic was a type of aristocracy of patricians with a popular assembly and the plebeian tribune representing the common people. However, the Senate, for the most part, controlled the Consulate and the higher magistracies. Consuls governed along with 300 Senators, who were elected for life. [3] In this way, the patricians held the predominance of power, and there was enormous inequality with the common people. Matters changed with the rise of Julius Caesar, who diminished the role of the senate. As a populist, he was first appointed a Proconsul and then became a member of the ruling trio. After military successes, he became a dictator and formed a hereditary dynasty, which was initially successful but fell apart due to the incompetence of later Caesars.

Monarchical Government in the Long Middle Ages

Iceland, a small, isolated country dependent on Denmark, established a parliament in 930 but, due to its size, failed to attract imitators elsewhere. Democracy also emerged in some fifteenth-century Italian city-states, but with these small exceptions, democracy with any form of wide suffrage was to vanish for over two thousand years. Throughout the Middle Ages, monarchs maintained that they were chosen by the will of God or 'divine right', a doctrine generally accepted by their courtiers.

Dynastic monarchies prevailed for centuries. Subjects were needed to grow crops, provide military service, and pay taxes. When a peasant revolt broke out, it related to a profound grievance, not the idea of democracy. The Catholic Church, also a monarchical power with territorial interests and widespread ecclesiastical jurisdiction, was able to enforce discipline on the faithful, as well as occasionally on kings.

The first celebrated and formal constraint on monarchical power in England was the Magna Carta in 1215, a charter designed to put a limit on the powers of the absolute monarchy and share some powers between the Crown and the powerful barons. It was to have a profound limitation on the powers of absolute monarchs. Many people today regard this as the first tenuous step on the road to parliamentary democracy, but this was in no way understood at the time.

The question arises that if true democracy could disappear for two thousand years, while society survived, could history repeat itself? To answer this question, it is necessary to understand how it developed over time after the Middle Ages in different countries, what setbacks it encountered, and how it can fail.

The Decline of Monarchies and Rise of Republics

The decline of the monarchies was accelerated by events in England, France, and America. In England, the royalists were defeated in a civil war. In France, a revolution led to the guillotining of the king. In America, a war of independence led to the creation of a republic.

The first significant reappearance of any form of democracy was in England. Tensions came to a head in the seventeenth century when a civil war broke out between parliamentarians and royalists, ending with the defeat and momentous beheading of King Charles I in 1649. The victorious parliamentary general, Oliver Cromwell, presided over a kind of united republic, the Commonwealth of England, but he was no democrat. He prorogued parliament and ruled as an authoritarian 'Protector', with the army for support, conducting a savage campaign to subdue dissent in Ireland. Nevertheless, in Britain, he is normally remembered as a parliamentarian.

In England, the Glorious Revolution of 1688 laid the foundations of parliamentary government and limited monarchy. The Bill of Rights in 1689, a document fundamental to the making of parliamentary power and a limited monarchy, laid down that laws could not be suspended by the Crown. Regular parliamentary elections, based on a limited franchise by property qualification, were mandatory, taxation required the consent of Parliament, and freedom of speech within Parliament was established, along with individual rights, reflecting the views of the liberal philosopher John Locke.

A century later, another Englishman, Thomas Paine, argued in *The Rights of Man* that true justice should support not only natural rights such as life, liberty, free speech, and freedom of conscience but also civil rights relating to security and protection.[4]

At this time, American revolutionaries had just fought a successful war of independence, aiming to replace the monarchy with a republic. Benjamin Franklin told George Washington that he preferred a republic "if you can keep it". Until 2025, this has never been in doubt, even in times of war. The Founding Fathers of the 1787 Constitution were familiar with democracy in Athens and Rome, as well as the writings of French Enlightenment philosophers. They were concerned about the dangers of mob rule, fearing the danger of rule by the masses. They were anxious, nevertheless, to widen the franchise beyond limiting it to men of property. Thomas Jefferson proclaimed that all men are created equal, though this excluded slaves and did not mention women.

The 1787 Constitution, although it made no reference to democracy, was framed around freedom, equality, and justice. Congress was divided between the House of Representatives, which elected representatives for each State based on their relative population, while the Senate gave equal representation to each State, which was seen as a brake on rule by demagogues. The president, elected by eligible voters, appointed senior judges, but the guiding principle was the separation of powers between the Legislature, the Executive, and the Judiciary. The Judiciary had considerable power since it interpreted the Constitution. Voting was restricted to white males over the age of 21.

The loss of the American colonies was to have serious repercussions in England. Despite the fall of the Government of the day, the Monarch, George III, was seen as partly responsible. He had regarded the rebellion as treacherous and refused to allow surrender. It was the last time a British monarch was involved in military decisions.

Swiss eighteenth-century philosophers of the 'French Enlightenment' paved the way for the French Revolution. Jean-Jacques Rousseau claimed that everyone was born free and equal, but society imposed ownership over resources and a division of labour, which caused conflict and social injustice.[5] Voltaire explained that human beings are not machines since they can exercise free will, but common sense is not common. His writing demonstrated the benign effects of religious toleration.[6]

Louis XIV, in the same century, declared "L'Etat, c'est Moi", meaning "I am the State". Such an absolute monarchy, endorsed by the accepted doctrine of divine right, was the model for European monarchies, which endured for many years. However, the French Revolution in the eighteenth century ended with the execution of his successor, Louis XIV, while the revolutionaries demanded "liberty, equality, and fraternity". After a promising start with the creation of a Revolutionary Assembly, which brought together representatives of the Third Estate, the revolution eventually degenerated into a reign of terror under Robespierre before it turned into the authoritarian rule of Napoleon Bonaparte, an enlightened despot. Nevertheless, the legacy of the French Revolution was to place liberty and equality at the centre of a representative system of government.

After the end of the Napoleonic wars in 1815, there was a period of conservative reaction against liberal and democratic movements, particularly in the Austrian and Russian empires. Britain, on the other hand, widened the franchise progressively towards a male democracy in a series of Great Reform Acts, as well as eventually increasing the powers of the House of

Commons at the expense of the House of Lords. In Ireland, the 'Liberator' Daniel O'Connell sought the emancipation of the Catholics, who formed most of the population. After a series of monster peaceful meetings throughout the country, he successfully showed the power of the people in the face of a formidable British Government.

In 1848, there was a series of upheavals throughout Europe against the prevailing systems, but no real permanent changes were achieved. Prussia emerged as a formidable monarchical State and defeated France in 1870. France then set up the Third Republic, a male democracy which lasted until the Second World War.

The new democracies, to some degree, adapted to the era of empires in the latter years of the century. The European powers of Britain, France, Holland, Belgium, and Germany vied with each other to extend their colonies across the world, particularly in Asia and Africa. The benefits included access to natural resources and cheap labour to transport them. Imperial Powers often ruled with considerable brutality, but sometimes introduced representative elements to their colonies. An extensive civil service was created to manage the colonies. The ability to control large areas of the world with a small number of their own nationals was limited but often assisted by a policy of 'Divide and Rule', while unfriendly local governments could be overthrown if required. Political parties, such as the Congress Party in India, played an increasingly influential role in their opposition to colonial rule. Thus, the seeds of democracy were, perhaps accidentally, sown and could survive when the empires eventually crumbled.

The Early Twentieth-Century Experiment in Democracy

The consequence of the First World War was the collapse of four traditional empires: The German Hohenzollern Empire, the Austrian Habsburg Monarchy, the Ottoman Turkish Empire, and the Russian Romanov Empire. Except for Russia, this opened the way for new parts of Europe to adopt democratic government. Tsarist Russia had fallen in 1917, and all traces of democracy disappeared when the Bolsheviks seized power in a coup in October of that year. The country was renamed the USSR, a Union of Soviet Socialist Republics, but it quickly turned into a dictatorship ruled by the Bolshevik party under Lenin and later Stalin.

In the aftermath of the First World War, it seemed that democracy would prevail in Europe and beyond, with the League of Nations playing a key role. However, the new German Weimar Republic, burdened with war reparations, was riven with division from the start, suffering hyperinflation and then the Great Crash of 1929. Germany was destroyed from within by the National Socialist or Nazi Party, using the democratic system in the 1930 and 1932 elections, without commanding a majority in the Reichstag, but nevertheless operated as a dictatorship.

Similarly, in Italy in 1922, a fascist dictatorship, headed by Mussolini, was initiated by harnessing democratic institutions. In Spain, democracy was overthrown in a civil war when General Franco emerged victorious in 1939. Japan also developed into an aggressive Fascist State ruled by an emperor. In contrast, the new Irish Free State of 1922 was successfully set up as a parliamentary democratic state. Following a civil war, the defeated party formed the government ten years later, a good day for democracy.

During the Second World War, many Western democracies, including France for seventy years, disappeared during the Nazi conquest. Democracy was reduced to a handful of states: the USA, Britain, and her dominions, together with a few neutral countries, such as Switzerland, Sweden, and Ireland. The war ended with the USSR's victory in the east, the success of the Anglo-American armies in the west, and the dropping of two atomic bombs on Japan.

In 1945, there was a brief illusion that liberal democracies would be restored across Europe. Europe, however, is divided into two very different ideological blocs. The victorious allies sought to spread democracy, while the USSR sought to spread its influence by military conquest. The USA and its democratic allies in Western Europe guaranteed the survival of democracy through the Marshall Plan, membership in NATO, and containment of the USSR in the Cold War.

Out of the bloody partitioning of India, India became a democratic state, but Pakistan only sporadically so. Eventually, Pakistan broke into West and East Pakistan, which were renamed Bangladesh, and initially set out on the course of democracy. The USA, Western Europe, and Japan became the standard bearers of democracy worldwide. With the breakup of the British and French Empires, many of these lands adopted democracy, too. Other European countries quickly followed suit. Spain returned to democracy after the death of Franco, and Portugal followed a few years later.

Liberal democracy became the major form of government worldwide. Its mode of operation varied enormously, according to the model chosen. But many countries followed the model introduced in Britain and France in 1918 and adopted a policy of universal suffrage, where all men and eventually women received the right to vote, irrespective of any property rights. The main exceptions were Muslim states governed by Sharia law, which significantly reduced the freedom of women, the centralised economies of the USSR, and the 'Sleeping Giant' of People's China before it emerged from its slumber in 1949. If the Allies had not won the Second World War, liberal democracy in Europe certainly could have disappeared forever. Victory made its existence and growth possible, but by no means guaranteed that it would survive indefinitely.

Democracy has been built on the cornerstones of Athens and Rome. The American Founding Fathers drew up the American Constitution, which became a role model available to all fledgling democracies. Parliamentary democracy in Britain and France also played an important role. But the City State of Athens needed to evolve to meet the requirements of larger modern nation-states. Whereas a consensus could be achieved relatively easily with small numbers, larger numbers necessitated a more organised approach to be effective. Representative democracy evolved to allow for the presence of political parties, which grouped together people with broadly similar views.

Could democracy disappear again, as it did for 2,000 years? The answer undoubtedly is 'Yes'. Certainly, it has received a serious setback with the election of Trump as US President in 2024. Many people now living in liberal democracies naively assume that they will continue to do so indefinitely. But, as history has shown, democracy has developed very unevenly with frequent setbacks. Most countries today that describe themselves as democracies adopted this system of government only since the end of the Second World War, and many citizens are dissatisfied with what has resulted. Democracy is vulnerable to its many opponents, who may seek its destruction. The idea that democracy will automatically survive is a dangerous myth. Democracy in any country will only survive by the will and determination of the people to defend it as their chosen system of government.

CHAPTER 3

Democracy and Fundamental Political Divides

As democracy evolved, parliamentary leaders sought to improve the stability of their governments. They needed to attract permanent allegiances by establishing common ground for their members. This was achieved through the creation of political parties, which quickly became central to the working of democracy.

An eminent sociologist, Max Weber, who advised on the setting up of the Weimar Republic in 1918, defined 'party' in terms of a group of people that can be differentiated based on their affiliations with other engaged members in the political domain. He did not regard them as divisive, distracting, or dangerous. Rather, they were the children of democracy, of mass franchise, of the necessity to woo and organise the masses. Political parties were machines to perform the mechanical functions of government. [1]

There may be two or more parties in a democracy. In the USA, the two-party system comprises a liberal reformist party, the Democrats, and a more conservative Republican Party. But a greater number of parties is possible and has developed elsewhere with different underlying structures.

Liberalism

Liberalism has been described as the dominant ideology of modern times. In the Age of Enlightenment, the English philosopher John Locke set out the foundations, based on a social contract, whereby every citizen has a natural right to life, liberty, and property, which were fundamental to good government. [2] These words were later paraphrased in the American Declaration of Independence. Human affairs should be guided by reason, rather than orders from the Monarch. The underlying principles should be freedom and liberty. Government exists to serve the people, rather than vice versa.

These ideas and beliefs influenced both the French and American Revolutions. This gave birth to the ideology of liberalism and instituted forms of government that attempted to implement it in practice. Freedom of speech, assembly, and worship became generally accepted in democracies. Importantly, it stressed the rule of law and promoted equality before the law. It demanded human and civil rights for all citizens. Generally described as the dominant ideology of modern times, it is now associated with the market economy, free trade, and freedom of the press.

An influential nineteenth-century Englishman, John Stuart Mill, did much to popularise liberalism. He emphasised the importance of individual freedom and the right to disagree, denouncing social tyranny or the tyranny of the majority, to be contained by constitutional checks. [3]

Conservatism

Conservatism is a cultural, social, and political philosophy. It seeks to promote and preserve traditional values. Its application varies from country to country. In England, where its members are called Tories, it has been associated with the nuclear family, organised religion, the military, property rights, and the monarchy.

It started with the ideas of an Irishman, Edmund Burke, who became involved in British politics in the eighteenth century. [4.] It has respect for authority and an independent judiciary. Gradual change and continuity are preferred to revolution, but it rejects the total laissez-faire approach of traditional liberalism in favour of protecting workers from exploitation. While Burke accepted that reform was necessary, he believed that it must be undertaken with the utmost care. He supported the American Revolution, but not the French Revolution. Writing in the twenty-first century, the British Conservative, 'Tory' chairman explains that it aims to protect and apply what is best in the existing State.[5] Economic growth is based on capitalism and individual enterprise. Competition is fostered by the 'invisible hand', as described by a Scotsman, Adam Smith, one of the founders of modern economic thinking, whereby supply and demand adjust quickly to changes in market conditions through the price mechanism.[6]

Left-Wing Thinking: Communism and Socialism

Left-wing thinking is based on the ideas of Karl Marx, who regarded capitalism as doomed to fail and would ultimately give way to socialism.[7] The overall aim of society was equality of all citizens, and this could be achieved by nationalisation of the means of production over a wide range of industries, such as transport, water, banking, and coal production. Communism believed that this could only come about through a class struggle and revolution. Marx was disdainful of democracy, which he believed was a defence by the bourgeoisie of their interests and needed to be replaced by the dictatorship of the proletariat, achieved through the class struggle.

Socialism is characterised by the social, rather than private, means of production. Social ownership can be public, community, collective, cooperative, or employee. It developed first in the 1820s and 1830s with the followers of Charles Fourier, Henri de Saint-Simon, and Pierre-Joseph Proudhon in France. In England, Robert Owen was highly critical of the poverty and inequality of the Industrial Revolution.

While socialists had the same ultimate ends as communists, they believed that change was possible peacefully. A distinct split emerged between communism and modern socialism. Under the policies of New Labour of Tony Blair, nationalisation and socialism were dropped, as were references to the class struggle. It favoured the expansion of health and welfare services while becoming supportive of business. It maintained restrictions on trade unions, which provided a strong sector of its support. Increasingly, it came to resemble the Democratic Party of the USA in the same way that the Republican Party of the USA increasingly came to resemble the Tory Party in the UK, admiring in due course the privatisation of nationalised industries, introduced by Margaret Thatcher in Britain.

Liberal Democracy

Liberal or Western Democracy is a blend of liberal thinking with the basic concept of democracy. It includes elections and multiple distinct political parties, with a minimum of two. It embraces the rule of law, a market economy, and private property. It advocates human rights, civil rights, civil liberties, and political freedom for all people.

It can take different constitutional forms, such as the constitutional monarchy of the UK or a republic, as in both the USA and France. It may or may not entail a written constitution and is normally based on universal suffrage. By the end of the 19th century, it had become not only a liberal idea but an ideology, supported by many other ideologies.

It has been argued by a German, who for a time was a member of the Nazi Party, that the term itself, 'liberal democracy', contains a fundamental contradiction. [8] Liberalism is concerned with individual rights, while democracy relates to collective decision-making. Be that as it may, liberal democracies have retained their popularity until recently, though it must be admitted that individual rights may not be upheld in times of war or national emergency.

Changes during the Second World War

During the preparation for and conduct of the Second World War, all participants ran their economies through a system of central planning. Materials, labour, and output were organised centrally as a necessity. During the war, a prominent Austrian economist, Friedrich Hayek, pointed out the deficiencies in socialist central economic planning, which should be avoided in peacetime. [9] It inevitably led to the loss of freedom, individualism, and democracy. Democratic capitalism should be based on a market economy, because the alternative, central planning, degenerates into totalitarianism. At this time, an American, Joseph Schumpeter, argued that growth was based on periodic inventions, which inevitably brought in a fundamental reorganisation of the industry by a process of 'creative destruction'.[10]

Western liberal democracies moved after the War to a more laissez-faire approach to running the economies, where the State intervened as little as possible, other than to control monopolies. Perhaps the greatest defence of democracy ever by Karl Popper was published in 1945.[11] It attacks the writing of Marx, Hegel, and Plato's philosopher king, pointing out the dangers of centralised planning and totalitarianism. It inspired one of his admirers, George Soros, to set up an 'Open Society Fund' from the considerable wealth that he had amassed. These funds were used to oppose totalitarianism and further liberal education in his native Hungary, for which he was reviled by Viktor Orban, who denounced it all as a Jewish plot.

During the 1950s in the UK, there was a swing to the centre. An influential book by a Labour minister,[12] moved socialism away from Marxism, while the Tories adopted more progressive welfare policies. The result was 'Butskellism', a combination of the ideas of Rab Butler, the Tory Chancellor of the Exchequer, and Hugh Gaitskell, the leader of the Labour Party. It was not destined to change radically until Margaret Thatcher became Prime Minister, slashing public expenditure and reducing taxes.

Illiberalism

Liberalism has traditionally been regarded as a virtue in democratic countries, since it values the classical freedoms outlined in Chapter 1. While many countries may ignore some of the freedoms in practice, they normally pay lip service to the idea of freedom.

In recent years, this has been called into question. Viktor Orban in Hungary has declared that the country is an 'illiberal democracy'. He stressed the need to protect people's dignity, provide freedom, guarantee physical security, maintain a "Christian culture", and avoid becoming a slave-like nation. Maintaining a Christian culture is clear, but how illiberalism achieves the other objectives is confusing. Illiberalism is often put forward by leaders who have a tendency toward autocracy.

The Greens

Taking their inspiration from Rachel Carson in America, a new movement grew in many countries, mainly around environmental issues, starting in the 1970s. In a world of well-established political parties, it has not proved easy to make major progress in terms of the number of parliamentary seats. The Greens seldom get more than 10% of the national vote, so their route to power has so far been by way of alliances with other parties. In an era of worries about climate change and concerns about sustainability, their views are receiving wider attention. Their voice cannot be ignored, and their influence has grown enormously, but many people resist the costs involved. Important green issues are considered in Chapter 11.

Libertarianism

An extreme form of liberalism, libertarianism, has come to prominence, particularly in the USA. It believes that the State should never encroach on individual liberties and never intervene at all in the regulation of the economy. It can morph into anarcho-capitalism. The best known of libertarianism is Donald Trump, who stated that he would represent their interests at their 2024 National Conference.[13] It is much favoured by tax evaders and money launderers, amongst others.

Fascism and the Far-Right

Fascism is an ultra-nationalist party, founded by Mussolini in Italy in 1919, demanding total obedience to the leader. The far right is a modern form of fascism, based on extreme nationalism, racism, and the use of violence to achieve political ends.

Given that there were many different parties, it was necessary to find a way to aggregate them and form an Executive, either from a single party or a coalition of parties, to manage the country. But there existed several different models as to how best to achieve this and form a government.

CHAPTER 4

Different Models of Liberal Democracy

Most people are familiar with democracy as it is practised in their own country. But several different models exist, which can fundamentally affect how democracy works in any given country.

Referendum Challenges

The most direct form of democracy is by way of referendum. Essentially, this resembles the Athenian democracy, modified to the needs of the Nation State, as opposed to the City State. The voters, whoever they may be, cast their votes, and the majority determines the decision.

Swiss cantons have used referendums for many years. Power is divided between the national government, regional cantons, and local communes, which allows greater local participation. Other countries, such as Ireland, use referenda for major changes, such as changing their constitution. Australia uses them, but failed to give the indigenous people the 'Voice' by having them recognised in the Constitution in 2023, despite strong Government backing. Probably, however, the best-known example is the decision of the UK on whether to remain or leave the European Union. But any form of referendum is necessarily time-consuming and expensive.

A fundamental issue for a referendum is that there must be a binary choice, and the voter decides yes or no. This gives rise to problems if the alternatives are not completely clear. In the case of 'Brexit', it was clear what was meant by 'remain'. But there was a range of possible 'leave' options, from remaining in the single market or customs union to a 'no-deal' Brexit, which made it difficult for voters to make a rational decision. Where decisions can be nuanced, a referendum may be overly simplistic. The normal practice now is for indirect democracy, dominated by political parties.

Parliamentary Democracy

Parliaments were established, where elected representatives could meet, talk, and exchange views. Some countries adopted democracy, having observed it in America, Britain, and France. Most countries adopted the two-chamber or 'bicameral' approach, though Scandinavia set up a single chamber, and the powers of the second chamber were limited, except for America.

Britain's House of Lords eventually could only delay legislation introduced by the House of Commons. Britain eventually introduced life peerages, who could use their skills to enhance performance, but too often those chosen were failed former politicians. The Monarch became the titular Head of State, undertaking functions performed by presidents elsewhere. The Irish Senate suffered similar weaknesses, but a proposal to abolish the Senate was rejected by the electorate in a referendum.

Some power was exercised by local authorities, provided they had the necessary sources of funds. Clear demarcation lines between the local and central government were essential. This was the fundamental issue that caused the American Civil War when the southern states wanted to retain their rights over slavery.

Many models were tried, with the key element being the role of the elected president. The role, powers, and tenure of the president are critical to the effectiveness of the democratic state. In some countries, the president is also the head of the government. Whenever excessive powers are granted to the president, the State could revert to an autocracy, if not a tyranny.

Parliamentary Parties

Early parliaments allowed members to vote according to their own conscience, which often destabilised the government. Like-minded people joined political parties, which vied with each other to form a government. In practice, the parties may not be truly independent and may be vulnerable to powerful lobby groups representing special interests.

In Britain and America, the electoral system favoured a two-party system, or 'First Past the Post', which created stability of government. It does, however, inevitably lead to the underrepresentation of minorities, such as the Liberal Party in the UK. In Europe, systems of proportional representation allow for a wider range of views and parties, which usually need coalitions to form a government.

Proportional Representation more accurately reflects the wishes of the entire electorate, since it allows greater representation of minority groups. Britain, for example, has not had a government that represents the majority of the people for a century. Minorities are heavily penalised and underrepresented.

But, where no party gains an overall majority, the Government must be formed through alliances, which can lead to serious instability in countries, such as Italy, where Governments may last only a year or so. Ireland adopted a unique system when it became independent over a century ago, called the 'Single Transferable Vote', which only exists in one other country, Malta. Several members of the same political party may be competing for the same seat with the same party manifesto, which encourages localised parish pump politics.

The system in the USA operates in a way very different from that envisaged by the Founding Fathers, who drafted the Constitution. They had designed an Electoral College to select the President. This was intended to be a debating chamber, where the respective merits of the candidates were up for discussion. It has provided a disproportionate influence on small States. George Bush in 2000 and Donald Trump in 2016 were elected to the Presidency, despite not having a majority of the popular vote. In practice, it reflects the wishes of the party that obtains the most seats, a decision that was a mere formality, until Donald Trump tried to overturn the election result in 2020 with his March on the Capitol.

Another serious issue is the limitations on any American President whose party does not control both the House of Representatives and the Senate. The Senate, which comprises two representatives of each State, was designed to act as a curb on demagogues, since sparsely populated States had equal representation with the large States. Much legislation in Congress needs to be passed by both Houses, so this can, in practice, prevent a President from effectively exercising the party mandate when the other party controls the Senate. In these circumstances, there can be a series of crises when the

President seeks finance. A similar chaotic situation can arise when the largest party cannot agree on who should occupy the important position of Speaker of the House of Representatives, as happened in 2023. The presidency may become a 'lame duck' presidency, where the president must rely on 'Executive Orders' rather than legislation. But these orders can easily be reversed by successors.

Another controversial aspect of the US model is the existence of the filibuster. Senators can speak for very lengthy periods on irrelevant matters to block new legislation that the Government has proposed. The filibuster can only be stopped by a three-fifths majority of senators present and voting. This device particularly favours Republicans, who traditionally have around half the Senate seats.

There are concerns about how political parties operate in practice. Nowadays, members of political parties may have difficulty voting according to their consciences. Party whips can enforce ever stricter discipline to ensure that legislation is passed. Dissenting members can face serious sanctions and potential damage to their political futures.

Prerequisites for Effective Democracy

If democracy based on the Athenian model is to operate effectively, then simple underlying assumptions must be followed. Citizens in most Western Democracies believe that the rules are just and are properly applied, although this may not always be the case. Serious breaches will inevitably lead to the undermining of the democratic process and loss of confidence in the system.

Where democracy breaks down, it is usually a result of failures in these government criteria, rather than a failure to create economic growth.[1] Governments must listen to their citizens' voices, engage their participation, tolerate their protests, protect their freedoms, and respond to their needs. The erosion of these factors, sometimes undetected, is examined in Chapter 15.

A Stanford professor has set out the criteria for democracy to succeed. There must be free and fair elections.[2] This necessitates the active participation of the people as citizens in civic life. Protection of human rights must be granted to all citizens. The rule of law must prevail, applied equally to all citizens. But first, what do free and fair elections mean in practice?

The first rule is that there must be clarity over who is eligible to vote, and an up-to-date register must be maintained. Nowadays, this is usually based on a universal adult suffrage without any property or gender qualification. Some countries may disallow those in prison or of unsound mind. There can also be disagreement about the age qualification: 18, 21, or another age. Usually, but not always, voters are restricted to those residents in the country, voting in person or by postal vote, if necessary. Voting by citizens resident overseas may not be restrained by living with the consequences and associated costs of their vote. Each voter is entitled to only one vote and should be encouraged to register. Citizens should not be disqualified on the grounds of poverty or race. There is some evidence that some voters were improperly removed from the register in Pennsylvania in 2024.

Secondly, there should be no manipulation of constituency boundaries to favour one party, class, or group. The distortions have happened even in America. 'Gerrymandering' originated with Governor Elbridge Gerry of Massachusetts in the nineteenth century, where boundaries were drawn up in the shape of a salamander to his advantage. There are fears now that voter identification rules may be designed to exclude poorer voters, who may not have a driving licence or bank account. Trump loyalists have been appointed to the Election Board in Georgia, a critical State in the 2024 presidential election. They then changed the law to allow the questioning of the result and deferred certification of the result. Right-wing groups have challenged the registration of more than 100,000 people in Arizona, Wisconsin, Georgia, North Carolina, Michigan, and Nevada since November 2020, without much apparent evidence.[3]

Thirdly, if elections are genuinely to be free and fair, voters must cast their votes in a secret ballot without any intimidation. Violence and intimidation have become commonplace in some countries in 2024. Sometimes it has been committed by criminal gangs, anxious to grow their influence, sometimes by the government party, and sometimes by far-right candidates. In such circumstances, voters are free not to vote, as they wish, and some may spoil their ballot papers. In some countries, such as Australia, non-voters are liable to be fined. Voting is compulsory in many South American countries, which results in a very high turnout.

Fourthly, the count must be impartial, accurate, and all ballot boxes must be counted. This is helpful if candidates can attend the count. Outside observers may enhance confidence in the process, where appropriate candidates may seek a recount. In 2024, Russia, Rwanda, and Algeria reported that over 90% of voters had supported the incumbent, while the Venezuelan declared result was widely disbelieved, casting considerable doubt on the validity of the official result. Increasingly, there are claims that the declared results are fraudulent, due to outside influence, especially from Russia.

Fifthly, voters must understand the issues involved, which means that they should have available to them the various options. A free press is vital, so that different parties can present the facts according to their views without untruths or deliberate distortions. Unfortunately, often this does not happen, as much deliberate fake news and stories are circulated through social media. Where the Government has control over the press or television, it is unlikely to give equal coverage to opposing parties. Such elections may well be free, but they are not fair. Unfortunately, there is increasing interference by Governments attempting to manipulate information, especially on social media, to prevent voters from making their decisions based on the real facts. Harassing political opponents or even detaining them without trial, as happens in Israel, totally undermines the proper working of democracy.

Sixthly, elections must be free from foreign interference. This is critically important in view of Russian attempts to interfere in elections all over the world to promote their own interests. This appears to be increasingly commonplace through the skilful use of social media. [4] One recent example is Moldova, which has taken in the highest number of Ukrainian refugees, relative to its size. Russia wants to prevent Moldova from joining the EU and maintain its influence there. [5] To this end, they have openly used bribes, intimidation, double voting, and misinformation, as well as instigating violent street protests in the 2024 presidential election and referendum. [6]It has been estimated that Russia has spent $100 million to buy votes by such means as topping up pensions from funds channelled via an oligarch.[7]

The 2024 Romanian referendum, considered to be a vote to apply for EU membership, was narrowly passed after what the President claimed was an unprecedented attack on democracy, when criminal groups tried to buy 300,000 votes.

Another case was Georgia. The Government proclaimed a 54% majority in the 2024 parliamentary elections, which was contrary to exit polls. Observers reported many irregularities, including the distribution of pre-marked ballot papers, the forced expulsion of observers from the polling stations, the violation of voting secrecy, and the exertion of pressure on state employees to secure their votes. The EU had major reservations about the result, but Viktor Orban endorsed it. While the pro-Russia Georgia Dream Party continues in power, it seems likely to be able to thwart the will of around 80% of the population, which favours eventually joining the EU. The president declined to accept the result of the election and urged citizens to make peaceful protests. Putin has emerged successful in what was not a fair election.

Seventhly, when the votes are accurately counted, the results must be correctly announced, and the losers must accept the result. This test was challenged by Trump in the 2020 presidential election.

Eighthly, the three elements of Government, the Legislature, the Executive, and the Judiciary, though connected, must be able to operate independently. This important principle is covered in more detail in Chapter 14. Finally, democracy may be suspended in times of war or national disaster, but should be resumed once normality returns.

Some of these fundamental tests have been broken in recent years in the USA. There have been allegations of Russian interference in elections, refusal to accept the results, and the independence of the judiciary has been called into question. In 2024, concerns about Russian interference in the European elections gave rise to concerns about the proper working of the system. European political groups said that they will demand swift action over Russian interference allegations and plan to debate the issue, fearing the scandal's impact on the June 2024 elections. This arose when an investigation by the Czech authorities uncovered what it said was a pro-Russia influence operation in Europe involving pro-Russian Ukrainian politician Viktor Medvedchuk and the Voice of Europe. The investigation showed that Moscow "has approached MEPs, but also paid, to promote Russian propaganda here", Belgian Prime Minister Alexander De Croo said during a debate in the Belgian Parliament. "A full and transparent internal investigation by the President of the European Parliament is now needed", said Renew Europe Group President, Valerie Hayer.[8]

Respect for Minorities: Northern Ireland

While the majority party can make all the decisions, it needs to respect the rights of the minority if the system is to function effectively. Opposition rights need to be protected and respected. Parties can be opposed to the government of the day, but still be considered part of the 'loyal opposition', an expression of respect used in the UK.

In extreme cases, abuse can lead to genocide, as has happened in parts of Africa and some Slavic states. Israel often ignores the rights of Palestinians, while Myanmar, which had fought for its democracy, shocked the world when it maltreated the Muslim Rohingya people. Minority groups need to buy into the system and participate with the majority party. Whenever the governing party abuses the rights of the minority, this is a recipe for disaster, as Northern Ireland has demonstrated.

When Ireland achieved its independence from British rule in 1921, the island was partitioned into two separate countries. The Nationalist part, predominantly Roman Catholic, formed the Irish Free State, while the Unionist North, predominantly Protestant, remained part of the United Kingdom. The two communities were educated separately, with most Nationalists learning to speak the Irish language and even playing different sports. Religion became a form of tribal identification. The Nationalists aspired to be part of a United Ireland, and indeed, a small number of militants forming the IRA or Irish Republican Army, were prepared to employ violence to achieve this end. From the outset, the Unionists held most seats in Stormont, the local Parliament. Catholics faced discrimination, particularly in employment and housing. There were allegations of gerrymandering, whereby political boundaries were manipulated to ensure Protestant control. Violence erupted periodically between the guerrilla Irish Republican Army and the police.

In the 1960s, a civil rights movement emerged to end discrimination. After an outbreak of civil unrest, the British army was called in to restore order. This led to thirty years of conflict, involving loyalist and republican paramilitaries, the State forces, and gruesome sectarian murders. 'The Troubles' claimed 3,500 lives and over 50,000 injuries.

The British and Irish Governments, with the help of American mediation, brought matters to a long overdue close in

1998, when the Belfast Agreement [9] was signed after thirty years of conflict. Both nationalists and loyalists were represented in the Government, disarmament took place, and agreement was reached to retain the status of Northern Ireland, unless both Northern Ireland and the Irish Republic voted to end it. The Stormont Assembly in Belfast would manage day-to-day political decisions.

Deliberative Democracy: Citizens' Assemblies

Politicians in many countries are accused of losing touch with their voters. Populists, such as Donald Trump and Boris Johnson, claim to know the 'will of the people', which may or may not be true, but is impossible to prove. While individual politicians have access to opinion polls and clinics with their own constituents, they can still lose touch with views on important topics. Recent research by the Electoral Commission in Ireland showed that 61% of voters believe that the people, not the politicians, should make the most important decisions. [8] Judging by the demonstrations in America, Britain, and other European countries, many voters believe that their Governments do not know the will of the people over Gaza, while they continue to arm Israel.

One attempt to resolve this problem is through Citizens' Assemblies. Typically, in Ireland, 99 citizens are asked to join an assembly to deliberate over some important subject. The citizens are requested to give up periodic weekends to discuss a given topic. Allowance in the selection is made for age, gender, and class. Members are addressed by experts on the topic, and a debate is facilitated to allow different viewpoints, before they eventually make recommendations to the Government.

Ireland adopted Citizens' Assemblies in 2016. The subjects ranged from abortion to loss of biodiversity and gender equality. Their lifespan ranged from a year to eighteen months in duration. The experience has generally been good, and their recommendations were usually accepted by the Government. Whatever the chosen democratic model, it had to work within an economic framework, so how the Government handled economic growth and distributed its rewards had an important bearing on voters' confidence in the working of the whole democratic system.

Citizens' Assemblies form part of a branch of politics, known as 'sortition', the selection of representation by way of lot. The original Athenian model was based on random selection to govern for a two-year period. Nowadays, it is normally based on stratified sampling to permit greater representation of minorities. It cannot be perfectly representative, due to the unwillingness of some citizens to serve, but, nevertheless, it is workable, somewhat akin to jury selection.

The system has the advantage of being transparent, promotes equality, and should diminish money and narrow party considerations, while it does not permit permanent representation, acting as an antidote to populism. It has some distinguished supporters, including Rory Stewart, a former British minister and current Yale academic, who can appreciate both its theoretical and practical advantages, considering it to be a possible model for the future, as a way of preserving representation.

Realignment

In the past, it was easy to explain political parties on a Left/Right spectrum, but this is now changing. Over time, the support for left-wing parties diminished as trade union membership fell. With the growth of the far right, however, there is increasing support for strongmen, in particular Putin, causing the central social democratic grouping to seriously decline in most European countries. New parties can spring up at short notice and spread their message through social media. They can quickly draw major support from traditional parties, as the Conservatives discovered in the 2024 General Election and subsequent local elections. In the current era, party allegiance is more volatile than in the past.

Sometimes it is difficult to decide whether a party is on the Right or Left of the spectrum. Many people would see Russia, which for years was on the extreme Left, as having moved to the extreme Right under Putin, with massive inequality and little regard for the welfare of poorer people. Perhaps that explains why it attracts support from European parties of the far right.

In Ireland, all significant parties gravitated to the centre. This included the two largest parties, which fought on different sides in a civil war a century ago. Labour played no role in the war and was less to the Left than in most European countries. Sinn Féin, which translates into 'Ourselves Alone', set out its stall on the Left and grew to become the largest party, growing rapidly in recent years on a populist agenda. However, it dropped support dramatically in the 2024 local elections, apparently due to a liberal approach to immigration, on which the party was fundamentally divided, as well as the party's handling of several internal scandals.

provide for enlargement, the need to become energy-independent with the development of clean sources, such as hydrogen, and the need to provide for its defence in the light of possible diminishing support for NATO, there is no shortage of challenges ahead and reforms needed.

Like the UN, the EU has attracted considerable criticism. Some people believe that there is a democratic deficit in its structure, given the considerable power exercised by its unelected executive. Others focus on its high cost of operation, waste, bureaucracy, and slowness of decision-making. There are allegations that it can fail to provide food in emergency situations. Questions have been asked about how members of parliament spend their time, since the majority of them have second jobs. Although these interests must be disclosed, clearly, there can be conflicts of interest, as well as diversion of members' time, both of which have eroded public confidence in the system. [4]

There are now concerns for its future competitiveness in comparison with the USA and China. A report by a former prime minister of Italy and President of the European Central Bank outlined major challenges facing the EU. Critical changes will require substantial investment and the encouragement of innovation, particularly in technology. In the absence of major improvements, the future of European welfare, its environment, and its freedom are placed at risk. [5]

Freedom of movement is also under attack, as countries wrestle with immigration. Germany introduced border checks in 2024. Another worry is the absence of strong, stable governments in the increasingly polarised France and Germany, which could inhibit necessary changes.

Another feature of current democracy is the rise in the number of people who do not vote, especially young Millennials. Most are very concerned about climate change, which could dramatically affect their future, but the growth of the Green Party agenda has been thwarted by agricultural and other vested interests. Many young voters are disinterested in politics and are cynical about any party addressing their issues around affordable housing, rising inequality, and little real growth in income. Affordability of housing, of course, is a problem all over Europe, but Ireland does not score badly. A survey by the IMF on the price of an average house relative to average income in 34 European countries found that Ireland was second best after Denmark. [10]Nevertheless, politicians have a conflict of interest in addressing the problem, since many of them are landlords. Decreased involvement and growing volatility are now features of the political system.

CHAPTER 5

Liberal Democracy, Economic Growth, and the Role of Banks

During the aftermath of the Second World War, economic growth became the primary goal of the protagonists in the recovery to restore the infrastructure and provide jobs for the citizens. Gross National Product or GNP became the norm to assess progress in the market economies, accepted with enthusiasm by politicians. In 1957, the UK Tory Prime Minister Harold Macmillan ran an election campaign with the slogan: 'You never had it so good'. Economic growth freed up funding available for them to offer to voters, either to increase services or reduce taxes. The high income tax rates of the 1960s declined rapidly. Voters could choose between the parties, which set out their proposals in manifestos at election time.

The Importance of Economic Growth

The Western democratic model became widely copied. After the fall of the Berlin Wall in 1989 and the breakup of the USSR, Eastern European States adopted market economics, providing new outlets for trade. Confidence grew that the Great Depression of the 1930s, which had generated enormous hardship, would never be repeated, but this growth was to be jeopardised by the behaviour of the banks.

Economic growth associated with democratic countries has greatly enhanced the popularity of democracy. Travel and tourism demonstrated to visitors how living standards could be enhanced through the adoption of a democratic system. People wanted to enjoy these benefits, causing liberal democracy to flourish, attracting increasing numbers of adherents and supporters. The era of globalisation provided a further boost for the system. Undoubtedly, many formerly poor countries benefited enormously from the outsourcing of activities, a practice that grew with the spread of the internet. India was one of the first to benefit, as skilled programmers, who had been recruited to sort out the problems of the 'Year 2000', were happy to return home, where they would be paid lower salaries than they had received in the USA. Over time, many other developing countries offered their services.

Confidence grew that economic growth could continue indefinitely at varying rates over time, since the ups and downs of trade cycles were under control. Through the judicious use of Keynesian economics and conservative regulation, the banking system appeared to be in safe hands. The 'Washington Consensus' targeted low rates of inflation, while international capital markets, the growth of globalisation, and new technologies could help avoid undue concentration of risks. But technology did not upset the system; rather, it was the behaviour of the banks.

Banking

Throughout history, there have always been periodic banking crises, usually accompanied by a stock market crash, the most famous recent example being in 1929. The initial driver is increased risk-taking by investors, aided by a drop in credit standards by the banks. The correction can be very severe and long-lasting, with panic selling flooding the market, since psychological factors, first identified in seventeenth-century Holland during the 'black tulip bubble'. [1]

In 2008, the world experienced an unexpected banking crisis due to reckless bank lending in the property market. Investors sought to withdraw their deposits, which ultimately led to a run on the banks and the collapse of many banks worldwide. Its origins stemmed from foolish lending by Savings and Loan Institutions, supplying the mortgage market in the US. 'NINJA' loans were advanced to customers who had no income, jobs, or assets, often with initial teaser rates of interest. Because loans could be sold on to other banks by way of securitisation, it duly spread widely as a kind of financial pandemic in the era where freedom of capital was encouraged across national boundaries. The eventual consequence was an era of austerity, where ordinary citizens suffered great hardship to pay for the disaster.

There are two types of banks with very different cultures: retail and investment banking. Retail banks, traditionally run very conservatively, take deposits from customers and provide loans to them. Wholesale investment banks are risk-takers, putting together deals and raising capital for their customers. After the Great Crash of 1929, the US Congress passed the Glass-Steagall Act, separating the banks into two different and distinct categories. However, with its repeal in 1999, it gave investment banks access to the vast deposits of the retail banks, and lending standards fell dramatically. So, how could basic lending standards collapse?

The answer was rooted in the new banking culture. Investment bankers traditionally received vast bonuses, based on short-term profit performance, leading to ridiculous and reckless competition in lending. Banking differs from traditional industry in that profits are impossible to measure in the short term, since an estimate for bad loans is difficult to forecast without perfect foresight. Many banks believed that serious falls in the property market were very improbable, so profits in the short term could not be accurately measured with any degree of certainty. Loan books were expanded by relaxing conservative limits, and foolish competition ensued, driven ultimately by a greed for bonuses.

The banking crash of 2008 did damage not only to individual reputations but also to their influence in the capitalist system. Free markets constituted a cornerstone of financial capitalism, and a major setback seriously threatened the popularity of democracy around the globe. Only one little-known economist had foreseen the possibility of such a crash.[2] Few people in the world of today believe the view of Karl Marx, that capitalism must eventually collapse through its inherent flaws. Nevertheless, damage has been done to confidence in capitalism.

In 2023, the collapse of Silicon Valley Bank sent ripples around both banking and the tech industries after President Trump had relaxed regulatory rules under pressure from the powerful banking lobby. The much-vaunted regulatory system was unable to prevent the collapse, following a run on the bank by depositors, as had happened many times in the past, but which happened very quickly with digital banking.

Another banking crisis in the future is not impossible. International banks and speculators can precipitate a collapse of domestic banks, as happened in Iceland in 2008.[3] Banks can still compete in a reckless manner in pursuit of profits and bonuses at the expense of prudent risk management. It seems that they were often willing to lend heavily against vastly inflated and possibly fraudulent real estate valuations, existing in the Trump group.

Credit Suisse, traditionally a highly conservatively managed bank, showed how brittle the present system is. Its risk management and oversight by management proved inadequate, and in 2023, it had to be taken over by its competitor, UBS, as part of a rescue managed by the Swiss authorities to avert a banking sector meltdown.[4]

Central banks will seek to rescue banks in trouble. It would be naïve to believe that they have all the answers to prevent a major future crisis. A prominent financial commentator has explained that, while the banking system is in theory private, in practice it is a ward of the State.[5] Bankers can still disregard the norms of prudence in the management of their banks, often with impunity. A crisis could arise in the unregulated shadow banking sector or perhaps through using derivatives, mathematically complex financial risks, described by Warren Buffett as 'financial weapons of mass destruction'. It may not be restricted to Western banks, as China has been experiencing a property bubble for some years.

As a former corporate lender, I found it hard to understand how such reckless lending could occur. In the late 1980s, on a trip to London, some senior bankers there tried to persuade me that restricting mortgages to 3.5 times income and 65%/75% of the property value, as was common in Ireland, was far too conservative. People needed somewhere to live in London, and they were happy to lend up to 100% of the value or more for furnishings. Prices must always rise, other than minor dips.[6] This argument sounded eerily familiar to me. I recalled that I had heard it from Irish farmers years before, when land was priced around IR£4,000 an acre, while yields were typically

IR100/200 per acre and interest rates were almost 20%. The crash in land values duly arrived. I smelled a similar bubble in London and rang a stockbroker to see if I could short-sell London property. I was told that this was impossible and far too risky. When the fall in London property prices came shortly afterwards, I reflected on the fortune that I might have made, but consoled myself with the thought that such a disaster could never occur in Irish banking. How wrong I was!

Unfortunately, the crash of 2008 undermined confidence in capitalism in the longer term. Well-paid bankers were seen to be able to pass on their risks to other banks and investors with personal impunity, calling people to doubt its fairness. People also questioned whether it was the best role model for sustainable economic growth. Once confidence in capitalism is eroded, democracy can quickly come under attack, since it is the usual political system under which capitalism operates. [7]

CHAPTER 6

Democracy Beyond National Borders: UN and EU

Once democracy had spread widely, it was natural that it should seek to transcend national boundaries. In the aftermath of the First World War, there was a universal hope that it would turn out to be the 'War to End all Wars'.

The League of Nations

The League of Nations, set up in 1920, was the first intergovernmental organisation whose principal mission was to maintain world peace. The founding force behind the creation of the League was the president of the United States, Woodrow Wilson, but despite this, America never joined. It started with 42 members and at its peak reached 58 members. It centred around a General Assembly and an Executive of 5 members, comprising Great Britain, France, Italy, and Japan, together with four members elected by the General Assembly for a 3-year period. It also established a Permanent Court of International Justice.

Italy resigned following its invasion of Abyssinia, and Japan resigned in connection with the Sino-Japanese War. Russia eventually joined but was expelled following its invasion of Finland. The German Weimar Republic also joined, but resigned with the rise of Naziism in 1933. It was largely unsuccessful in its main aim of preventing war, unsurprisingly, when the protagonists included its Council members. It failed to prevent the Chaco War between Bolivia and Paraguay and did not become involved in the Spanish Civil War. Members started to resign, and it became increasingly irrelevant, as it failed to halt the Nazi expansion into Europe.

It did, however, manage to set up some important organisations addressing specific issues. These included the predecessors of the World Health Organisation (WHO), the International Labour Organisation (ILO), and the High Commission for Refugees (HCR). It also helped draw attention to issues, such as epidemics, slavery, and child labour. In addition, it strengthened the concept of collective security, which was to lead to the creation of the North Atlantic Treaty Organisation (NATO) and expanded the rule of law globally.

The United Nations

During the Second World War, the Allies decided to set up a replacement for the defunct League of Nations. A Charter was drawn up, reflecting President Roosevelt's Four Freedoms: Freedom of Speech, Freedom of Worship, Freedom from Want, and Freedom from Fear. It was signed by 50 States, but expanded to 193 members in an era of decolonisation. Only one country, Indonesia, has ever resigned, while no country has been expelled.

Its stated purposes are maintaining international peace and security, developing friendly relations among nations, promoting social progress, better living standards, and human rights. It has more recently added achieving sustainability to its aims. Its principal organs are the Security Council, the General Assembly, the Economic and Social Council, the International Court of Justice, and the Secretariat. It has multiple specialised

Agencies, including the World Bank, the World Health Organization (WHO), the World Food Programme, the United Nations Educational, Social and Cultural Organization (UNESCO), and the United Nations Children's Emergency Fund (UNICEF).

Power ultimately resides in the Security Council, comprising five Permanent members, being the Second World War victors, the US, UK, France, Russia, and China, together with 10 non-permanent members elected for two-year terms. All countries have a single vote in the General Assembly, which makes recommendations to the Security Council, but in practice, it is only a debating chamber.

Like its predecessor, the League of Nations, it has little effectiveness when one of the permanent members is involved in war, as was shown during the Cold War and currently in the invasion of Ukraine. Questions have now been asked about whether it is failing in its primary goal of keeping world peace. Its mediation in conflicts in the Middle East and Vietnam proved to be ineffective, and increasingly it turned its attention to interventions in conflict areas with the presence of observers or lightly armed troops. In most cases, these have been successful, though they notably failed to prevent genocide in Bosnia.

Its social and economic achievements, which absorb the bulk of its budget, have been more successful with a reduction in world poverty and hunger, increased education, advancing women's rights, reducing disease, and lowering infant mortality. Its efforts to resolve the 2008 banking crisis by imposing heavy austerity measures on the most indebted countries through the International Monetary Fund (IMF), an independent body within the UN, are more controversial. [1]

Its critics accuse it of wasteful spending, excessive bureaucracy, and occasional corruption. It has serial offenders who have taken loans without implementing the promised reforms, such as Argentina, Pakistan, and Egypt, together with smaller countries such as Angola, Ecuador, and Jordan. [2] While there is some truth in this, its net benefits have exceeded its shortcomings. The major challenge facing it is climate change and obtaining agreement on reducing carbon emissions, a daunting task that has provoked much disagreement. A major forum for discussion will be ecological sustainability in areas where the extinction of animal and plant species is feared, together with the problem of ocean pollution. Failure would precipitate major problems for the entire world and prevent it from delivering on its motto 'Peace, Dignity and Equality on a Healthy Planet'.

There are now increasing concerns that the existing liberal international system is slowly coming apart and could degenerate into anarchy. The primary aim of keeping peace has failed in both Ukraine and Gaza. Several of the UN's key institutions are becoming moribund, with the World Trade Organisation in stasis for five years. The IMF is torn between the green agenda and ensuring financial stability, while trade wars are now a reality.

Regional Groupings: The European Union

The European Union was the first and most important regional group. The EU started after the Second World War as an attempt to promote peace through economic union, comprising 27 States and an approximate population of 450 million people, nearly 6% of the world's population and 18% of global GDP. Its cornerstone is a Customs Union, paving the way for a Single Market. Voting operates with a qualified majority, which provides protection for smaller States. Ten more countries are aspiring to join. Iceland has announced a referendum to join the EU in the face of US tariff threats, while only the UK has left.

The Customs Union is based on the theory of comparative advantage, as was first set out more than two centuries ago by David Ricardo.[3] Both trade parties should benefit if tariffs are abolished. Consequently, members have received large economic benefits from free trade, a major advance on the traditional mercantilist world, which fostered protection by way of tariffs.

In the early days, the EU performed poorly with dismal economic growth and slow decision-making, earning it the description of 'Éuroschlerosis'. This was to change fundamentally with the abolition of internal barriers to trade and the creation of a Single Market with 27 member states. It is centred on four freedoms: Free movement of goods, capital, services, and people. This is designed to increase competition, labour specialisation, and economies of scale, allowing labour to move where it is required. It is estimated to have increased the GDP of member states by 9%.

There is disagreement about its future development. Federalists want to see an ever closer union and alignment of rules, but others prefer a looser arrangement of member states. Some want to see membership expand, while others prefer to allow a period of digestion to achieve smoother cooperation among existing members. There are currently eight applicants wishing to join, including Ukraine and several Balkan countries, with the first applicant being Moldova. Given the need to

Eurosceptics believe that the EU undermines national sovereignty and the nation-state. It is attacked as elitist, while lacking democratic legitimacy and transparency. It also encourages high levels of immigration, which is disruptive. There are Eurosceptic parties in most European countries, such as Hungary, Slovakia, and Romania. However, the temptation to leave may be tempered by the UK experience. The EU's failure to condemn outright the Israeli bombing of civilians in Gaza has diminished its reputation in the Arab world, as has its failure to fully support Ukraine.

The 2024 European Elections and Their Consequences

Concern for future directions in the EU is growing. The support for the far right has grown rapidly in recent years. For example, in Portugal, support for Chega ('Enough'), an anti-immigrant, anti-Islam populist party, has increased from 1% in 2019, when it was founded, to over 18% in 2024 [6] and over 22% in 2025. Other European countries have shown a similar pattern in varying degrees.

The French President, Emmanuel Macron, a prominent and unapologetic globalist, fears for the future of Europe if it does not tackle three crucial issues: the threat of Russian aggression, slow economic growth relative to both America and China, and the rise of far-right parties.[7] He could have added the need to finance an ever-growing budget. It is unnecessary to adopt Orban's far-right policies to "Make Europe Great Again", but action and firm leadership are needed.

Despite France's historic opposition to far-right parties resulting from the Second World War, Macron fears for the erosion of the fundamental principles of liberal democracy, such as freedom of the press, independence of the judiciary, cultural diversity, and academic freedom. Jihadist atrocities in France led to more people demanding a crackdown on crime. In Germany, which had also feared a resurgence of Nazism, there remains concern about defence against Russia and the excessive reliance on Russian oil, which encouraged the growth of AfD, particularly after Chancellor Merkel welcomed over one million immigrants.

In the 2024 election, far-right parties won 184 seats, compared with 111 in 2019. Before the election, there were only three countries with a right-wing government (Hungary, Italy, and Slovakia). Far-right groups have now become the largest group in two more countries (France, Austria) and are equal in Holland, where left-wing parties also prospered. It became the second largest group in two further countries (Germany and Romania). AfD in Germany forced the Socialists into third place, despite AfD comments expressing admiration for the SS, Hitler's paramilitary group, which was responsible for numerous atrocities and was involved in several scandals. It is particularly well supported in the former East Germany. The Greens in general lost support, as did Viktor Orban's party in Hungary. Although there are many splits in their ranks, such as support for Ukraine, the far right will definitely become a greater threat to EU harmony in the future.

It was not a good election for democrats. Centrist parties still control the Parliament, albeit with a smaller majority. Provided that they can provide a united front and sort out their general differences, they can still manage the overall direction of the EU. Nevertheless, far-right parties performed well in many countries, which could have enormous consequences. [8] Early indications are that the EU will adopt a more right-wing approach to immigration.

Macron's response of calling a snap French election, hoping to halt the growth of the Far-Right, was misjudged. Marine Le Pen's National Rally Party won the most seats, followed by the New Popular Front, comprising far-right to left of centre parties, leaving Macron's centrist Ensemble Group dwindling in third place. But this was not the end of the matter.

In the absence of a clear majority, a second round was required shortly afterwards. With tactical voting by the left wing and the Central parties, the result was that the Far-Right was reduced to third place behind both the left-wing and centrist parties. The result was a 'hung parliament', which makes decision-making problematic. But, nevertheless, it sent out a strong warning about the growing strength of the far right. It remains to be seen whether or not a stable and lasting Government comprising numerous and diverse factions can be formed to support President Macron. The main unifying factor is a strong dislike of Marine Le Pen's party, with its anti-EU attitude and dubious commitment to democracy. Opposition parties eventually brought down the previous Barnier government.

The growth of the Far-Right in Germany was shown in the 2024 State elections, particularly in what was formerly East Germany. In Thuringia, AfD, whose leader has been convicted for using Nazi slogans, became the biggest party, which was the first time this happened in any State since the Second World War. In neighbouring Saxony, it finished strongly as the second-largest party. Similarly, in Austria, the right-wing Freedom Party emerged with more seats than any other party.

Although no party has suggested leaving the EU or the euro, anti-EU sentiment may increase significantly, which could adversely impact the development of EU policies and its expansion. It makes it more difficult to achieve change at a time of rising insecurity and growing protectionism around the globe. Intimidation, suppression of freedom of speech, and abuse of the right to protest do not sit easily with democracy.

It seems probable that Marine Le Pen, leader of the strongly performing French National Rally (formerly National Front), is a potential future French President and Moscow sympathiser. In 2025, she was sentenced to imprisonment for embezzling EU funds to pay herself and her staff, while being prevented from standing for office for five years. Unless she successfully appeals, she will be prevented from standing for the presidency in 2027.

Another key woman is Georgia Meloni, leader of Brothers of Italy and Italian Prime Minister, who will play an important role behind the scenes. A further person, who may feature, is Geert Wilders, leader of the Netherlands' Party for Freedom, which has a strong anti-Islamic stance and is part of the Dutch government coalition.

One particular concern is the continuation of support for Ukraine. When President Zelenski addressed the European Parliament, he was greeted by a standing ovation from all those present, with the exception of two Irish MEPs, neither of whom was subsequently re-elected. Many members of the far right are closet supporters of Russia, although they are unlikely to declare their allegiance publicly. There may be pressure to review EU foreign policy in general, while difficulties in enforcing regulations in Hungary, Italy, and Slovakia could also increase. With Hungary holding the initial EU presidency in 2024, this was a major concern, particularly after Orban quickly made an early visit to Russia, without obtaining prior EU approval, to discuss 'peace' in Ukraine.

Ireland, which held local government elections simultaneously, had a 49% turnout. The campaign was marred by abuse, violence, and intimidation, as occurred in other countries. Mainly, this came from right-wing groups, who targeted immigrant candidates in particular,[8] but Ireland's system of proportional representation makes it more difficult for extremists to be elected. There is no mainstream far-right party yet, so there is no far-right Irish MEP. However, anti-immigrant candidates had a minimal impact in the local elections. Concern has been expressed by the Irish President, Michael D. Higgins, over the intimidation of public library staff by right-wing opponents in connection with books not agreeing with their beliefs. Also, the appearance of masked anti-migrant protesters outside the house of the Taoiseach has been widely deplored.[9]

Other than Greenland, an Associate Member, which resigned over fishery disputes in 1985, no member of the EU had resigned before Britain did so. The experience is instructive. It is not easy to unscramble eggs, but future defections cannot be ruled out with an increased number of Eurosceptics in the European Parliament.

The Brexit Fiasco

The UK Prime Minister, David Cameron, announced that a referendum would take place on the continuation of membership of the European Union as a sop to his Eurosceptic right-wing members. Since most other parties backed the policy to remain, although the Labour Party, under the left-wing Jeremy Corbyn, did not canvass actively, it was widely expected that the electorate would vote to remain. Only UKIP, the United Kingdom Independence Party, with few members, but backed by the influential *Daily Express* tabloid newspaper, urged the people to vote to leave, while many members of the Tory right-wing and the Democratic Unionists also supported 'Leave'.

Astonishingly, there was little economic analysis in government white papers, which could have explained the implications of leaving. Many voters did not understand the difference between the Customs Union and the Single Market. Where there is no hard data, politicians fill the vacuum with their own 'facts', designed to woo voters in their direction.

The referendum took place on 23 June 2016. 'Leave' won by a very small margin. So, Britain left the EU with effect from 31 January 2017. Britain had refused to join the original European Union and was subsequently refused admission on two occasions before it eventually joined in 1973. Two years later, a referendum on continued membership showed that a majority of 67% wished to stay in the EU. Attitudes had clearly changed.

The result threw up some anomalies. Scotland and Northern Ireland had both voted to remain but were forced to leave. The upshot was that direct democracy had overturned the will of Parliament. The slogan gained widespread publicity that "Brexit means Brexit", but important matters had received scant attention, such as whether Britain should leave the Single Market and the need to avoid an internal border with the Irish Republic. The influences on voters will be examined in the next chapter.

The Leave campaign had argued that it would be easy to negotiate a trade deal with the EU, whose members wanted to sell their cars and wine to Britain. Boris Johnson had claimed that Britain could 'have its cake and eat it', which proved to be hopelessly naïve. 'Divide and Rule' was not possible, since the EU showed a united front, preventing cherry-picking by the UK. The voters had been told that there would be enormous prosperity through savings from leaving, since they would no longer need to pay membership fees and would be freed from costly regulation. This, too, proved to be wide of the mark.

The new premier, Theresa May, previously a 'Remainer', rapidly became a hard-line 'Leaver', dismissing the possibility of the country remaining a member of either the Customs Union or the Single Market. With a limited parliamentary majority, she was obliged to depend on support from the DUP, a Northern Ireland Evangelical party determined to stop any border on the sea between Britain and Northern Ireland, but which represented less than 1% of the UK population. Her party was badly divided, and after three attempts to get her bill through Parliament, she resigned in June 2019.

The next Prime Minister, Boris Johnson, adopted a very aggressive attitude towards the EU. When he sought to prorogue or suspend Parliament, seeking to avoid parliamentary scrutiny as is normal in a democracy, he was prevented from so doing by the Courts. The judges were denounced by the *Daily Mail* as 'Enemies of the People' after they insisted that the law must be followed and that Parliament could not be circumvented. Johnson insisted on making demands that the EU could not accept, since they would undermine the Single Market. The main sticking point was the Northern Ireland Protocol, an arrangement to avoid a hard border between

Northern Ireland and the Irish Republic, which had been put in place by the Good Friday Agreement in 1998 to end conflict between the unionist and nationalist communities. Eventually, a formula was found, and the Withdrawal Agreement was ratified in January 2020, three years after the decision to leave the EU had been made.

Within months of signing, Boris Johnson announced that the Protocol was to be abandoned. The jingoistic right wing of the party harked back nostalgically to 'Britannia Rules the Waves' and felt that it could now 'waive the rules'. This caused serious reputational damage to Britain with allegations of bad faith and the traditional accusation of 'Perfidious Albion'. Ian Paisley junior, a member of the DUP, a Northern Irish party that had never signed the Good Friday Agreement, claimed that Boris Johnson had promised to tear up the Protocol even before he agreed to sign it.[10] The assertion was confirmed by Dominic Cummings, his chief advisor at the time, before the matter was eventually resolved by yet another British Prime Minister, Rishi Sunak, in 2023, agreeing to the Windsor Framework, very much on the lines proposed by Theresa May four years earlier.

The economic consequences of Brexit for the UK have proved to be severe, estimated at a 2/3% reduction in the growth of GDP. Economic growth is amongst the lowest in Europe, exacerbated by low productivity, tight budgetary constraints, and rising inequality, without any clear strategy to redress the problems. There is unrest in the over-extended National Health Service, which did not receive the extra funding promised by the 'Leave' campaign. Nor has the number of immigrants and asylum-seekers diminished, a factor which later encouraged the growth of the far-right populist Reform Party.

On the ground, there was chaos in the port of Dover and lengthy delays for lorries, together with long queues at customs and passport control. Some businesses found form-filling too time-consuming and ceased trying to trade with the EU. In general, the red tape was retained, eventually becoming red, white, and blue tape to conform to the regulations of other trading partners. Given the absence of any contingency planning, none of this should be surprising.

Farmers could not get migrants to harvest their crops. Supermarkets ran short of certain vegetables. The number of immigrants was not reduced, as had been predicted by those who relished 'taking back control'. The expected investment failed to materialise, while the City of London lost business. A major British microchip designer chose to float its shares in America, rather than London. It was followed by other companies that moved their primary stock exchange listings to the USA.

The forecast that in 'Global Britain' London could become Singapore-on-Thames, based on international trade and economic globalisation, proved to be a fantasy. The trade agreements made were little more than 'stick and paste' copies of EU agreements, while no trade agreement was reached until May 2025, after Rishi Sunak, the Tory prime minister, announced that this was no longer a priority.[11] For some people, London became Leningrad-on-Thames, where Russian oligarchs laundered their wealth.

Unsurprisingly, the economic performance of the UK compared unfavourably with that of Euroland. Over eight years after Brexit, the problems for businesses in Britain remain, as the costs of red tape for both importers and exporters are immense. Many companies, as a consequence, particularly in the food and plant industries, have ceased trading with the EU, rather than meeting the requirements of the Single Market. [12]

The whole saga has been a sad reflection on the workings of democracy in Britain. It seemed that at times the Ship of State was being steered too close to rocks by captains mindful of promises made to voters before the referendum. Unfortunately, voters were not made aware of the facts at the time of the referendum, but instead were showered with wild, unsupportable promises.

By ignoring the wishes of the people of Scotland and Northern Ireland, the whole question of the future of the Union has come into the spotlight. If they were forced to leave the EU, they probably would have wished to remain in the Single Market and Customs Union. A 'Hard Brexit' imposed serious economic costs on them, but under Theresa May's 'Brexit means Brexit', a tautology with no obvious meaning, rapidly became a Hard Brexit. The deep divisions amongst both MPs and the electorate deepened, as the bitterness increased, when opponents of Brexit were dubbed 'Remoaners'. A Government, even though it had a large majority in Parliament, was hopelessly split on how to implement the result. Attempts were made to steamroll Parliament, and the judiciary was attacked. A treaty made after lengthy negotiations was quickly reversed, causing serious reputational damage to the nation.

Negotiations were not helped by reckless promises that the process would be quick and simple. The British people might indeed want to 'Get Brexit Done', but totally unrealistic demands and jingoistic slogans could not succeed with the EU negotiators. Reality had to be faced at the end of the day. At an early stage, Boris Johnson assured the public that "Brexit means Brexit" and that they would make a "titanic success" of it. That may be so, but it should be remembered that the vast majority of the passengers on that unfortunate ship drowned!

The basic question: How did a great nation bring itself to a point of such wilful self-harm?[13] One commentator believed that there was an element of self-pity. Britain had helped to win the Second World War, but had not received adequate recognition or thanks. This, combined with an air of superiority, led to a strong distaste for the EU. Another factor was a rejection of the status quo, where Britain was lagging behind its neighbours in terms of economic growth. It was a rebellion that led to the rejection of the status quo, often found in the age of punk culture, which had survived for many years. Punk, imported from America to London in the 1970s, was not based on reason, but stood for anti-authoritarianism and not 'selling out'.

Sixty percent of both men and women aged between 50 and 64 years voted to leave. They could remember the era, if not of empire, at least when Britain was a leading world power. The Falklands War of the Thatcher era was well within their memory, as was the jingoistic triumphalism which accompanied it. The Leave campaign urged voters to 'take back control' and no longer act as 'a vassal'. They would become prosperous again once they could reject the shackles of bureaucracy, enjoy free markets, and make their own trade agreements. There was no shortage of journalists to spread these views, irrespective of their accuracy.

In the end, it was a strange and unlikely coalition. On one side was the 'red wall' of Northern English voters who hankered after their manufacturing past and the prosperity which it brought before the age of globalisation, but traditionally had always voted for Labour. On the other side was a group of affluent Tory right-wing politicians who nostalgically cherished a belief in England's glorious colonial past. Britain had never been invaded since the Norman Conquest twelve hundred years earlier. Many of these Tories, however, could afford to indulge their fantasies because they were independently wealthy and so could avoid the economic pain that would come with Brexit failure.

Brexit had not been a victory for British nationalism, but rather that of a very narrow English nationalism. English nationalism, which has its roots in Shakespearean England, sits uneasily beside Scottish or Welsh nationalism and has an ambiguous relationship with 'Britishness', now that the Empire no longer exists. [14] The views of the Scots and Northern Irish, who had voted overwhelmingly to remain, were totally disregarded. Only the interests of the diehard Northern Irish DUP were considered. The Welsh had voted narrowly to leave, with the help of many English citizens, based on blatant misinformation, which purported to show that the EU had neglected their financial interests and was destroying their industry. In fact, generous EU funding had been made available to them. The potential damage to the port of Holyhead on the Irish Sea was also conveniently ignored.

Brexit has led to very serious consequences, but it may have more fundamental consequences for British society. One well-known British journalist has suggested that it has sunk Britain's political class, synonymous with the Conservative Party, which was the predominant party of government for many years. [15] They always had a strong representation from the aristocracy and upper middle class. They emerged as the leaders of the 'Leave' campaign, purging the party of 'Remainers', but were heavily discredited by the reckless promises made and seemed destined to remain out of power for a considerable period of time. Their opponents described the fiasco as an 'Eton Mess', named after a dish originating in the well-known establishment school. The ruling political class may have changed for the foreseeable future.

Many Tory politicians, who forecast that Brexit would lead to the breakup of the EU, are likely to be disappointed. The DUP and some Tories had also believed naively that Irish self-interest would result in Ireland following Britain out of the EU. In fact, it may have done irreparable harm to the future of Great Britain, which should become clearer in the future, when the extent of national dissatisfaction becomes better understood. The promised savings from leaving have failed to materialise so far. Not many countries are likely to follow in the light of the Brexit experience. Most European countries can see the advantage of cooperating amongst themselves and becoming part of an international force in world affairs, which none of them could do individually. While Britain lost, the European Union emerged stronger.

A poll by Statista in May 2024 showed that 55% of Britons felt that Brexit had been a mistake. But no political party has advocated rejoining, fearful of restarting more bitter internal divisions. In the 2024 general election, it was again mired in scandal, as several close associates were investigated for betting on the date of the election with the benefit of insider knowledge. The upshot was a massive defeat for the Conservative Party. In contrast to Europe, the British general election showed a swing to the Left-Centre. Several prominent Brexiteers did not stand for re-election, while others lost their seats.

The Conservatives lost 160 seats, mainly to the Labour Party, but were also damaged by the Liberals and Nigel Farage's

Reform Party, an extreme right-wing nationalist party, whose members are often seen sporting 'Make Britain Great Again' badges. In their worst result since 2008, the Tories have become riven with internal divisions and lost considerable talent over Brexit, whether members fled or were deselected. It seems destined to move increasingly further to the right of the political spectrum. [16] The next election will be a test for the Conservatives in the light of rising support for the Reform Party, which made enormous gains at the expense of the Tories in the subsequent local elections. If the Reform Party were to gain substantial support, democracy in Britain would face the same challenge as it does in the rest of Western Europe.

Britain, although democracy has been weakened during the leadership of Johnson, has withstood the challenge of populism and restored its democratic credentials in 2024. The turnout was only 60%, compared with 67.3% at the last general election, which could partly have resulted from stricter voter identification rules, as well as general dissatisfaction with political parties. The Labour Party gained over 200 seats, despite receiving only 34% of the votes, an increase of less than 2% five years earlier, and also lost five seats to pro-Palestine candidates. The underlying reason was not so much a growth in the support for Labour, which received three million fewer votes than Labour received under Jeremy Corbyn, as the British first-past-the-post system of democracy. However, the results were analysed, and it was certainly not a ringing endorsement of Brexit. Thinktank UK concluded that 78% of Labour voters would vote for a return to the EU. It seems that an element of 'Begret' has set in.

It appears that the European Union is more successful than the United Nations in achieving democratic agreement and cooperation from its members in different countries. It has the advantage of having fewer members and considerable financial muscle. Thus, when Poland and Hungary breached their rules on the independence of the judiciary, it was able to withhold the payment of grants to them. It also succeeded in enforcing the rules on Brexit, despite efforts by Britain to divide and rule.

Euroscepticism needs to be kept in perspective. A 2025 poll showed that 74% of EU voters believed that their country had benefited from EU membership, the highest level of satisfaction ever.[17] 89% want to see greater unity in tackling global challenges, such as climate change, and 62% want the EU Parliament to take on a more prominent role.

The Brexit fiasco, with its theatrical features in Parliament, has drawn attention to the possible deliberate misleading of voters. The current Tory party leader, Kemi Badenoch, admitted that the party had made too many promises that could not be honoured. It also resulted in serious and enduring damage to relationships between Britain and individual EU States, especially Ireland. So, it is important to understand the kind of information that influences voters and where it originates when they place their mark on a ballot paper.

CHAPTER 7

Influences on Voters

Communication is the way individuals pass on their views to their fellow citizens. To the extent that anyone can pass on his or her views, their influence can be enhanced. How this happens has changed dramatically over time, most especially in recent years.

In Plato's era, communication was purely by word of mouth. The first great invention to change this was Caxton's printing press in the fifteenth century, which enabled views to be transmitted widely. It has been argued that the French Revolution could never have occurred without pamphlets to spread the word. Now, there are many forms of media available.

In a village community, the citizens in the past usually sought advice from their local dignitaries, such as priests, doctors, teachers, and lawyers, while banks could also influence them. In Ireland, the strongest of these parties was the priests. The 1937 Constitution was drafted to comply with Catholic teaching, but now that has totally changed, partly due to the misconduct of individual priests and partly due to the way in which the Church handled them. Efforts by the Church to influence voters on issues such as abortion have failed. Now, with declining congregations and vocations, its influence is much reduced. Surprisingly, Pope Francis intervened in the 2024 US Presidential Election by urging voters to choose between the lesser of two evils, identified as policies on abortion and immigration.

In Britain, the Church of England, technically the Established Church, has little influence in practice. The Russian Orthodox Church, once driven underground and dubbed by Marx as the 'opium of the people', seems now to comply with Government wishes. It approves of the war in Ukraine, and so priests who pray for peace, rather than victory, are dismissed from their jobs. In India, the world's largest democracy, the Government is strongly influenced by its predominant religion, Hinduism. The one religion that has the greatest influence globally is Islam, which is adopted by some states in its entirety, often promulgated by Sharia Law, which is at odds with many democratic principles.

Business has traditionally been a supporter of right-wing parties, providing them with funding to advance their views, frequently assisted by a group of powerful lobbyists. It was therefore surprising to hear Boris Johnson in the Brexit debate stating, "F*** Business". Multinationals, especially, can impose their views by threatening to withdraw from host countries and take the highly paid jobs with them.

Modern Media

One major influence now emanates from the media, both traditional and modern. In the past, the Press, newspapers, and magazines were the source of information for most citizens, with the later addition of radio. During the twentieth century, television became an important addition. In extreme cases, content can be straight disinformation, which is commonplace in totalitarian states. As Oscar Wilde put it over a century ago: "In the past, men had the rack. Now they have the Press". Modern media can also set the agenda for the public. They determine what issues are to be discussed and also slant the views presented before the citizens. Given the fact that many of them are owned by wealthy moguls, this can lead to relatively little importance being given to topics such as equality.

With the decline of advertising revenue in local newspapers, voters may become further removed from this source of their information, finding themselves obliged to rely on national media for their news. News reporting should be truthful and accurate. If not, there may be severe penalties, as Fox News discovered in 2023 when it was obliged to settle a defamation case for $787 million. It had pandered to its listeners who believed that the 2020 election had been stolen from Donald Trump by defective voting machines.

In America, ownership of the media is extremely concentrated. Ninety per cent of all media are owned by just eight corporations. They, in turn, are owned by wealthy Americans, who have a strong influence on what is seen, heard, and read by the citizens, which has implications for the freedom of the Press. America does not rank in the first 40 countries on freedom-of-press indices.[1]

Usually, people choose the paper that most closely mirrors their own views and prejudices. But often they are unaware how their views are formed by the way the paper reports 'the facts'. Aware of their power, politicians court reporters assiduously and canvas them for their support, especially large groups, such as the Murdoch Group. It would seem likely that the Brexit referendum was strongly influenced by the Press. Interestingly, every city that had a university voted to remain, and some academics emigrated after the result. Highbrow papers, such as the *Financial Times* and the *Economist*, presented the facts from an economic perspective, stating clearly that remaining would promote greater economic growth than could be achieved by leaving.

But the tabloid Press ('the Red Tops'), which had a much larger readership, was supporting the leave option and appealed to prejudices, rather than reason, as advocated by Plato, with scant regard for its accuracy. One advertisement, widely displayed on the side of buses, claiming that the National Health Service could spend an extra £350 million a week, received good coverage. No sooner than the result was announced, it was firmly stated that this pledge could not be honoured.

Politicians and the Media

Politicians who fear unwelcome criticism may simply refuse to give interviews to journalists, whom they consider to be hostile. But they can also pressurise the media to report favourably on their policies. This can be a dangerous practice, since freedom of expression is a fundamental democratic principle. The BBC has a long history of impartiality, but its views may differ from those of the government, and they have been threatened with a cut in its funding by a former Tory Government.

Two recent incidents illustrate the conflict with freedom of expression. In 2023, a popular freelance soccer commentator tweeted a particularly strong criticism of the Government's immigration policy. Tory backbenchers were furious and demanded that he be sacked. The BBC chairman, a prominent Tory party donor, suspended him, raising a national furore. But Governments in the UK cannot dictate to independent bodies on how to manage their businesses. The commentator was reinstated a week later.

The other incident was the curious pulling of an episode on 'Wild Isles' by the renowned naturalist Sir David Attenborough, showing it only on BBC Player. In it, there were strong warnings about the destruction of nature, together with the threats of extinction to many animal and plant species. Critics claimed that the reason for its withdrawal was that its content was unacceptable to Tory right-wing elements, but this was strongly denied by the BBC.

Another tool for politicians is data analytics, whereby the views of the electorate can be ascertained using computing to examine vast amounts of data. This was used to great effect by Dominic Cummings, advisor to Boris Johnson, in the 2019 UK general election. The issues for voters were identified as funding of the NHS, education, safer streets, more infrastructural spending, and, above all, lower immigration. The Tory manifesto focused on these issues, resulting in a gain of 48 seats Tory landslide, which gave them a majority of 48. Great swathes of traditional Labour supporters, particularly in the Midlands and North, changed sides. But promises, if not delivered, can quickly change voters' intentions. Three years later, after a series of scandals, accusations of sleaze and poor economic performance, the Tories' popularity fell dramatically, with opinion polls showing them to have fallen 20% behind Labour. The party was deeply divided on many issues after the leadership had changed three times in rapid succession.

A new form of medium appeared around this time, Social Media. This was to transform the operation of the industry functions and had a profound effect on the behaviour of politicians. It is taken up in Chapter 17.

Military

The military, especially the army, has traditionally played an important role in Latin America, Africa, and elsewhere. This may be by direct participation or indirectly with the threat of a coup. Autocrats who have the support of the Military are difficult to dislodge by democratic means.

Money

Money has a significant role in the relationships between politicians and voters, often not for the better. At its lowest level, a voter might seek to influence a planning decision by offering cash to a local politician. Bribery and corruption are outlawed, but can take place out of sight.

Fundraising by politicians may raise ethical issues. In the 1960s, Fianna Fáil, the Irish Government party, introduced a scheme named 'Taca'. Five hundred businessmen were invited to subscribe £100 each to attend a dinner, where Government ministers were present. More recently, they had a table in a tent at the Galway horse races, where property developers mingled with senior politicians. Now there are stringent rules, both as to the maximum donation and their disclosure. Many countries now ban overseas contributions to political parties to try to prevent interference by Russia and other foreign countries in their elections.

Politicians seeking votes may be able to provide significant benefits to their supporters, such as directorships in public companies and, in the UK, elevation to peerages. More questionable still is the awarding of Government contracts to their friends, which in Britain during the pandemic raised serious controversy. Under EU law, any significant contract must be put out to public tender, which places a barrier to favouritism. The granting of contracts to oligarchs in Russia is particularly notorious. In Poland and Hungary, well-remunerated jobs were often found for political supporters.

In the USA, the situation changed fundamentally in 2010, when the Supreme Court made a controversial decision that any restrictions on political contributions were in breach of the citizens' right to free speech.[2] President Obama warned that it gave special interests and lobbyists even more power in Washington. It opened up the way for Elon Musk and other major donors to impact policy in a major way. Large corporations and billionaires may exercise enormous, often excessive power, while expecting something in return for their big donations. This may be to make the 'super-rich' even 'super-richer' or facilitate the use of tax havens. The Republican Party has been able to achieve large tax reductions for the rich. There are serious worries that such largesse can damage the democratic system. [3]

One trenchant critic of the system, as it currently operates in America, describes it as 'legalised corruption'. [4] In the Trump presidency, there is increasing concern about the influence of the richest man in the world, Elon Musk, who has a following of twenty million followers on social media. [5]

Elsewhere, there is increasing concern about the support from people who hide their wealth in secretive offshore tax havens. Trump's decision to allow anonymity for shareholders in shell companies will give this practice a further boost. This murky industry has grown rapidly since the 1990s and provides its users with anonymity, as they plan for their personal safety in doomsday disasters ahead. [6]

The havens are usually used to avoid tax and have enormously benefited oligarchs, whose wealth may not have been accumulated legally. In particular, they are used by drug dealers and other criminals. Ireland has identified €350 million of suspected money laundering, which it cannot use due to the inherent anonymity. It would be most undesirable if such people were to have an influence on politicians with their lavish donations. [7]

Greater transparency about major donors is important. In Ireland, concern has been expressed about funding of the Sinn Féin Party, given its close association with the IRA, which has a history of bank robberies. In 2024, there were worries that donors close to Israel could influence US policy on Gaza. Also in 2024, in England, it was revealed that the largest donor to the Conservative Party had made strong racist comments.

The misuse of cash or benefits can seriously undermine the proper working of democracy. Clearly, it varies enormously from country to country. Whether any form of bribery or corruption is permitted in practice depends not only on the legal system but also on the prevalent culture. There can be a fine line between normal lobbying and corruption. The best defence is a free and vigilant press.

The way autocracies seek to influence is fundamentally different from that of democracies. What matters is uncritical support of the autocrat, as he seeks to gain or maintain power. The culture imposes few restrictions on how government is conducted, such as those that exist or are believed to exist in democracies. Ideology is irrelevant, and a disdain for democratic Western values is a distinct advantage.

Fear

One factor that has come to prominence in the 2024 US Presidential Election is fear. This may be based on real dangers or the exaggeration of problems. A party that believes it could gain votes by generating fear amongst the electorate may strive to inflame basic worries of citizens on matters such as immigration. Russia also uses fear, along with money, to influence elections in other countries.

CHAPTER 8

The Clash of Cultures: Autocracy and Liberal Democracy

Liberal democracy had been gaining influence as a system of government after the Second World War. But when the Berlin Wall fell in November 1989, rapidly followed by the collapse of communism in Eastern Europe, it seemed that liberal democracy had defeated the USSR once and for all. This proved to be a misguided hope, as the spread and fortunes of democracy can ebb and flow.

The Recovery of Autocracy

The USSR, the Union of Soviet Socialist Republics, was always a misnomer, when a hundred years ago Lenin introduced one-party rule through the Communist Party. In the 'Great Terror', Stalin sought to purge all possible opposition, using famine, imprisonment, torture, violent interrogation, and arbitrary executions. Gorbachev relaxed the rules, introducing 'Glasnost' or openness and 'Perestroika' or restructuring to stimulate economic growth.

This relaxation has been reversed by Putin, restoring one-man rule. There has been a fundamental shift since shortly before he was elected in 1999, when he promised "to protect freedom of speech, freedom of conscience, freedom of the mass media, ownership rights, these fundamental elements of a civilised society". The following year, when he had been elected, he proclaimed, "We have proved that Russia is becoming a democratic State."[1]

The USSR was and Russia is a totalitarian, centralised, dictatorial system, requiring complete subservience of all citizens to the State. It is somewhat akin to the future of the world foreseen by George Orwell in 1949 in his novel *1984*, but more malignant. [2] 'Big Brother' is indeed 'Watching You', but now has the assistance of modern technology that even Orwell could not have envisaged. There is no press freedom, and the media slants all news to fit in with Government propaganda with total disregard for human rights. There is no freedom of speech, freedom from fear, or freedom from want, as advocated by President Roosevelt in 1941. A more recent work of fiction, which won the 2023 Booker Prize, an annual award for the best novel published in the English language, showed how a totalitarian life today could impact family life. It set out a vivid and terrifying picture, which reminded me of a trip I made to Russia in the 1980s, but very much worse.[3]

Rather than the writing of Karl Marx, the underlying philosophy is that of Thomas Hobbes, who was writing in the aftermath of the Civil War in seventeenth-century England. He claimed that the natural basic state of humankind is one of anarchy, with the strong dominating the weak. Life for most people was 'solitary, poor, nasty, brutish and short'. One natural right is self-preservation, which can be achieved by submitting to Authority, which he described as 'Leviathan', a large and dangerous sea serpent.[4]

One group that adopts this policy in Russia is the very wealthy oligarchs, whose acceptance of Hobbes can lead to totalitarianism. [5] The leaders usually adopt a Machiavellian approach to politics. Party loyalty is well rewarded with gifts of positions, which enable the holders to exploit monopolies. Equality, as outlined by Karl Marx, has vanished in a society whose wealth distribution resembles that of Tsarist Russia. Vladimir Putin is probably wealthier and more powerful than any Tsar ever was.

Anyone opposing the regime does so at considerable personal risk, even if they are resident abroad. Alexei Navalny and Sergei Magnitsky were to pay the ultimate price with their lives in Russian jails. Whenever and wherever opponents can be found, they are in mortal danger. Russian agents tried to poison a dissident living in Salisbury in England, who was not the first such victim and is unlikely to be the last. [6] Another was removed from a Ryanair flight, which had been forced to land in Belarus.[7] Ireland, though a neutral country, is always an advocate of small nations and strongly supports Ukraine in the war against Russia. Putin reminded the world when, in September 2022, he showed Ireland on a map, indicating how much of the country would be destroyed by a single nuclear bomb.[8]

Opposing Autocracy: Bill Browder and Sergei Magnitsky

Perhaps the most vivid danger of opposing the regime has been recounted by an American-born British financier, Bill Browder. Bill Browder was the founder and CEO of Hermitage Capital, a very successful hedge fund, investing in Russia. But, as an activist investor, he made enemies of powerful oligarchs, exposing their corruption in the international press. [9]

In 2005, his visa was revoked, and he was deported from Russia. In due course, it became clear that the Russians wanted to destroy Browder's reputation. They seized the Russian subsidiaries' corporate documents and seals, which were then used in illegal misappropriation of these companies. Over the next three years, there were police raids on his office, which removed company seals, followed by thefts from various companies. This was supplemented by false court judgments, the involvement of ex-convicts, senior police, and tax authorities' complicity in the theft of $230 million of taxes, which had been paid by Hermitage to the Russian budget.

Browder's young tax lawyer, Sergei Magnitsky, who had helped to investigate the €230 million tax rebate fraud against Hermitage, declined to leave the country, believing that he had done nothing wrong. He was arrested and detained in dire, inhumane conditions, but he steadfastly and courageously refused to sign a false confession to perjure himself and his client. He suffered serious and painful ill health, but was refused any medical assistance. Finally, almost a year after his arrest, he was beaten to death by riot police while handcuffed to a handrail.

From then on, Bill Browder set about obtaining justice for his dead friend. Three years later, in 2012, the United States Congress passed the Magnitsky Act, banning those responsible for his death from obtaining US visas and freezing their assets. Canada, followed by a further 33 countries around the world, passed similar legislation.[10] The EU now has equivalent legislation.

The other strand of enquiry was to follow the stolen money. This was not only a difficult, laborious task, but also a dangerous one. The search featured Russian mafia bosses, honey traps, and several mysterious, sudden deaths of key figures. Fortunately, the corrupt policemen and officials left many footprints from their lavish lifestyles. The Russians decided to contest the freezing orders through the courts in New York. Incredibly, they managed to retain the services of a renowned lawyer, who specialised in money laundering. He had also acted for Bill Browder and so had in his possession a lot of his information, including personal data.

But this was not the end of the matter for Bill Browder. The Russians were determined to get hold of him. In May 2018, on a trip to Madrid, he was arrested by Spanish police, who had an Interpol 'red notice' authorising his arrest and further extradition, deportation to Russia to face spurious charges of fraud. Fortunately, he was able to put a tweet out to his friends, politicians, and journalists, advising them of his predicament. This resulted in massive political and media attention, which ultimately led to Interpol declaring the arrest warrant invalid within the next hour, and he was promptly released. Following this setback, the Kremlin tried him in absentia, sentencing him to a lengthy prison term in Russia.

Later in July 2018, at the Helsinki summit, Putin proposed to Trump an exchange of twelve Russian officials accused of interfering in the American presidential election for twelve Americans, including Bill Browder. Trump found the offer "incredible and very interesting". The US Senate rejected this outrageous idea by 98 votes to nil. It seems that offending Putin involves considerable personal risks to fundamental human rights, since autocracies do not readily accept criticism.

Alexei Navalny

Alexei Navalny exposed the corruption of the regime, after which he was arrested. He had produced professionally made videos, circulated on YouTube, which exposed Putin's Black Sea residence with its hookah lounge, helicopter pad, vineyard, and an oyster farm. On his return to Russia in 2021, he was imprisoned in conditions described as torture and later was isolated in a 'special regime' Siberian prison colony, where he was to die in mysterious circumstances in 2024. The jailing of his lawyers in 2025 indicates clearly that no dissent will be tolerated in Russia and any attempted opposition will be ruthlessly suppressed, with those involved facing imprisonment, torture, or murder.

In the face of enormous odds against him, Navalny showed great courage in exposing corruption. After his poisoning, he returned voluntarily from Germany to Russia, well aware of the risks involved. He started writing his memoirs after being poisoned and finished the book from his prison diaries.[11] He loved both his family and his country, for which he was prepared to die. He was a strong believer in proper law, justice, and democracy. His patriotism, optimism, and determination inspired millions of Russians and provided them, at least for a time, with a ray of hope. In 2025, it was disclosed that some of his lawyers who had remained in Russia had been imprisoned.[12]

Since 1989, the former USSR has regained much territory and influence. It had absorbed both Crimea and Georgia through military invasion, which met minimal resistance or even token Western condemnation. It now has full access to the Black Sea, as well as the Mediterranean. It was not until it started what it described as a 'military exercise' against Ukraine in 2022 that Russia faced serious resistance.

A Jewish German philosopher, Hannah Arendt, writing in the aftermath of Nazism, explained that totalitarianism thrives in an atmosphere of desperate hope and desperate fear, rather than balanced judgment and measured insight. It relies on support from the masses, but this may be obtained by the elimination of opponents and suppression of unfavourable comments. If faceless bureaucrats mindlessly follow orders, they do not need to be monsters to commit atrocities, as Adolf Eichmann showed in Nazi Germany. [13] If true democrats do nothing, autocracy can arrive quickly. Writing in 1955, a decade after the end of the Holocaust, she was also highly critical of the way the Israeli government was treating the Arabs. [14]

Nor is Russia the only autocracy. The West was encouraged by the general relaxations after the death of Mao Tse Tung, but this changed dramatically after the attack on students in Tiananmen Square in 1989. Subsequently, China became the manufacturing capital of the world in the era of outsourcing. Westerners presumed that it would become more open and democratic with increased wealth. This has now changed, since China is seen as a threat to American dominance. There is now a concerted effort to persuade American multinationals to 're-shore'. Above all, there are worries about China's collection of information from its use of sophisticated technology and growing artificial intelligence.

President Xi has increasingly come to resemble Putin with an autocratic leadership style, evidenced in his treatment of protesting demonstrators in Hong Kong in 2020. Early in his political career, he tried and imprisoned over one million opponents on charges of corruption. He does not tolerate dissent or free speech, persecutes minorities, and has extended his rule indefinitely. While he has not caused suffering on the scale of Mao with his 'Great Leap Forward' and 'Cultural Revolution', he has caused significant hardship for opponents. Militarily, China is now a threat to democratic countries, particularly Taiwan and Japan, while it now controls Tibet. The challenges of China have become belatedly recognised with its technological power and considerable financial muscle in developing countries, particularly in Africa. They have persecuted Tibetans for centuries, but what is less well known is their treatment of the Uyghur people in the north-west of their country.

North Korea also threatens to expand by war. In the last twenty-five years, autocracy around the globe has threatened to expand territorially and increase its sphere of influence. The support of Russia, China, and North Korea for undemocratic regimes is of concern, particularly since they are all contemptuous of the rights of individual citizens. Both Russia and China have supplied arms to the military junta in Myanmar for use against the rebels, who are fighting for the restoration of democracy in their country. Both countries are fundamentally opposed to and contemptuous of any democracy. So, they are happy to support regimes run by strongmen or military forces.

There is widespread distaste for America and Western values throughout the Middle East, as was evidenced by the attack on the Twin Towers in 2001 by Al-Qaeda. Islamic extremism crosses many national borders. While regimes may profess an affinity to the West and buy their arms, some are happy to support Russia over Ukraine. Many of the Middle East Gulf States are dictatorships, sometimes adopting strict Sharia law, while others are more liberal. Today, due to their oil wealth, they have enormous power internationally.

Respected Authoritarian Rulers

Occasionally, some authoritarian rulers become widely admired. Two such figures are Marshal Tito and Lee Kuan Yew. Josip Broz Tito was to emerge as the leader of communist Yugoslavia in 1945, following a distinguished military record during the First and Second World Wars. Since he had a Croat father and a Slovene mother, he was generally accepted by the various racial groups. He ruled independently of Russia and created a decentralised federation, operating a model of self-governing socialism, whereby firms were run by worker councils, while all workers received an equal share of the profits. His model was widely accepted by his people, and prosperity ensued. However, he had no accepted successor, and after his death in 1980, the country eventually fragmented, descending into ferocious inter-ethnic wars. It was only after his death that it became apparent how enormous his success had been for his people.

Another politician, who worked in a mixed-race country, was Lee Kuan Yew, who worked in Singapore, a land with few natural resources. He became Prime Minister in 1959, shortly before the country gained its independence from Britain, and continued until 1990. Throughout this time, he ruled as a benevolent dictator, despising populism and focusing on long-term economic and social planning. He encouraged meritocracy and created one of the least corrupt countries in the world. It became a major manufacturing and financial hub in the Asia Pacific region, with a very open economy and a high average income. His legacy endured after his death. The economic success of the country, which was achieved in no small measure by the leadership of Lee Kuan Yew, is still widely admired today. His son, Lee Hsien Loong, succeeded him and carried on the same tradition. Recently, there have been several corruption scandals, relatively minor by modern standards, as the economy faces economic challenges in the post-globalisation world. [15] The family dynasty came to an end in 2024. What makes these two leaders exceptional is that they invariably put the public interest ahead of any personal benefit. One produced internal peace, and the other substantial economic growth.

The Ebb and Flow of Liberal Democracy

The popularity of liberal democracy has ebbed and flowed throughout history. The tide was low in the Second World War, when fewer than a dozen democracies still existed. Other than the UK and USA, there were Commonwealth countries, such as Canada, Australia, New Zealand, and arguably South Africa, together with a few neutral countries, such as Switzerland, Sweden, and Ireland.

Numbers increased rapidly after the war in an era of decolonisation. The high-water mark was reached after the fall of the Berlin Wall in 1989 and the subsequent breakup of the

USSR. Confidence was shaken over the Vietnam War, and when the West invaded Iraq, based on false information about weapons of mass destruction. A further setback came with the war in Afghanistan, when the Americans were forced to withdraw in 2021. They had sought to persuade the rival warlords to provide education for women and introduce other democratic values. This all disappeared with the return of the Taliban and Sharia law.

The tide in recent years has been ebbing for a variety of reasons. Haiti, one of the world's poorest countries, has had an unstable political history. Following the 2021 earthquake, basic services broke down, and it is now considered to have an authoritarian regime. In the Middle East, democracy failed in Syria, which became a brutal dictatorship, backed by Russia, until it was overthrown in 2024. The atrocities revealed a rule of terror, evidenced by torture and the world's largest mass grave of the century. Civil war, which had a history of religious conflict, emerged in Lebanon and brought its democracy to an end. Parts of Africa, where corruption is rife and strongmen rule, have long struggled to maintain democratic standards.

In the Philippines, democracy has been eroded with an increasingly coercive military and police force in the war against drugs, together with systematic attacks on the political opposition. Human rights have been eroded in the war against crime in El Salvador, where arbitrary arrests are commonplace. Researchers attribute the threats to democracy in El Salvador, Honduras, and Guatemala to weak financial regulation. Institutional corruption and the growing influence of criminal gangs. [16]

Respect for Democratic Politicians

It has been known for some time that the public has a low regard for politicians in general. Recent research commissioned by the Electoral Commission in Ireland revealed that 69% of voters agreed with the statement that most people seeking office are generally interested in their own importance, power, and perks of office. [17] Their ability to land lucrative jobs, however incompetent they may have been, when they retire, gives rise to cynicism. Revolving doors open up in the private sector for businesses that value their connections. They make wild election promises in their manifestos, which are disregarded once they are returned to office. They are trusted about as much as second-hand car salesmen.

There are also concerns that they focus excessively on the short term in their efforts to get re-elected and are slow to tackle issues, which are important in the longer term, such as climate change. A young Tory politician, Rory Stewart, explained it over ten years ago.[18] He went on to become a cabinet minister, but declined to serve under Boris Johnson, before eventually resigning from the party. He is now a political commentator and academic. He believes that the typical politician is seen as a mixture of a snake, a monkey, and an iguana.

Politicians always profess to have an answer and will never admit that they do not know. Some 84% of people in Britain believe that politics is broken. Too often, they ignore the wishes of the highly educated electorate and do not trust the public. Internationally, it has oversold the benefits of the system, which does not readily work in countries that are culturally fundamentally different, such as Afghanistan.[19] Its basic justification is that it delivers effective, prosperous rule of law, while it reflects the ideas of liberty, equality, and the dignity of the individual.

The fact that democracy provides economic progress and social harmony does not guarantee that it will endure, particularly when its defenders are held in low regard. It is time to examine how successfully they address the challenges facing them and why democracies often fail.

CHAPTER 9

Reducing Inequality

Equality has always featured prominently as an issue in countries striving for democracy. In the French Revolution, the slogan was "liberty, equality, and fraternity". The American Founding Fathers emphasised freedom and equality. Many countries today stress equality, though they may have different interpretations of what it means and how it should be achieved.

Equality of Opportunity

For Conservatives, particularly in America, traditionally the emphasis has been on equality of opportunity, rather than wealth or income. Self-improvement was a fundamental American value. Immigrants were welcome and encouraged to avail themselves of the opportunities of the New World. A poem composed in 1883, mounted on the Statue of Liberty, illustrates this cherished value of the American Dream: "Give me your tired, poor, your huddled masses, yearning to breathe free, the wretched refuse of your teeming shores. Send those the homeless, tempest-tossed, to me. I lift my lamp beside the golden door".[1]

Setting out equality of opportunity as a value is one thing, but applying it in practice is another, because not all citizens start life off equally. Some may be disadvantaged physically or mentally from birth. Others may inflict disadvantages on themselves through addiction to drugs or alcohol. Poverty creates a trap for families from which it is difficult to escape.

Children from poorer families are at a significant disadvantage, often being required to earn money to support the family and thus have less time for education.

In today's world, education is key to advancement. A third-level student has a better chance of making money than a child with minimal education. Exceptions are always possible, but generally opportunities in a world of high technology require literacy as a prerequisite. Wealthier families have greater access to private education, where they can develop skills more easily than their poorer counterparts.

Genuine equality of opportunity does not exist in many modern democracies. Children born into families where crime, drug abuse, and poverty prevail may have little opportunity to attend school on a regular basis. It is usually hard for them to earn an income greater than that of an unskilled labourer when they reach adulthood. Children, whose parents aspire to a third-level education, tend to fare much better with more doors open to them. For others, the American Dream may be more like an American Nightmare, as they struggle to survive on very limited means.

Rapidly Rising Inequality of Pay

The rewards granted to senior businessmen have attracted widespread criticism, particularly in America, where the pay of US CEOs relative to that of ordinary workers has increased dramatically in recent years. In 1965, the multiple was 20, rising to 366 in 2020 and an astonishing 400 in 2021. From 1978 to 2020, CEO remuneration increased by 1,460%, while that of a typical worker only increased by 18.1%.[2]

As stated at the start of the book, Senator Bernie Sanders claims that America is now an oligarchy. [3] Just three billionaires between them have more wealth than the combined bottom half of the population. The top 1% own more wealth than the bottom 92%, and have access to private education and top medical care. They are much more likely to receive a college education than the poor. So there is much inequality in the standards of living.

The poor have difficulty surviving on an inadequate minimum wage, which has not been increased since 2009. Some 60% live from paycheck to paycheck. Adjusted wages have not increased in 50 years, despite huge increases in productivity. Eighty-five million people are uninsured or underinsured. Roughly 500,000 people go bankrupt every year due to the cost of medical bills and the consequences of staying away from work. Sixty thousand die each year because they cannot obtain the medical care they need. The child poverty rate is among the highest in any major economy, disproportionately affecting black and brown families. The plight of the poor in America is alarming and compares unfavourably with that of their peers in Canada or Western Europe. Given the power of the rich to influence the media and political parties through large donations, nothing is likely to change anytime soon.

Another concern in recent years has been the tendency of top businessmen to award themselves large pay increases, while their workers receive minimal increases or even cuts. In the US, the scale of bonuses for bosses can be astonishing, while ordinary workers receive no bonuses. Their contracts can reward them well for failure, as they are heavily compensated for loss of office. Some even receive enormous increases, while shareholder returns drop. [4]

In Ireland, 18 long-standing bosses of the largest publicly listed companies in 2022 received average remuneration of €1.61 million, representing 39 times the average salaries and a fall of 10% from the previous year due to declining stock markets. [5] Later, it was disclosed that CEOs of Irish-listed companies earned 30 times the average pay of their staff, which seems modest in comparison with the USA.

In the USA, there is little sense of change towards greater equality. The Democrats had proposed a doubling of the national minimum wage in 2024, but the victory of Donald Trump makes any significant change unlikely. The board of Tesla awarded the CEO, Elon Musk, a massive $56 billion pay package. But this was nullified by the Delaware court, the premier US business court, on the grounds that the board members were insufficiently independent of the CEO. Musk's response was to move the incorporation to Austin, Texas, where he expected more sympathetic judges. If he is correct, no doubt the super-rich should agree with the legendary frontiersman, Davy Crockett, who claimed that some people were born in Texas, while others came as quickly as they could. [6]

Within countries, there can be large variations in the spread of inequality. Texas, with its pro-business and socially conservative culture, has considerable poverty. The Lone Star State ranks in the bottom 10 US States for educational attainment, has the highest proportion of people with no health insurance, and has one of the highest rates of child poverty, at about 20%. [7] The EU Eurostat in 2024 reported that 21% of its population were at risk of poverty, with large regional variations.

A seminal work has explained the growth of inequality worldwide. [8] It is based on British and French data, since this is more available than elsewhere, but also describes other countries, including the USA. The central tenet is that inequality will continue to grow over time, so long as the average return on capital exceeds the average rate of growth.

The data shows that the level of inequality varies over time and by country. For example, in times of war, governments are obliged to increase levels of taxation to finance their defence. During both the First and Second World Wars, levels of inequality dropped sharply. The Government centralised the management of production, resisting any profiteering by businesses, and controlled wages. In the inter-war years, inequality was sharply reduced, as rents stagnated, while the Great Crash of 1929 took its toll on inherited wealth. At the same time, civil servants, professionals, and salaried managers expanded the middle class.

After the war, in an era of reconstruction, levels of inequality returned to their traditional levels, before rising dramatically in the 1980s. There was greater demand for well-educated workers, as advances were made in technology. Such fortunate people could command high salaries, as could others in certain niches, like investment banking and the law. Minimum pay stagnated for unskilled workers, who were unwanted, as their jobs migrated abroad in the era of global outsourcing. The declining influence of trade unions meant that they no longer had much protection. There is no evidence that the trend of the rich becoming ever wealthier at the expense of the poor has changed.

Politicians could correct this by means of taxation. It is obscene that a successful businessman pays a lower rate of tax than his secretary, as can happen in the USA. Income can be taxed progressively, with the rich paying greater rates of tax than the poor. Regressive taxes, where the poor pay proportionately more of their income, such as the poll tax proposed by Margaret Thatcher in the UK, are repugnant. Wealth, too, can be taxed, sometimes by Estate Duties, payable on death, and at other times by periodic wealth taxes. Finally, capital gains can be taxed when assets are realised. But redistributive tax has not happened in a significant way, indicating that the reduction of inequality is rarely a major government priority.

A further cause of increased inequality is the avoidance of tax by the super-rich. Many wealthy individuals have protected their wealth by changing their country of residence and domicile to tax havens with the assistance of their professional advisors. In this way, they can avoid paying tax in their country of origin and only minimal amounts of either capital or income tax in the tax haven. Consequently, billionaires can build up vast fortunes and further distort inequality. The number of super-rich in Ireland, with wealth exceeding $50 million, has more than doubled in the last decade, rising from 655 to 1435. [10] Many prominent Irish businesspeople, with the notable exception of Michael O'Leary of Ryanair, are domiciled outside the country.

Global Inequality

The evidence from the 2022 Global Inequality Report [11] shows that worldwide, the richest 10% take 52% of the income and 76% of the wealth, while the poorest 50% have 8.5% of the income and 2% of the wealth. Generally, capital inequality is greater than income inequality. The 2024 Nobel Prize in Economics was awarded to three academics studying the issue. They pointed out that the richest 20% of the world's countries are now around 30 times richer than the poorest 20%.

There are substantial variations in inequality prevalent in different countries. Western Europe is the most equitable area, followed by East Asia and then North America. Those areas at the other end of the spectrum in ascending order of inequality are the Middle and Near East, sub-Saharan Africa, Latin America, and Central Asia, including Russia. Autocracies fare much worse than the norm, usually with a very large share being taken by the top 1%. African countries, Iran, Turkey, and above all, Russia score badly. China is slightly better, but is well short of Western Europe. The USA is the worst-performing of the Western democracies, with the concentration of both income and wealth increasing significantly in recent years.

The super-rich often argue in a self-serving way that everyone benefits from their wealth through trickle-down economics. This must ring very hollow for those suffering at the bottom of the ladder. The rich are getting richer, and the poor are mostly getting poorer. Clearly countries abandoning democracy cannot do so with the expectation of a more equitable distribution of either income or wealth, which would face trenchant opposition from the wealthy The only real winners would be a potential dictator and a small band of oligarchs, who would probably try to advance their own interests and that of their families at the expense of the wider public.

During the first fifteen years of this century, considerable progress was made in reducing the gap between the rich and poor countries, helped by increased school enrolment and improved healthcare, but in the last decade, this convergence ceased. [12] Rich countries had other priorities, such as climate change and energy disruption. Economic growth in many poorer countries was minimal, and problems were exacerbated by protectionism and declining mineral prices.

China has been a role model, but its ability and willingness to invest in poorer countries have declined. It has its own problems, since a quarter of its population still lives on less than $2,500 per year, while it faces increasing tariffs around the world. The situation in most of Africa and parts of Latin America is dire. It is estimated that 700 million people are extremely poor, and 3 billion can be described as poor with little prospect of change in the near future, particularly after Trump withdrew foreign aid.

An almost universal issue is gender inequality, whereby women receive less income and fewer opportunities than men. Mary Robinson, the former president of Ireland and UN Commissioner for Human Rights, has been a fearless champion of the cause, but little progress has been made, despite the fact that most countries, outside the Muslim world, pay lip service to the issue. In many countries, particularly those with right-wing parties, especially the US, there has been a reaction against 'woke' measures, and gender equality has received a setback.

The Swedish Model of Social Democracy

The Scandinavian countries are the most egalitarian in Europe in terms of gender, income, and wealth equality. In Sweden, although there has been some decline in recent years, the top

10% receive only 30% of the income, the bottom 50% receive 23% and the top 1% 10% of the national income. In the eighteenth and early nineteenth centuries, Sweden was a most inegalitarian country. The current distribution of wealth remains less egalitarian than its income distribution. Nevertheless, it is a shining example to many other countries, if equality is a serious intention, rather than an empty political platitude.

The country has a strong welfare system and taxes its citizens much more heavily than elsewhere. It is a social democracy, rather than the other Western European liberal democracies, which have a more laissez-faire capitalist bias. Equality of income or wealth is not incompatible with democracy. Where economic growth is not the overriding objective in a democracy, greater equality can be achieved if it becomes a priority.

The problems created by inequality have grown in recent years with the rising significance of inherited wealth. People in advanced economies are set to inherit 10% of GDP currently, up from 5% during the middle of the twentieth century.

CHAPTER 10

Satisfying Basic Human Needs

Given the fact that many countries are abandoning traditional liberal democracy, it may be helpful to assess the major challenges facing democracy and how effective it is in dealing with them. These challenges include how well it satisfies basic human needs, as well as how it can approach concerns that cross national boundaries, such as climate change and pollution of the oceans, together with the war in Ukraine and Gaza.

A Hierarchy of Needs

Human beings have needs with different levels of importance, described by the American psychologist Abraham Maslow as a hierarchy of needs.[1] The most fundamental needs are physiological, which are key to human survival. People need air, water, food, heat, sleep, clothing, and shelter. Most of these needs are largely satisfied in modern democracies. The main deficiency in Western Europe is shelter, since homelessness is widely experienced. The quality of food and clothing may vary with wealth, but the basic need is normally fulfilled. Real hunger is a relative rarity, but it has emerged as an issue with recent inflation and rising fuel costs. Obesity seems to be more of an issue than starvation. In recent years, with rising energy costs, heat may also be an issue, but in the temperate climate of Western Europe, this is not life-threatening.

However, in the Sahel or sub-Saharan Africa, the situation is very different. Repeated military coups, civil war, and tribal violence are commonplace. Marauding gangs of Russian mercenaries and Islamist extremists strike widespread terror. Extreme violence also persists in Sudan, Haiti, and Honduras. For the population, the basic need for security and other physiological needs inevitably remains unfulfilled. In these circumstances, satisfying higher needs becomes of lesser importance.

On the next level is the need for safety. Safety at the national level can be endangered by war or natural disasters, such as earthquakes, while crime may be an issue for society at large. On a personal level, physical violence, child abuse, and ill health are commonplace. Lastly, economic security cannot exist when citizens have no job or other form of income.

Security at local and national levels can be a really important issue, since it enables citizens to relax both by day and by night without being permanently on their guard, fearing for their own safety. [2] Since the Metropolitan Police was formed two centuries ago in London, most countries have police forces to protect their citizens. Police forces in democracies are expected to behave with impartiality and never indulge in bribery or corruption. If there are 'no-go areas', the law cannot be enforced, and the situation degenerates into anarchy or falls under the control of drug barons, as can happen in some South American *favelas.* When confidence in the police has fallen, as it has in London frequently due to the criminal behaviour of some of its members, politicians need to take urgent action.

Most democracies do not allow their citizens to take the law into their own hands. The exception is the USA, where guns are freely available and many citizens have at least one gun, even deadly high-powered automatics, for their own protection. This has led to numerous atrocities, where gunmen have attacked schools and shopping malls, slaughtering innocent children and passersby. Owing to the existence of a strong gun lobby, the situation is likely to persist for some time. Security is also required at the national level to protect the country from foreign invasion. For many years, democracies sought to involve all their citizens through a system of compulsory military service. But if democracy is to survive, the armed forces, in the absence of an emergency, should keep out of politics.

The importance of a widely respected security is critical for democracy. If citizens feel unsafe, they can abandon the many valuable freedoms and turn to an autocrat who may purport to provide them with security. At a higher level, again comes love and social needs. These may be fulfilled not only by partners and family, but also by wider friendships. Club membership can play an important role in this regard, bringing together people with a common interest. Self-esteem is especially important for children as they grow up, as well as for adults. Racism damages esteem and love at both the local and national levels.

The next level is cognitive, which centres on the use of the brain to solve problems. It also includes curiosity, foresight, and creativity. Fundamental to every society is the educational system. The top level is the need for aesthetic pleasure and ultimately self-actualisation. Society may sometimes destroy things of beauty, but it should encourage the arts. Self-actualisation, however, is personal, and the only role of society is not to place barriers to achieving it.

Democracy, compared with other forms of government, has a singular advantage in satisfying these needs. If any Government fails in this task, it can be voted out of office. Dictatorships can and do ignore many of them. Their citizens may not have their basic physiological needs satisfied, and sometimes be faced with starvation. Many are unlikely to have a sense of security, living in fear of the army and police. Education may not be readily available, especially for women and girls, but can break down completely in times of strife or economic hardship.

No democracy, however prosperous, can succeed in satisfying all needs at a price which young middle-class citizens can afford. In Ireland, opinion polls show dissatisfaction with the current situation. The country spends only 3.95% of its national budget on housing, compared with an EU average of 6%.[3]

Homelessness is a problem and can have many causes, but primarily it is the lack of an adequate income to pay market rents or meet mortgage repayments for house buyers at an affordable price. Developers may seek to hoard sites, rather than build. Inadequate amounts of land may be designated for building in the appropriate locations, and vexatious planning appeals may hold back construction. During the pandemic, sources of supply for critical materials rose rapidly in price and were often unavailable. In times of full employment, there is a shortage of construction workers. The upshot is that there is a serious shortage of houses being built.

Ireland spends more per head on health than most other European countries, but the hospital service has patients lying on trollies for extended periods. Staff shortages for both consultants and nurses provide a constant challenge. While advances in modern medicine have enormously increased life expectancy, the associated cost may often be prohibitively expensive.

Very few countries can be wholly satisfied with their health systems or their ability to house everybody. Many are also dissatisfied with the rate of economic growth, which fundamentally affects the level of resources available to governments. As an example, it may be useful to consider one country. Ireland's overall performance is assessed here and compared with other countries.

Ireland has an advantage over most other countries when it comes to economic growth. First, it has a very small armed force to maintain. Since gaining its independence from Britain a century ago, it has adopted a policy of neutrality, and, given its island location, invasion by foreign powers is improbable. While this policy is now under review, expenditure on defence remains low. Secondly, many American and other foreign multinationals are located here. Their rate of growth is much larger than that of domestic businesses, and their contribution to the finances of the State is very considerable. Overall competitiveness is strong.

Each year, IMD, the International Institute for Management Development, produces a world competitiveness index, covering 84 countries and measuring 36 indicators. In 2023, Ireland rose from eleventh position to second, trailing only Denmark. [4] It ranked first in economic performance, third in both government and business efficiency, but only ninth in infrastructure. Government efficiency includes measures around social cohesion, the distribution of wealth, and freedom of the press. Business efficiency includes a measure of social responsibility. It is reassuring to find that Ireland compares favourably with most other countries.

Infrastructure

Infrastructure development has always attracted critics in Ireland. One example is the announcement by two major technology companies that they could not consider Ireland as a suitable location for a major investment due to infrastructural problems. It is widely agreed that the country has suffered at least a decade of underinvestment in critical infrastructure.

The management of projects is weak, leading to serious cost overruns, the latest of which is the catastrophic cost overrun in the construction of a children's hospital in Dublin. The current estimate for a Dublin maternity hospital is over ten times the original estimate. The construction industry suffers from low productivity. [5] It is strange that major construction projects in the private sector are tightly controlled, while in the public sector, there are enormous overruns, despite the fact that they often use the same construction companies. The reason can only be attributed to poor management. [6]

A special report by investigative journalists has drawn attention to many deficiencies in the system. [7] There are concerns about the level of cost consciousness, but it is hard for most citizens to know if major projects provide value-for-money. However, they may have strong views on smaller projects. Both the Minister for the Environment and many citizens were shocked when it was discovered that a bicycle shed at Government buildings for eighteen bicycles cost over €355,000. Similar criticism greeted the disclosure of a security hut costing over €1.4 million.

Overseas investors are concerned with transport and housing, but the two major concerns are energy and water.

There has been no single power plant constructed in Ireland in the last decade, but demand has grown rapidly, particularly from pharmaceutical manufacturing and the data centres, which account for more than 20% of Ireland's electricity consumption. Amber warnings of possible energy failures are growing more frequent. The country urgently requires to upgrade its grid and is heavily dependent on imported energy. Progress on the transition to wind power proceeds at a glacial pace. It seems that ambitious EU carbon emission targets are at risk.

Transport and housing are areas in need of attention. Road usage needs to be changed from motor to cycle lanes, while expanding public transport. The housing stock is grossly inadequate for a growing population. Inordinate delays in the availability of houses are also caused by the failure to connect water and electricity in a timely manner. The problem is exacerbated by a naturally high growth rate of population, compared with other EU countries, and substantial immigration. Increasingly, problems are emerging with the provision of clean water. In 2024, it was discovered that the presence of chemicals in drinking water exceeded the permitted EU levels.[8]

A current problem is the planning system, which is not fit for purpose. Vexatious objectors can unreasonably delay major projects, making them unviable, in the hope of being bought off. Above all, there is a shortage of staff at An Bord Pleanála, where appeals are heard, and long backlogs have emerged. The Irish National Competitiveness Council considers that deficiencies in infrastructure are of serious concern and are damaging the country's international competitiveness. [9] A new

Department of Infrastructure was announced in 2024, which may help to redress the underlying issue

Short-Termism

There is surprisingly little clamour from politicians for infrastructural projects for a simple reason. They cannot be finished in the five-year electoral cycle, so usually they need people to suffer costs or inconvenience in the short term. It is much easier to lobby for current expenditure projects when re-election is an issue.

Short-termism is a common problem in most democracies. Politicians are reluctant to ask people to undertake short-term costs for long-term gain. They may deliberately undermine important long-term commitments in favour of short-term electoral advantage. The UK Tory Government, for example, in 2023 promised to issue another hundred drilling licences in the North Sea, which could create thousands of new jobs, rather than adhere to their climate change policy. The Opposition Labour Party cut its green budget by almost 90% a few weeks later. Autocracies may be able to act more quickly, but whether their projects really benefit their people is generally questionable.

CHAPTER 11

Achieving and Maintaining Transnational Cooperation: Global Warming and Protection of the Oceans

In the era of globalisation, problems can no longer be confined within national boundaries. The increase in global warming threatens the future of the planet, but it cannot be tackled by one country operating in isolation.

Global Warming

Transnational cooperation is needed to tackle climate change. The evidence of climate change, the long-term shifts in temperatures and weather patterns, has been studied by scientists for years. August 2023 was the third successive month that broke all previous temperature records around the world, followed by the warmest September on record. The frequent fires and floods in many countries have done much to convince the sceptics. Europe is the fastest-warming continent, around double the global average. It experienced widespread flooding, severe heat waves, and lower snowfall in 2023.[1.] 2024 was subsequently declared to be the hottest year ever. The 1.5% increase in average temperature for the first time breached the Paris Agreement warning level.

Most of the increases in temperature since 1950 are due to human activity. In particular, the burning of fossil fuels, intensive agriculture, and deforestation release large volumes of greenhouse gases, trapping heat and causing temperatures to rise. Temperatures have already risen by about 1° degrees Celsius over the last century.

The consequences of existing global warming are devastating. Melting Arctic glaciers, due to growing sea temperatures, create a rise in sea levels and widespread flooding, causing massive housing damage in affected coastal regions. Meanwhile, the coral reefs of the Indian Ocean and the Great Australian Barrier Reef are vanishing. Many species of animals have already suffered extinction, and this trend will intensify if no action is taken. The United Nations in 2024 estimated that 20% of all migratory species are at risk of extinction. Food insecurity will lead to enormous population shifts. Some areas of the world may well become uninhabitable.

Another problem is the enormous decline in the insect population, attributed to climate change, habitat loss, pollution, intensive farming, pesticides, and fertilisers. The implications are serious for the food chain and birdlife, as well as the loss of pollinators, which could result in a loss of biodiversity. There are serious concerns over the likely impact over time of a strong El Niño, the cyclical warming of the Pacific Ocean, in 2024. Coming on top of existing global warming, the results will likely be catastrophic, especially for poorer countries. In addition to drought and flooding, there could be serious damage to food security and widespread outbreaks of disease.

Bill Gates has explained the scale of the problem: 52 billion tons of greenhouse gas are being released into the atmosphere each year and need to be reduced to zero. [2] He outlines the solutions that already exist, and the breakthroughs needed with further investment. He explores new forms of energy, such as hydrogen and the further development of atomic power. His proposals cover heavy manufacturing, agriculture, transport, and domestic housing. The energy will cost more, carrying a 'green premium', but this seems to be reasonable if the planet is to be saved. Carbon capture, where carbon is captured and stored underground, is a recent development with potential.

The UN Synthesis Report of March 2023 warns of the dire consequences of inaction but believes that the target of a 1.5^{0} °C reduction set out in the 2016 Paris Agreement is achievable and that carbon neutrality, which is having a balance between emitting carbon and absorbing carbon from the atmosphere in carbon sinks, by 2050, is possible. Shortly afterwards, the World Meteorological Organisation cast doubts on the target being attainable. The Global Institute forecast that under current policies, temperatures would rise by 2.7 °C by the end of the century, leaving 20% of the world dangerously exposed. Meanwhile, Europe continues to be warming twice as fast as the rest of the world. Ireland is well behind its carbon emissions reduction target. The problems continue to escalate, as 2024 has been declared to be the hottest year ever.

The COP28 summit, held in the UAE in 2023, made a small amount of progress. There was a strong commitment to renewable energy and an agreement to provide financial support to poorer countries. There was agreement on the 'need for deep, rapid and sustained reduction in greenhouse gas emissions'. But there is no commitment yet to phase out fossil fuels by 2050, and many countries remain well behind their targeted reductions.

The challenges are daunting. Energy sources must be efficient, sustainable, and secure, with good access, according to the International Agency. This entails changing the infrastructure to provide the appropriate energy mix, flexibility, and backup capacity. Success requires a tripling of global capital on renewals, a doubling of energy efficiency improvements, and agreement on the financed contribution from emerging economies. For Ireland alone, which is facing increased flooding, the cost is expected to exceed €150 billion by the end of the decade. [3]

The hundreds of billions of dollars being poured into clean energy annually in America remain well below the level needed to reach climate goals. Returns on investment in wind and solar often lag those from oil and gas. Companies such as BP and Shell have now scaled back plans to pivot away from fossil fuels. [4] In Britain, following the 2023 offshore wind farm auction, no licences were issued because operators found that the energy price offered was too low. The switch to alternative energy is still proceeding very slowly. Worryingly, there is mounting opposition to the introduction of green changes. Some people are still climate change deniers, others resist paying higher taxes or energy prices, while others again resist the hassle of installing new equipment or simply any change.

Asian countries, such as India and China, are realistic, but opposition is strong in parts of Europe and the USA, meeting widespread resistance amongst right-wing groups. In France, Marine Le Pen is opposed to wind farms. In America, Trump derides electric cars and plans to leave the Paris Agreement again, joining only three other countries: Iran, Yemen, and Libya, as well as reversing many of the Biden Presidency reforms, such as those controlling methane emissions. In the UK, Prime Minister Rishi Sunak slowed down progress to change, deferring the zero net carbon date and the ending of sales of fossil fuelled cars, while he even refused to introduce 'diktats' requiring citizens to separate rubbish into different bags.

The EU, on the other hand, is open to reform. The European Green Deal is designed to tackle climate change, reduce carbon emissions, and achieve climate neutrality by 2050. It sets out a roadmap, which aims to provide a cleaner environment, cheaper energy, smarter transport, new jobs, and a better quality of life. Targets range from waste reduction, protecting resources, to healthier food, to renovating housing. Legislation covers land use, aviation fuel, and carbon reduction schemes. It aims to reduce carbon emissions by 55% by 2030.

The challenge lies with the enforcement of the Green Deal. The early indications are that, although the roadmap is laudable, it is very unlikely to be achieved. EU members must accept the inevitable short-term costs, which necessitate persuading the electorate. Too often, countries ignore regulations that do not suit them. In 2023, the European Court of Justice stated that Ireland had persistently breached the EU Habitats Directives over two decades. Time is allowed for readjustment, after which heavy fines are levied. Perhaps pressure for change could come from ethical investment funds, which are growing in importance. If investors insist that only projects that operate to the highest climate standards are considered, longer-term considerations may be forced on those projects seeking funding from the private sector.

In 2023, the EU introduced a biodiversity strategy for 2030. This is a comprehensive, ambitious, and long-term plan to protect nature and reverse the degradation of ecosystems, leading to further serious obligations on its members. As the American politician Al Gore pointed out in 2021 at COP26, climate change and biodiversity are inextricably linked, since we need to solve the climate crisis to protect nature, but also protect nature to solve the climate crisis. It is particularly important to avoid the wanton destruction of carbon-absorbing plants and animals. These include the kelp forests, mangroves, and salt marshes, as well as preserving whales. A 2024 landmark decision by the Court of European Rights stated that the Swiss Government had violated its citizens' human rights by not doing enough to stop climate change.

Oceans: Overexploitation and Pollution

Serious pollution and environmental damage are commonplace in both freshwater and marine environments. It has been reported that over 90% of protected river habitats in Britain are blighted. [5] The main causes are farm pollution, raw sewage, and water abstraction. A 2025 court case by angling interests against the government may belatedly force water authorities in the UK to take the problems more seriously. Thankfully, over time, there have been some overdue improvements in rivers running through European capital cities, such as the Thames in London and the Seine in Paris.

In Ireland, the Environmental Protection Agency has stated that 34% of water bodies are at risk of not meeting water quality targets. The rivers fall within the control of local authorities, so that the problem can be tackled if the political will to do so exists. Similarly, the seabed is being ravaged by excessive, indiscriminate trawling, dredging, mining, and pollution, doing serious damage to Special Areas of Protection and Special Areas of Conservation. This, too, could be addressed if the necessary legislation is introduced and enforced. Pollution in the oceans is more complex, since no country has exclusive jurisdiction over them, and transnational cooperation is required. Debris from unwanted spacecraft and sunken oil tankers adds to the problem.

A worrying universal problem is how to protect the oceans from overexploitation and growing pollution. The oceans cover 70% of the surface of the planet, but two-thirds of it lies outside national boundaries. Given its vast area and enormous depths, it is estimated to contain 95% of life on the planet. Almost every country in the world is affected by the welfare of the oceans and seas. Countries with a shoreline are directly affected, but inland countries usually see them as a source of fish and nourishment. Unfortunately, they are facing more severe challenges than ever before.

One estimate of the large species, such as whales, has diminished by 90% since 1850, while large and medium stocks have fallen by 60%. Norway, Japan, and Iceland still permit whaling, despite the threat of extinction and the fact that they are significant absorbers of carbon dioxide. Although the total mass of humans on Earth is about 0.4 gigatonnes, it is nevertheless responsible for 2.7 gigatonnes of life that has disappeared. [6]

The UN Food and Agriculture Organisation considers that 94% of all fish stocks are either fully exploited or over-exploited, with over-exploitation accounting for 34% of the whole. Action is required if fish stocks are to be preserved and increased. This will necessitate rewilding the oceans, which can be achieved only by restoring their habitats or leaving them alone to recover.

Conservation activists have been successful in reversing some of the damage done by overfishing, proving that it can be done if the will is there. The EU has successfully restored the stock of hake in the North Atlantic to sustainable levels.

Overfishing often entails the killing of juvenile undersized fish, which have had no chance to spawn. A start can be made nationally by banning the most dangerous fishing methods that destroy the ecology of the seas. In the south of England, the use of fleets of trawlers was damaging the livelihood of the local scallop and shell fishermen, but when trawling was banned, matters improved very quickly. In the Mediterranean, Turkey has followed suit. In Belfast Lough, native Irish oysters are being restored after an absence of a century. Nevertheless, illegal fishing, such as that practised by Chinese fleets off the coast of Africa, showing scant regard for protected species, still persists.

Another great success has been the recovery of the almost extinct Atlantic oyster, an important part of marine ecology, since it feeds on algae. The Solent in the South of England was a major source of oysters, but had become excessively polluted and was subject to damaging dredging. Ecologists obtained a stay on dredging, which led to a rapid recovery of the species after restocking, an experiment eventually copied elsewhere. [7]

It is also possible to set up marine conservation areas, where the area is under the control or protection of one country. [8] This has happened in the Ascension Islands, a former British colony, together with St. Helena, Hawaii, an American state, and the small population of Tristan da Cunha, initiated by the islanders themselves. Marine conservation areas are important for the tourist industry and have been nicknamed 'The Jurassic Parks of the Sea'.

Fishing has been estimated to have been in existence for about two million years. Initially, it, along with hunting and gathering, was necessary for human survival for seasonal subsistence purposes. But over time, this has changed out of all recognition.. A famous early angling author claimed that the water is more productive than the earth. He went on to state that fishing, unlike 'Mathematiks', can never be fully learnt, [9] a doubtful practice in today's world. With a mixture of curiosity, observation, and technology, mankind has sought to change the ground rules and exploit the opportunities arising.

It was traditionally thought that fish stocks were inexhaustible, although overfishing has existed for many years, with growing human populations. Initially, it was experienced with cod and herring, but now, more widely, stocks have suffered as many existing species are threatened with extinction. The International Council for the Exploitation of the Seas has recommended that the Irish Sea be closed for herring fishing in 2025.

National feelings can result in serious conflict, as was evidenced by the 'Cold War' between Britain and Iceland in the 1970s, when Iceland sought to extend its fishing limits. The industry has been transformed in the last century and a half, as shortages have become widespread. Owing to the use of heavy seine nets, diesel power, and refrigeration, enormous catches became a reality, while factory fishing has developed over the last twenty years. As giant trawlers and factory ships increase their activities, matters can only deteriorate. Even the smallest fish are exploited for fishmeal, while they also take out vast swathes of seaweed, which absorb carbon.

A further serious matter is pollution. Air pollution claims many lives worldwide every year, but at least countries can tackle the problem in their own jurisdiction. Increasingly, rivers bring detritus from the land into the oceans, making sea pollution more complex. Raw sewage is often dumped into the sea to avoid the cost of processing it with expensive equipment. There can be ecological disasters from oil spills, shipwrecks, and the dumping of treated nuclear waste. The scale of the problem can be enormous. It has been estimated that Norwegian salmon farms release approximately 17 million tonnes of organic waste annually into the ocean, equivalent to over three tonnes per head of its human population.

Abandoned fishing nets can entangle fish, as well as seabirds. These nets also contribute to marine plastic and microplastics. Other boats simply jettison garbage into the sea. Recently, people have become more aware of the damage caused by plastics, but despite more recycling, much of it ends up in the ocean. It may be broken down by sunlight and is now known to enter the food chain. Detritus from tornadoes and tsunamis can all end up in the oceans. The normal principle that the polluter pays is rarely applied, so there is minimal incentive to tackle marine pollution.

A looming problem now is deep ocean mining. The technology now exists, and many businesses are anxious to excavate a range of valuable minerals beneath the seabed. Licences are heavily promoted by Trump, which could have enormous ecological implications. It is likely to cause serious pollution and damage to life on the ocean bed, although this may not be immediately apparent. [10]

National conservation measures can help, leading by example and publicising the problem locally. Advocacy groups, such as Oceana, devoted to protecting and restoring the oceans, play an important role, but if the issues are to be effectively redressed, there must be transnational cooperation, possibly tackled through a United Nations Agency. The problem is that any country could refuse to cooperate, and so minimise the efforts of environmentally conscious nations.

The European Union has started to introduce conservation measures and requires members to designate protected marine areas. It started with an area of 10% in 2020, but it aims to increase this to a target of 30%. Since it is estimated that only 13% of the oceans are protected today, this could have a significant impact. Daunting though that the task may be, there is no alternative to international agreement if the oceans are to be cleaned up and overexploitation of stocks brought under control.

Some progress has been made with plastic recycling in many countries, but about 400 million tonnes of plastic waste are generated each year. A United Nations body believes that this could be reduced by 80% by 2040. [11] Countries need to make deep policy and market shifts using existing technologies to enable reuse, recycling, reorienting, and diversification of products. Such a change, however, is unlikely to happen without the agreement of the major plastic-producing nations.

Open-pen Salmon Farms – An Example

Salmon farming is a relatively new industry that has a devastating impact on the oceans. Enormous pens are placed in the sea, and both Atlantic and Pacific salmon, despite being migratory fish, are artificially grown in them in conditions like battery hens. It is an issue of particular interest to me. As an activist opposed to open-pen farms, in 2022, I set up a group 'Save Ballinakill Bay', which now has over two hundred members, opposed to a licence being issued in a Special Area of Conservation, located in the heart of Connemara, a major Irish tourist destination.

At first glance, salmon farming may seem like a good idea, providing nutritious food in the oceans to help satisfy world needs and generating a small number of jobs in remote coastal villages. Increasingly, however, scientists are questioning whether the product is, in fact, safe to eat, while many jobs disappear with automation. But the industry also has damaging consequences for the marine environment, due to the transfer of untreated biological waste into the sea.

Two investigative Norwegian journalists paint a disturbing picture of the industry.[12] The Norwegian Government saw it as a replacement for declining oil revenues and a source of exports and taxes. Critical researchers were isolated, discredited, or silenced, as had happened in Canada, and their findings were deemed 'erroneous'. Huge fortunes were made, and young 'salmon billionaires' developed a powerful influence on policy-making. There were serious fish welfare issues with salmon subjected to thermal delousing, resulting in high levels of stress and multiple deaths. Grossly disfigured Frankenstein-like fish were discovered in pens. It can require 1.3 kilos of fish feed to produce 1 kilo of salmon, so it is depleting world fish stocks, while the effect on ecosystems is devastating. The *New York Times* compared their book with Rachel Carson's *Silent Spring* for the oceans.

The reality is that salmon farmers are doing much to lead to the extinction of the wild salmon, an iconic fish for thousands of years. The fate of the salmon from an Irish perspective has been recorded around the fate of Ireland's biggest river, the Shannon.[13] The ravages of electrification and industrialisation have proceeded for a century with scant regard for environmental considerations. Other problems are pollution from farmers and businesses, as well as river obstructions, such as hydroelectric dams without adequate fish passes. Worldwide stocks have declined, often very quickly, and much of the cause may be issues far out at sea, such as global warming resulting in loss of feeding grounds, pollution of the oceans, and large-scale illegal fishing. But, if countries wish to see the king of fish survive, it is imperative that they do not permit damage on land and inshore, which will aggravate the problem.

There are several serious problems with open-pen salmon farming. A central Issue is that the farms generate large volumes of sea lice, which attack outward migrating juvenile wild salmon and sea trout, which are coastal feeders. To counter this problem, salmon farmers use high volumes of chemicals. These, along with faeces and uneaten food, drop to the floor of the ocean, rendering it barren and destroying all marine life there. This problem often passes unnoticed, since it is only visible to divers.

Escapees are another potentially serious problem. If they interbreed, they can damage the genetic strain of the wild fish. The consequences of a major escape are serious. In 2020, the Chilean Regulator fined the world's largest salmon farmer of Atlantic salmon, the Norwegian MOWI, over $6 million following the escape of 690,000 fish in 2018 for what the watchdog described as "irreparable environmental damage". In 2023, an alarm was raised when 3,500 escapees from another MOWI-controlled farm were found in 35 different Icelandic rivers, as far as 400 kilometres from the original point of escape.

A further danger is disease, which spreads rapidly in confined spaces, resulting in mortality rates as high as 40% in warmer waters, a rate that would not be tolerated in terrestrial farms.[14] The extent of the pollution is colossal. It has been estimated that a moderate-sized farm generates the same amount of pollution as a town of roughly 16,000 with no sewerage system.[15]

Economists describe the costs incurred by businesses but not borne by them as 'externalities'. The normal rule that the polluter pays does not apply in this industry, because nobody owns the sea beyond their territorial waters, and no State has jurisdiction beyond 200 miles. It has been estimated that open-pen salmon farmers foist onto the community 40% of their total costs, which would not be tolerated in most industries.[16] Much of these undesirable consequences could be avoided if production took place on land, which is technologically feasible, but more expensive.[17] Salmon farmers resist this, preferring to offload their costs on the ill-informed public.

Another consideration is the damage done to the marine food chain. With the growth of the industry to supply the feed, enormous trawlers hoover up small fish all over the world. This has devastated the local fishing industry around the globe, from Peru to West African countries, depriving the locals of their inshore fishing and an important source of food.

Most countries, other than Norway and Scotland, are severely restricting open-pen salmon farming, as knowledge of the environmental damage they cause and their lack of sustainability spreads. Ireland, which has a totally inadequate regulatory system, is alone in encouraging and even subsidising them.[18] The industry relies on 'free riding' by the imposition of heavy costs on the community in pursuit of short-term profits, which is most definitely not sustainable. The overall damage caused by the industry was summed up by an 84-year-old shareholder at a MOWI meeting. He accused the company of polluting nature, wildlife habitat, ecosystems, and "threatening the future of future generations". The speaker was Thor Mowinckel, the founder of the business. [19]

Protecting the Oceans

While many countries acknowledge the importance of preserving marine life in our oceans, it is difficult to introduce and enforce the necessary legislation. Local lobby groups, such as Coastwatch and Fair Seas, have done good work in publicising the problems, but urgent action is needed at both national and transnational levels. It is difficult to reach an international agreement when strong vested interests come into play. The Japanese fought hard for whale fishing until many species were almost extinct. National Governments show little interest in the stocks of fish outside their own waters. So enormous factory trawlers are permitted to destroy all marine life on the ocean floors, where they often operate. A documentary by the naturalist David Attenborough exposes the horrors of unrestricted trawling. [20]

The EU has a fisheries policy, which allocates quotas for different species amongst member states. But it has failed to reduce the rapid decline of many stocks. The central issue is enforcement, which is problematic when catches are landed in foreign ports. For countries with a small fisheries protection fleet, such as Ireland, it is difficult to intercept large foreign trawlers at night. Another problem is the dumping of 'bi-catch', when a more valuable species is encountered, a gratuitous waste of scarce fish, driven by financial greed. It seems that the decline in fish stocks is likely to continue.

There is also a UN Convention on the Law of the Seas, to which over a hundred countries have signed up. It too suffers from enforcement problems, even if an agreement can be reached over contentious issues. In 1995, a UN Fish Stocks Agreement was published with a view to conserving stocks. But it has fewer signatories than the Convention on the Law of the Seas. More recently, in June 2023, the UN adopted the Treaty of the High Seas. The key is to protect the ocean, promote equity and fairness, tackle environmental degradation, fight climate change, and prevent loss in the high seas. These are all laudable aims, but what will be achieved in practice remains to be seen.

The oceans are difficult to regulate and even harder to police. Pirate fishing is all too common. Many ships operate under flags of convenience, sometimes employing slave labour. As well as fishing, they can be used for crimes, such as money laundering and drug smuggling, which encourages a culture of lawlessness. Fishermen may ignore quotas and catch preserved species, often using illegal equipment, such as long drift nets, the Chinese being amongst the worst offenders.

Factory ships dump unwanted nets and other equipment at sea to the detriment of wildlife. A further complication is the need to protect underwater cables from sabotage, which could affect fish stocks in the vicinity. If nothing changes, many species of fish will become extinct in the very near future.

Spreading the Burden

A fundamental issue is how the costs are spread. Many large economies, such as China, India, and the USA, are major polluters. Poorer countries should not be expected to pay for the past mistakes of rich companies. But obtaining agreement on how the substantial burden is spread is a daunting challenge. It must be admitted that transnational cooperation in tackling important issue has not been effective. The problems have only belatedly been recognised, but obtaining agreement on reforms with different nations having widely diverging interests is very difficult. Challenging targets have been set, but these do nothing unless they are translated into short-term goals and unpopular decisions are made, which are strongly opposed by powerful sectoral groups, such as farmers and fishermen.

When communal assets are in limited supply, it is necessary to decide who gets what. Similarly, when externalities arise, it is important how these costs are distributed. For too long, economists have failed to provide a solution. The traditional example was expressed as herdsmen sharing common grazing land. If any herdsman overstocks the land, this creates hardship and tragedy for everyone in the absence of any enforceable instruction. An economic Nobel prize-winner proposed a solution. [21] If the problems were explained to the herdsmen and if they knew each other's stocking level, then they could understand the issue and come to a solution without any external direction.

This has been the approach of COP 28. The first immense issue is the principle of who pays. There has been some basic progress on this matter. It has been accepted that the poorer countries bear little responsibility for the growth of dioxide and that, therefore, payment should fall mainly on the richer industrialised countries. But beyond that, the problems remain more intractable in a world where cross-border issues loom large. At stake are powerful vested interests supporting fossil fuels, particularly from countries producing fossil fuels, which may form their biggest source of overseas revenues.

Another is the serious issue of 'free riding'. Countries hope, especially if they are small players, that they can have minimal impact on the outcome and that they should be excused from contributing or make only a minimal contribution. Free riders want all the benefits with none of the costs. If America, which twice abandoned the Paris Agreement under Trump, persists in its refusal to participate, it is difficult to see how a solution can be reached.

It will not be surprising if global warming causes ever-increasing problems. There is growing concern amongst oceanographers that climate change could have a devastating impact on the North Atlantic. Beneath the waves, the Atlantic Meridional Overturning Circulation, which includes the Gulf Stream, acts as a planetary conveyor belt, bringing nutrients, oxygen, and heat from tropical waters while moving colder waters south. But research shows that climate change may cause it to slow, leading to a disastrous collapse, which would take a long time to reverse, and a serious decline in temperature in the Northern Hemisphere. [22]

As with satisfying basic human needs, sound long-term planning is critical. But in democracies, it is notoriously difficult to gain the attention of politicians on matters arising beyond the next election. Awareness of the issues has grown with publicity generated by private organisations, such as the Mary Robinson Foundation for Climate Change, which has highlighted the enormous problems caused by drought and flooding in underdeveloped countries and the need for climate justice. Nevertheless, change to date has proceeded with glacial speed, while the problems have worsened.

COP 29 met in 2024 in Baku with a view to reaching an agreement on the spreading of the burden between rich and poor countries, an almost impossible task in view of Trump's election as US president. Unsurprisingly, it ended in a mood of frustration, though a $300 billion deal was agreed to help wean developing countries off fossil fuels. [23] Major achievable goals were not agreed upon, nor was agreement over the split of funding, while fossil fuel producers resisted efforts to limit their growth. Some cynics considered it to be an expensive waste of time. Nevertheless, the Irish Minister for the Environment expressed confidence that further funding would become available in the future. [24]

However, there are some grounds for optimism, not only for climate change improvements and clean air, but also for pollution generally.[25] A Stanford professor has asserted that no miracle is needed, since existing technologies are currently available. Fossil fuels can be discontinued, and nuclear energy is not required. Energy needs can be supplied by a combination of wind, solar, and water power, which includes hydroelectricity, tidal and ocean current electricity, wave energy, geothermal electricity, and geothermal heat. Grid transmission and storage need to be improved, while increased efficiency in general is required, as well as the electrification of transport systems. The main outstanding issue is hydrogen cells for long-distance shipping and aircraft.

Unfortunately, it is not simply an issue driven by technological change. Geo-economic rivalries also have a role to play. Territorial expansion, wars, and competition over minerals cannot be ignored, as geopolitical considerations take primacy over remedies for climate change. [26]

CHAPTER 12

Achieving Peace

Making peace and avoiding war where possible have always been central planks of democratic government, whether national or transnational. Since the end of the Cold War, there has been much research into 'democratic peace'. Its origins date back to the philosopher Immanuel Kant. His republics, i.e., liberal democracies, have no reason to fight one another. [1] Modern researchers generally agree. Some put it down to having a common culture, while others stress the institutional separation of powers, together with various checks and balances.

Ever since President Woodrow Wilson in his 1917 address to Congress, the US has sought to make the world 'safe for democracy'; subsequent US Presidents have repeated this message. How does it stack up in the light of the war in Ukraine and the war in Gaza? Although neither of them is a war between two democracies, the wars reveal the attitudes of large democracies toward making peace.

The War in Ukraine

When Russia invaded Ukraine in 2022, it took the world by surprise. It had generally been assumed that following the fall of the Berlin Wall, Russia's new boundaries had been redrawn for all time and Russian imperialism was dead. Even their invasion of Crimea and Georgia in 2014 did not alter this viewpoint. But Ukraine was different, particularly when its citizens put up a strong resistance. To capitulate to Putin would be to abandon any form of the idea of a law-bound international order and, quite possibly, lead to the slow death of liberal democracy.

Putin's avowed intention of 'the military exercise' was to protect Russian-speaking Ukrainians and rid the country of 'Nazis'. Yet his behaviour is reminiscent of Hitler, who had occupied the Sudetenland of Czechoslovakia to protect its German-speaking citizens, almost in due course leading to the end of liberal democracy in Europe. [2] Ukraine is not only a valued source of food and minerals, providing good access to the Black Sea, but also a geopolitical buffer to any invasion from Western Europe. [3] The world has finally woken up to discover that Putin's apparent intention is the restoration of the USSR and might not stop there.

Putin was playing his own brand of Russian roulette. Under the Putin kleptocracy, he and his chosen oligarchs have accumulated enormous fortunes, while the peasants struggle in poverty with a shorter expectation of life than is normal in Europe. He has tolerated no dissent while expecting blind loyalty from the army and support from the Russian public. He has relied heavily on convicts and mercenaries for troops, but, above all, he totally underestimated the courage and resistance of the Ukrainian people. Russia has suffered enormous losses of troops and equipment.

When Yevgeny Prigozhin, who led the mercenaries, criticised the Russian military before seizing the town of Rostov, shooting down a few Russian military helicopters, and then marching towards Moscow, Putin described them as mutineers and stated that they must be punished. However, shortly afterwards, a deal was brokered, allowing the mercenaries to retreat to Belarus or join up under the official Russian army. Nobody was immediately punished, though

Prigozhin was strangely killed in a plane crash some weeks later. Nevertheless, Putin lost face after he had forfeited the unwavering support of the army. Despite declining morale and the deaths of many mercenaries, Putin can ignore the massive costs and appears to have little wish to bring the war to an end, if it damages his power in Russia.

The EU has instituted economic sanctions on exports of arms to Russia, but these are easily circumvented by third-party countries, which are well disposed towards Russia. So Russia remains able to arm itself with weapons from the West and China. After three years, Russia appears to be gaining the upper hand. The Ukrainians are short of key weapons, such as long-range missiles and drones, as American support diminishes, while their front-line troops are suffering from exhaustion. When some NATO members sought to allow Ukraine to use long-range missiles to attack military targets in Russia, Putin threatened them with an attack, hoping presumably to split the alliance with a divide-and-rule policy.

The summer 2024 counterattack into Kursk in Russia temporarily strengthened the position of Ukraine. The decision by France to supply Ukraine with Mirage jets in 2025 should make a difference. The use by Russia of North Korean troops is worrying and threatens to widen the war. Putin has threatened the UK and USA, following their permission to allow Ukraine to use their weapons to attack Russia, and then launched intercontinental ballistic missiles against Kyiv. America cannot be considered to be an honest broker, since Trump considers that Russia could have claimed the whole of Ukraine.

However, the failure of Putin to support Bashar al-Assad, who had for years been a close ally of Russia and ruled Syria as a cruel, brutal tyrant, against a rebellion in 2024 could indicate that Russia is overstretched militarily. Following the election of Donald Trump as President, this will probably lead to a significant boost to Putin and a major setback for the Ukrainians, as he has no love for democracy.

As Churchill had observed, Russians respect military strength and despise any form of weakness. It is unlikely that Putin himself would survive defeat, so he is reluctant to get drawn into peace talks on any realistic basis. In the meantime, the long-suffering Russians expect victory, and any contrary view is brutally suppressed whenever it emerges.

The War in Gaza

Democracies must be able to protect themselves from foreign attackers, as Europe and the USA did in the Second World War. So, Israel was entitled to defend itself from the savage, barbaric, and rightly condemned attacks by Hamas in Gaza. But the situation is complex when the attack comes from densely populated urban areas. The retaliation against urban guerrillas should be proportionate and avoid civilian deaths, as far as possible, while always complying with international law.

The plight of the citizens of Gaza has been known for many years. Stephane Hessel, a former French Resistance fighter and diplomat described their situation in 2010 in a bestselling international booklet· *Time for Outrage.* [4] Although he was a Jew and supporter of the Israeli State, he was outraged by the treatment of Palestinians, who had historically comprised the majority of the population, both in Gaza and on the West Bank. He believed that their human rights and international law had been breached by Israel. Gaza resembled a prison, more than a city, where the citizens have to be well prepared if they are to survive. Even then, the material destruction and loss of human life were immense. Hamas' terrorism was an almost natural form of exasperation against the violence, which the citizens were obliged to suffer. Nevertheless, Hessel stated that Hamas' terrorism was not acceptable, but predicted with remarkable foresight that it would end badly.

A former executive director of BT Selem, the Israeli Centre for Human Rights in the Occupied Territories, claimed that for over seventy years, the Palestinians have not been treated as equal people. Some hostile enemies claim that they should not be considered to be a distinct people, a charge similarly made against the Jews in the past. Nobody in Israel has yet been held accountable for crimes against Palestinians. [5] There has long been criticism of the United States' support for Israel and ignoring the plight of the Palestinians. The occupation of the West Bank has been described as a drift to fascism and in breach of international law. [6]

Netanyahu and Zionism

The war should be understood in its historical context. For over two thousand years, Jerusalem has been considered a holy city by Jews, Christians, and Muslims, but has experienced much turmoil and conflict. Periodically, the Jews were expelled, but they always sought to return. [7] In 1917, Britain, under the Balfour Declaration, sought to create a State in Palestine, much to the disappointment of Arabists, such as Lawrence of Arabia, who had led the Arabs for the Allies in the First World War. The State of Israel was duly set up in 1948, despite the resistance of the local people.

The treatment of the indigenous Palestinians has been deplorable. Periodically, they resisted unsuccessfully with a series of 'intifadas'. A Sunday Times journalist described it as a betrayal of the Middle East and condemned the hypocrisy and interference by the West on the side of Israel, revealing the horrific truth of reality on the ground. [8] The explanation of the slaughter of Red Crescent aid workers in 2025 did not stand up to scrutiny. Ever since the decision to set up a Jewish State was made, the West has always sided with Israel against the Palestinians, but this has been taken to a new extreme by Donald Trump.

The right-wing Israeli Government under Benjamin Netanyahu has, for years, been undermining democracy in pursuit of its Zionist expansionist agenda. Unfortunately, there is still support among the Jewish community for the war, which many people around the world consider to be a disproportionate response to Hamas and Hezbollah. This has resulted, unsurprisingly, in some antisemitism.

Netanyahu dismisses any criticisms as antisemitism. But there is a difference between antisemitism, which cannot be reasonably defended, and opposition to Zionism, which reflects the wish to expand the Israeli national territory. Religious extremists would like to see Gaza absorbed by the State of Israel. Those who subscribe to Zionism believe that the Israeli people are the chosen race, entitled to occupy the ancient territory of Palestine as their homeland, based on the teachings of the Old Testament. They might achieve this goal by way of military invasion. There are reports that many Israelis similarly want to create new communities in Gaza.

Netanyahu tried to become an authoritarian leader to further Zionism. He attempted to overhaul the judicial system and control the appointment of judges, limit the Supreme Court's ability to annul legislation through judicial review, and enable parliament to override decisions made by the court. This had met with widespread resistance, being considered a fundamental threat to their democracy. [9] He dismissed his defence minister, who opposed these reforms, despite enormous demonstrations against the government. A general strike was announced, while the military expressed strong disapproval. Under pressure from the public, Netanyahu was forced to back down and reinstate his defence minister. The Gaza war has overtaken these events, once a national government was formed. Nevertheless, despite large civil demonstrations, he persisted when he tried again in 2025 to take control of the judiciary.

Israeli intelligence about Hamas appears limited, given that the attack appeared to come as a surprise. They seemed to be more concerned with the PLO and mounting international support for a two-state solution for the Palestinians. They had received warnings and Hamas had been spotted assembling crowds on the border, but these were all ignored. It was revealed that Netanyahu himself had received the news very early on the day of the attack, long before it had been initially reported. In these circumstances, it is amazing that the army was so slow to respond and protect the kibbutz people. The military accepted that there had been failures of security, but Netanyahu refused to accept any responsibility.

Israel's War Aims in Theory and Practice

Netanyahu reacted, albeit too slowly on the first day, to the Hamas outrage. He stated that it was a time for war and promised that it would be a long war, which would continue until Hamas was totally destroyed. This could take a very long time, since history has shown that when the leadership of terrorist groups is killed, they rapidly find successors. When Israel claimed to have killed the last Hamas leader, Sinwar, they still refused a ceasefire. They also assassinated the leader of Hamas' peace negotiators, who was then replaced by a more extremist leader.

The Israeli Defence Force adopted a brutal and ruthless policy of 'no water, no electricity, and no food', attacking hospitals, schools, and ambulances. The devastating destruction and horrendous human suffering were conveyed to millions of households around the world by vivid television pictures. [10] One, in particular, showing a Palestinian strapped to the front of an Israeli military vehicle, prompted international outrage and accusations that he was being used as a human shield.

A report by an Irish doctor with Médecins Sans Frontières depicted the dire conditions facing Palestinians on the West Bank. Over 650 citizens have been killed by settlers. There was no safe place for them to go because they were afraid to travel and could be stopped at numerous checkpoints. A system of apartheid is in place, under which there are severe limitations on where Palestinians may travel. They may be subject to arbitrary detention and regular harassment, often handcuffed with their hands behind their backs and blindfolded for prolonged periods by the IDF, which constitutes a form of torture. [11]

The Israeli response is disproportionate and certainly is in breach of acceptable humanitarian behaviour. The use of explosives in pagers and walkie-talkies used against Hezbollah in Lebanon and the targeting of civilian residential areas is also illegal. The justification that it was done to assist 10,000 displaced Israelis pales into insignificance, amounting to less than 1% of displaced Palestinians. In the first week of the war in Lebanon, over 1.2 million citizens were displaced, and when a sixty-day ceasefire was announced, deaths already exceeded 3,000.

Despite widespread international condemnation, Israel does not behave like a normal democracy. Without restraint from the USA, it has been permitted to commit genocide, war crimes, ethnic cleansing, and, in general, crimes against humanity. The Arabs there have very limited rights. It has invaded and occupied neighbouring lands, disregarding the wishes of the local population, while allowing its citizens to kill the local inhabitants. It is reminiscent of 'Lebensraum', whereby throughout history, the German people occupied the lands of neighbouring Slavic people to provide living space for Germans. It has weaponised the police to carry out far-right Zionist policies. [12] Understandably, Arabs are seeking to prevent Israeli settlements on the West Bank.

Currently, settlers are harassing Palestinians in the Occupied Territories of the West Bank and burning their properties with no adequate police protection provided. The UN has reported almost 500 deaths caused by settlers with the backing of the IDF during 2023, at least 100 of them preceding the attack by Hamas. It had long before the war shown scant respect for the law by 'detaining' Palestinians indefinitely without trial or access to defence, sometimes subjecting them to violence. Horrendous allegations of physical, psychological, and sexual abuse have been reported. [13]

Palestinian journalists have been subjected to continuous harassment. Some of them have been detained for up to four months with no charges brought against them. They are subject to serious mistreatment and can be prosecuted under draconian laws. It appears that Israel wishes to destroy the Palestinian narrative. Freedom of speech has been denied. [14] Foreign journalists are only admitted to Gaza if they are accompanied by the IDF.

Since Netanyahu has stated that the war will continue for many months until all the Israeli war aims are met, the suffering of Gazans seems destined to continue indefinitely. He has dismissed the inner war cabinet, increasing his own control. Two of his senior ministers are illegal settlers on the West Bank. He has even deplored the temporary pauses introduced by the military to allow for increased food aid. He is willing to risk an escalation of the war into Lebanon and Iran. [15] He has suggested that Gaza should become some kind of island and that its 2,000.000 citizens be deported to an unspecified destination. His approach does nothing to achieve the release of the hostages.

On the ground, Israeli soldiers have been aggressive. When three escaped hostages appeared on the street, waving a white flag and stripped to the waist to show that they were unarmed, they were shot dead by trigger-happy soldiers. It seems that prisoners are rarely taken. They have attacked vehicles providing aid, claiming without substantiation that they were carrying Hamas fighters. They also fired on a clearly marked UN truck, although they subsequently admitted that this was 'a mistake'. A dual-national Turkish-American, protesting against Jewish settlements on the West Bank, was shot dead by the Israeli Defence Forces. [16] Given its international dimension, this shooting attracted more widespread condemnation than the continuous killings of innocent citizens by the IDF in both the West Bank and Gaza.

Israeli moves are increasingly provocative to Iran, first by assassinating a Hamas leader in Tehran and then by retaliatory attacks on Iranian military targets, which could draw the USA into a wider regional war in the Middle East. It has been suggested by a former senior adviser to the UN Secretary General that Israel, which wants to permanently change the balance of power in the Middle East, will attempt to achieve this by imperial expansion, annexing Lebanon, the West Bank, and Gaza. [17] This overriding objective seems to be doomed to failure, since it would not be accepted in these lands or the wider Arab world. It would also be opposed by Western democracies and many Jews, both in Israel and around the world, especially in the UK, where the Jewish community has courageously condemned the killing of Palestinians by Israel when they renewed the war. The attack on military bases in Syria in an opportunistic pre-emptive strike after the overthrow of Assad was quickly condemned by the UN. It is consistent with the wish to change the balance of power and could further damage peace in the area.

For over a decade, Netanyahu has had a serious conflict of interest due to a fraud case against him, which has now commenced on a phased basis. Many Israelis blame him for having provoked Hamas with his continued new settlements on the West Bank. And, according to early polls early in the war, 76% wanted to see him replaced as Prime Minister. Over 70% of Israelis are critical of his response to Hamas, should withdraw from Gaza, and declare an immediate ceasefire, according to a former prime minister and IDF chief of staff. [18] He managed to postpone the fraud case for years, claiming that it should not proceed, when the country was at war. If he is found guilty of fraud, it could end his political career.

The View of the United Nations and International Organisations

Before the end of 2023, the UN reported that over two million Gazans had been displaced and 40% of their homes damaged or destroyed. The Secretary General of the UN has made it clear that hospitals, schools, and clinics should never be targeted. Crucial life-saving supplies, including fuel, food, and water, must be allowed in, demanding immediate humanitarian access. The UN has described the situation as a humanitarian disaster of colossal proportions.

The UN has also accused Israel of relentless and deliberate attacks on medical personnel and facilities. It has condemned the deliberate destruction of the healthcare system, amounting to a war crime and crimes against humanity, constituting extermination. The Israeli army has fired on UN peacekeeping soldiers in Lebanon, wounding several of them, as well as forcing entrance into UNIFIL positions with their tanks. This constitutes a clear breach of international law. Israel ignores UN requests, and the IDF has told the UN to remove troops from Lebanon. Israel has banned the UN Secretary-General from visiting the country, showing its contempt for world opinion. The UN has warned against possible crimes against humanity in the absence of medical supplies and food. They have left people in no doubt, describing the situation as 'apocalyptic'.

The World Health Organisation has stated that hospitals must never be targeted, that the largest hospital was in a dire state, and was becoming a mass cemetery. It has been reported that 36 hospitals in Gaza have been reduced to just 11 partially functioning hospitals, of which only one is located in northern

Gaza. The situation could further deteriorate with famine and disease, especially cholera, from drinking dirty water. The EU has accused Israel of using starvation as a weapon of war.

Genocide

It is not surprising that the charges of war crimes and genocide have been levelled against Israel by South Africa and other countries. The International Criminal Court has issued arrest warrants on both Netanyahu and his defence minister, as well as three Hamas leaders, despite American lobbying on behalf of Israel, evoking an angry response from Israel. In 2024, the International Court of Justice ruled that the settlements in East Jerusalem and the West Bank were illegal, and that the occupation of these territories amounts to long-term annexation, which has undermined the right of the Palestinian people to self-determination. The ICC had given an emergency order for an immediate cessation of the war.

The late Pope Francis has added to the condemnation of Israel, describing the Israeli conduct of the war as immoral and disproportionate, while calling for an investigation into the charge of genocide. Shortly afterwards, the human rights organisation, Amnesty International, also stigmatised the war conducted by Israel in Gaza as genocide, as did the Human Rights Council, criticising, in particular, the stopping of water supplies.

The Israeli response has been disproportionate. Since Hamas killed less than 2,000 Israelis and retained only about 100 hostages, it would seem that full vengeance has already been exacted. Certainly, it amounts to considerably more than 'an eye for an eye and a tooth for a tooth', a traditional Hebrew doctrine. Over 3,000 Lebanese have been killed, which amounts to 20 deaths for each Israeli death. Displaced people between Gaza and Lebanon amount to over 3,000,000, or 100 times an estimated 300,000 displaced Israelis. It has been estimated that the population of Gaza has declined by over 6% since the start of the conflict in 2023, consisting of more than 50,000 dead, excluding 10,000 missing, presumed dead, 113,000 injured, and 100,000 forced into exile, but these numbers could be seriously understated. Many of those remaining are in urgent need of medical attention, especially women and children, while thousands more face starvation. Attacks on civilian targets continued remorselessly throughout the peace fire negotiations.

Reactions around the Globe

While sometimes criticism is muted by those who recall antisemitism in the Second World War, the vast majority of people, especially the young, are demanding a permanent ceasefire, as shown by a vote in the UN General Assembly, which was vetoed by America. Although a majority of EU States supported the motion, the EU, as an entity, remains divided, ignoring the urging from Ireland to support a ceasefire, and, in common with America, has expressed no serious demand to end the fighting. There is now widespread international clamour for a cessation of the killing and adequate compensation paid, while the Palestinians continue to live in terror. [19]

Many members of the Jewish community are also highly critical of the Zionist policy of the Netanyahu government. The American Senate majority leader, Chuck Schumer, condemned the violence and daily horror visited on the Palestinian people.

He condemned the subjugation and displacement of the Palestinians in the West Bank, while he called for new elections. [20] There are disturbing reports of the loss of press freedom in its treatment of journalists. [21] Netanyahu and his allies have repeatedly undermined public trust in independent journalism by smearing the motives of individual reporters. They are obliged to comply with military regulations, with the threat of criminal violations for any breaches. It has been reported that Israel has imprisoned 47 journalists, the second-highest number anywhere in the world after Hong Kong. [22] But Hong Kong no longer accepts the rule of law, with journalists and judges constantly subjected to intimidation. [23] This is a serious attack on freedom of speech, is incompatible with democracy in both jurisdictions, and has been condemned by Pope Leo XIV, who has called for the release of imprisoned journalists in the interests of freedom of speech and the Press.

Ultimately, a solution can be found only if both sides can find lasting peace. This must allow self-determination for Palestinians, who have not received justice from the State of Israel. Accepting a Two-State solution, rejected out of hand by the current Israeli Government, as a compromise, would necessitate distancing themselves from their extremists and agreeing to appropriate mediation. It could provide at least a long-overdue start.

The decision of Ireland, Spain, and Norway, followed by Slovenia, to recognise the State of Palestine met with predictable Israeli criticism. The EU has not yet recognised the State of Palestine and has been accused of double standards by Arab countries, since it accepts the sovereignty of Ukraine, but not Palestine. This may change following a strong Dutch intervention after Israel increased the use of starvation and aid as weapons of war. Israel claims that recognising Palestine is rewarding terrorism. Ironically, the State of Israel was created with the assistance of its own terrorist organisation, the Irgun. Some people consider recognition to be premature and counterproductive, but this is hard to accept. It has been over a decade since Stéphane Hessel disclosed the dire situation of the citizens of Gaza. Little progress for the people of Gaza has been achieved under Governments led by Netanyahu.

A six-week ceasefire was declared in January 2025, but Netanyahu announced that the war could restart at the end of this period. Israel continued to breach the ceasefire by killing Palestinians. Trump has urged them to abandon it totally, unless the remaining hostages are released immediately, thereby further endorsing the Israeli policy of genocide. Yet the Government ignores international and domestic pressure, led by the military, to restore a lasting ceasefire, fearing a split in the coalition.

It would be a strange irony of history if Israel, whose people had suffered terribly in the Holocaust, were to resume a genocide against the Palestinians. A former Israeli Prime Minister has stated that the proposed New' Humanitarian' City in Rafah would be a concentration camp for Palestinians and that forcing people into camp would amount to ethnic cleansing. Israeli settlers have attacked Palestinian camps on the West Bank, which Netanyahu wishes to annex with American support, even though this act would be in breach of international law. Israel has declared an intensified imperial territorial expansion in both the West Bank and Gaza, backed by a barbaric policy of mass starvation and continued genocide, despite worldwide condemnation. This amounts to a strategic blunder and a moral outrage. [24]

A peace process is long overdue. The history of the Palestinian people has been set out years ago.[25] The colonisation and ethnic cleansing of Gaza have been continuous since the foundation of the State of Israel in 1948. The majority of the Palestinians were forced to forego their democratic rights in a system of apartheid, as was practised in South Africa. They have been exploited ever since, a process which has intensified since the attack by Hamas. [26] The world pressured the Boers to change apartheid. The Palestinians should not be treated as an inferior people, and global pressure should do the same with the present Israeli Government.

The Current Situation: A Personal Viewpoint

I enjoyed working on a kibbutz in Israel as a student and made many friends there. Since then, the Zionist settlements on the West Bank installed by Israel have understandably provoked retaliation. Israel's reputation as a civilised, law-abiding country has been severely tarnished, increasing its isolation on the global stage, and has inevitably given rise to further unwanted antisemitism.

During the pandemic, I read the bible from cover to cover, which provided me with a better understanding of Judaism, though I would have difficulties with some of its teachings. Fundamentally, I do not accept that the Israelites are God's chosen people and that they should be permitted to occupy the whole of Palestine through imperialistic conquest. It is perhaps not surprising that events chronicled thousands of years ago contain some controversial elements. For example, neither slavery nor extreme violence, such as putting one's enemies to the sword and killing all women and children, can have any place in Gaza or elsewhere. The Old Testament contains much wise teaching, but I find it problematic to claim that the bible should always be taken literally, and believe that many Jews today would agree. The interpretation should be adapted to the circumstances of the current world.

There have been attempts to find a solution based on the figure of Abraham, who is recognised by Muslims and Christians, as well as Jews, for whom he is the founding Patriarch. But many people now would not accept Abraham as a suitable role model. It is stated that he was concerned about his own well-being and that of his pretty wife, Sarah, when he went to Egypt. So he passed her off as his sister and put her to work in the sex trade, from which he amassed a fortune. [27]

If a solution based on the legacy of Abraham is ruled out, Northern Ireland could provide a useful role model. It is not, of course, an exact parallel, since no war was ever declared there. Casualties were much lower, amounting to 3,700 deaths, together with 47,000 injuries, of which 25,000 were women and children over the thirty-year conflict. Nevertheless, two serious adversarial groups eventually put aside their differences with the help of skilful and patient mediators. The Palestinians have been seeking their right to equality for more than a century, but democracy is currently endangered for Israelis, as well as Palestinians.

The USA remains Israel's closest ally and has not put serious pressure on Israel to end the war. Shortly after the ICC ruled against Israel, Netanyahu was invited to address the joint Houses of Congress, which constituted a record fourth time by any foreign leader. In his speech, he described his friend Joe Biden as a 'Proud Irish-American Zionist'. In view of America continuing to supply arms to Israel, the failure to condemn

Israeli atrocities, and ignoring international law over the West Bank, there is a ring of truth to this description. It does not seem that Biden was prepared to criticise Netanyahu, at least in public. Despite a strained relationship between Biden and Netanyahu, whom Biden described as a liar, America continues to supply arms to Israel, while also providing it with unconditional political and diplomatic support.

The Implications for Democracy and Possible Future Wars

Those countries that continue to supply arms to Israel must also be considered to be complicit in genocide. America's image as the leading advocate of democracy around the globe has been severely damaged. So too has the reputation of the EU countries, which were unwilling to condemn Israel. The respect for democracy as the ideal form of government has received a serious setback, particularly in the Muslim world. It seems that democracies are unwilling to protect the development of a fledgling Palestinian country, preferring to support their major allies and protect their own national interests. Democracies, seeking to defend their system of government, must be wary of the support that they can expect to receive from America, in view of their track record.

It is likely that further wars will break out in the future, whether predictably or not, between countries unknown. It requires a courageous pundit to predict who the parties might be. One of America's most respected political scientists undertook this onerous task in 1996 in a book that generated considerable controversy at that time. [28] But the attacks on

Hamas and Gaza have led some countries to reopen links with the Taliban. As in the Twin Towers attack in 2011, it seemed that a real threat between Western democracies and the normally divided Islamic world had become a distinct possibility. America's prevarication over Gaza has led some countries, such as the UAE, to reopen links with the Taliban, further adding to the religious divide.

It is possible now to forecast some trends, particularly after the US slashed international aid, such as the rise of China and Russia, together with the relative decline of the USA, especially amongst long-term allies, who question its future reliability. Israel under Netanyahu wants to control the Middle East. Each country is determined to protect its sphere of influence, but what might be the outcome for world peace is difficult to guess. America, Russia, Israel, China, and North Korea would be a formidable new Axis of Imperialist Powers.

America, too, could initiate wars, in view of Trump's threatened military intervention in both Greenland, with its vast mineral resources, and Panama. His claim that it is for security reasons appears to be spurious, since it has enormously reduced its troops there over recent years in existing US bases. This would turn America into a traditional colonial power, seeking to expand its territorial interests by military might. His treatment of Palestinians must inevitably provoke a strong reaction from the Arab world. If Trump rules as a fascist dictator, war could be the result.

But the wider tectonic changes from the speedy resurgence of Russia remain elusive, with endless possibilities. War could break out in the Balkans or in the turmoil of the Middle East. There might be another Jihad attack on the West. Muslim nations may seek to protect their co-religionists, suffering from discrimination in India. Iran could attack its traditional enemies. Finally, war could break out in Eastern Asia, where India and Pakistan could rekindle their war over Kashmir. [29]

One professor of European thought has pessimistically predicted that liberalism will not survive and the world will revert to a state of nature, as outlined by Thomas Hobbes. [30] It is hard to refute this pessimistic conclusion, but it is impossible to forecast where wars will occur with any degree of confidence.

The situation is complicated since the two leading aggressors, Netanyahu and Putin, have strong personal reasons to continue their wars. Furthermore, the USA has lost its ability to act as an honest broker in Gaza. What is, however, clear is that the United Nations, judged by its recent record and the continuation of vetoes on the Security Council, is ill-equipped to deal with them. The resolution of the Gaza war is, arguably, the greatest challenge for democracy internationally. Trump is likely to increase support for Israel, unless Saudi Arabia manages to exert moderation. Failure in Gaza could result in a loss of support for democracy around the world.

CHAPTER 13

How and Why Democracies Fail

Democracies can fail for varied reasons. The most dramatic way that a democracy fails is by way of a coup d'état. Coups normally occur without any warning. Occasionally, they may be bloodless, but usually they are accompanied by violence. They may be instantly successful or take a long time to reach their goals. Below are three very different styles of coup.

Coups

In April 1967, a coup took place in Athens, the home of democracy. The military was concerned that a left-wing government might leave NATO. Overnight, the army occupied the city. Tanks appeared suddenly on the streets, and key positions were secured. Radio and television stations were taken over. Individuals considered to be dangerous, including the prime minister and his probable successor, were arrested. It was a carefully planned, bloodless coup, and the Colonels were to remain in power until 1974, when they were ousted following the mishandling of the Turkish invasion of Cyprus.[1]

Many years earlier, a coup in Europe had a very different outcome. In 1936, Franco and other generals in Spain attempted a coup, which was partially successful, against the left-leaning republican government, in the name of the Nationalist Party. Thousands of people from abroad enlisted on either side. Germany and Italy backed the Nationalists, and Russia backed the Republicans. After numerous atrocities, the

Nationalists entered Madrid in 1939 and proclaimed victory. Hundreds of thousands of republicans fled to refugee camps in France. Those remaining faced persecution. Franco remained in power until his death in 1975, when the country transitioned back into democracy.

In 1973, Chile, which traditionally had been regarded as one of Latin America's most stable and successful democracies, was experiencing economic turmoil with hyperinflation. The democratically elected socialist government of Allende was overturned in a coup led by Augusto Pinochet with the backing of the USA. [2] The regime was characterised by the systematic suppression of political parties and the unprecedented persecution of dissidents, including throwing opponents out of helicopters. The mindless slaughter has been compared to Nazi Germany. [3]

Chilean human rights groups estimate that more than 40,000 citizens were politically executed, disappeared, imprisoned, or tortured. An estimated 200,000 citizens were also driven into exile. Draconian cuts in the standard of living arose from the economic policies advocated by the US Chicago School of Monetarists. The end came in 1990, when a civilian government was elected. Pinochet was later indicted for human rights violations, but he was never convicted. Margaret Thatcher astonishingly denounced his detention as outrageous, unlawful, and inhumane.

During the Cold War almost three out of every four democracies failed due to coups: in Latin America: Argentina, Brazil, Chile, Peru, Uruguay, the Dominican Republic, and Guatemala; in Asia: Turkey, Pakistan, and Thailand; in Africa: Egypt, Nigeria, and Ghana; in Europe: Greece. [4] Coups in Africa have been widespread over the last five years: Burkina Faso,

Sudan, Guinea, Chad, and Mali all became targets. The most recent cases have been in Gabon and in Niger, where the new military leaders wish to replace the traditional relationship with France with one with Russia.

In many parts of Africa, there is rising dissatisfaction with democracy, as it is currently practised. Corruption, violence, and extreme poverty are widespread. For an outsider, it is difficult to know if the reason is an unwillingness to accept the voting result, genuine dissatisfaction with misgovernment and corruption, the military seeking power and enrichment, or the influence of an outside country, searching for mineral wealth or some other strategic advantage.

Most of the Middle East Gulf States, in reality, are dictatorships, often showing a complete contempt for the values of liberal democracy. For example, in 2018, James Khashoggi, a Saudi dissident journalist, was tortured and murdered by agents of the Saudi government when he entered the Saudi consulate in Istanbul to obtain a visa. He was ambushed by a 16-member squad of Saudi assassins, who dismembered and attempted to dispose of his body once they had killed him. While Saudi Arabia's sports sponsorship is generous, its appreciation of democratic norms of behaviour in the Middle East dictatorships remains woefully deficient.

But, as has been evident for many years, democracies can also die from the acts of elected leaders, who subvert the process that brought them to power. [5] The Ship of State, named 'Democracy', may be heading for the rocks, steered by an autocrat, while those on watch either have fallen asleep or been forced off the deck. This surprising development is equivalent to an internal coup and will be taken up in the case of Britain below and subsequently in Chapter 15. The latest example of an internal coup was by Trump in 2025 America.

Coups may end with a countercoup and democracy restored following victory at the polls, where elections are permitted, as happened in Greece and Chile. In Spain, it ultimately fell after the death of the leader. Occasionally, they may end due to pressure from the people, as could happen in Thailand. The most surprising reversal in recent years was when the USA voted to terminate its democracy by voting in Trump, a fascist, in 2024 as its president. In Ireland, the military has always avoided any involvement in politics.

The assassination of any politician may not bring down the government, but it damages democracy. In the past, American presidents were periodically murdered in office. In the Brexit campaign, a Labour Party politician was killed, while in 2024, an attempt was made on the life of Robert Fico, the President of Slovakia. In Ireland, demonstrations of masked men outside the homes of politicians are an unwelcome, intimidatory step in this direction.

Arms and Threats of Violence

The support of undemocratic regimes in undermining democracies is a matter of serious concern. Both Russia and China have supplied arms to the military junta in Myanmar for use against the rebels, who are fighting for the restoration of democracy in their country. They are also happy to support regimes run by a strongman or military forces, opposed to democracy.

Communist China has reversed the thawing of regulation following the death of Mao Tse Tung and now threatens to invade Taiwan. President Xi has increasingly begun to resemble Putin with an autocratic leadership style. He does not tolerate dissent or free speech, persecutes minorities, and has extended his rule indefinitely. North Korea also threatens to expand its territory by war. In the last twenty-five years, autocracy has both expanded territorially and enormously increased its sphere of influence.

The challenges of China have become belatedly recognised with its technological power and considerable financial muscle in Third World countries, particularly in Africa. They back up their financial muscle with soft power, in contrast to Russia, which they hope to spread by a kind of osmosis, whatever the facts may be. They have persecuted Tibetans for centuries, and their suppression of dissidents in Hong Kong during 2020 received widespread coverage. What is less well known is their treatment of the Uyghur people in the north-west of their country. The Uyghurs are a mainly Muslim ethnic group, comprising around twelve million people, who have sought independence from China, which regards them as terrorists. Many have been detained in 're-education' camps, and hundreds of thousands sentenced to imprisonment. Prisoners attempting to escape risk being shot. Some are pressed into forced labour in the rich cotton-picking land. Women are subject to mass sterilisation. The former US Secretary of State, Anthony Blinken, has accused China of genocide and crimes against humanity.[6]

Different democratic governments have faced serious criticism in recent years for various reasons. Germany has been blamed for becoming overly reliant on Russian gas. President

Macron in France, trying to raise the pension age, thereby reducing the financial burden on future generations, has been met with riots and strikes. Britain has struggled with the fallout of Brexit. America has been deeply divided during and after the first Trump presidency, attracting criticism over the way it has treated detainees in the Guantanamo Bay camp during the War on Terror. Even democracies, which have emerged after a long struggle for freedom, like Myanmar, can treat minorities badly, as they did with the Rohingya Muslims.

Forty years ago, many people looked to Japan as an economic role model. But in recent years, no country seems to be able to match China in economic growth, which is needed to underpin democracy. Those countries seeking rapid economic growth now have a role model other than democracy to explore. Ten years ago, China embarked on the Belt and Road Initiative, essentially its way of creating a modern Silk Road of infrastructure, linking China to Asia and Europe. Consequently, it is often in a strong position to dictate terms when Third World countries have taken out large loans for essential infrastructure.

The Chinese political model, if followed, would be a promise of improved welfare, together with the loss of individual freedom, especially freedom of speech, which has been so highly valued by liberal democrats. But the problem remains of how to identify Plato's philosopher king who can deliver this solution without becoming a tyrant. The Marshal Tito's and Lee Kuan Yews of this world are in short supply.

Boris Johnson: A Failed British Internal Coup

Britain, the world's oldest democracy, has a proud record of democratic government and has produced Winston Churchill, one of its greatest defenders.

Following the resignation of Theresa May, Boris Johnson was elected leader of the Conservative Party. He was a surprising choice for prime minister in the post-Brexit world. His private life, like that of Donald Trump, was colourful and controversial. He was dismissed from his first job as a journalist for inventing quotes. He was sacked again from the shadow cabinet for lying about his private life. His former boss at the *Spectator* magazine stated that "He was unfit for national office because he cares for no interest, save his own fame and gratification, was morally bankrupt, and that he would not recognise truth if he met it on an identity parade". [7]

His style of leadership was very similar to that of other populists. As described in Chapter 6, he indulged in anti-EU rhetoric and attacked the institutions that he perceived to be his opponents, including the judiciary, the BBC, and Parliament itself. He also threatened senior civil servants who provided unwelcome advice. On the other hand, he could legitimately reward friends or large party donors with life peerages or a valuable government contract, a more dubious practice.

His handling of the COVID pandemic was also controversial. Similar to Trump in America, economic growth took precedence over human lives. Evidence to the UK parliamentary investigation into the pandemic was that Johnson believed that old people should be allowed to get COVID and die, while accepting their fate. Ignoring warnings from senior advisors, Johnson was slow to recognise the pandemic, and state systems were dysfunctional. [8]

Despite a large parliamentary majority, his party was hopelessly divided, with many moderates unwilling to risk a trade war with the EU. He seemed to be a prisoner of his own extreme right-wing views. Some of his party members simply resigned their seats, including his own brother, who must be one of the very few resigning politicians wanting to spend less time with their family! Others, many of them highly respected, including a nephew of Winston Churchill, were deselected from representing the party at the next election. Like Trump, appointments to the cabinet seemed to be based heavily on personal loyalty, rather than ability.

The Government appeared to lose its moral compass. Between 2020 and 2022, the Tory party was rocked by a series of scandals, some with a financial element and others with pure sleaze. [9] Boris Johnson sought help from a party donor for an expensive makeover to his Downing Street flat. He failed to establish the facts about a luxury villa lent to him in Mustique. A former minister committed an egregious breach of lobbying, for which he was paid £110,000 per annum.

Other scandals were sexual. A former Tory MP was sentenced to two years' imprisonment for sexual assault. Another was suspended for making unwanted advances to a former member of staff. A former minister was found by a High Court judge to have raped his wife. Another MP was suspended over allegations of sexual harassment and cocaine abuse. Another admitted to watching pornography in the House of Commons. The Deputy Chief Whip admitted groping two men in a private club.

Yet more scandals erupted over events which occurred during the COVID pandemic, when politicians seemed to believe that they were not bound by lockdown rules. Dominic Cummings, a close advisor to Johston, was found to have made lockdown-busting trips to north-east England. The Health Secretary resigned when it emerged that he had broken social distancing rules by kissing his aide in his office. The most significant problems were the parties thrown at Downing Street, known as 'Partygate', where politicians declined to follow the social distancing restrictions, introduced to fight the pandemic. Following an investigation carried out by a senior public servant, it was found that widespread rule-breaking had occurred. Fines were imposed on Johnson and others. In 2023, the Deputy Prime Minister also resigned following findings that he had bullied civil servants.

Boris Johnson was eventually forced to resign as Prime Minister. He was replaced by a close ally, Liz Truss, whose premiership lasted only 49 days, while the nation was mourning the death of Queen Elizabeth II. She embarked on a risky 'Big Bang' economic expansion programme, reminiscent of the 'Barber Boom' fifty years earlier. [10] Making a big bang dash for growth and disregarding the warnings may easily lead politicians to slip and fall flat on their faces, as indeed Liz Truss, a right-wing admirer of Donald Trump, did. A currency crisis developed, and she was forced to resign.

The scandals resulted in a collapse of support for the party in the opinion polls. Johnson, like Trump in the USA, refused to observe the rules and norms of political behaviour. Usually, the Tory Party would rein in its leaders, but they failed to do so in this case. He and his right-wing allies had taken over control. The populist government was finally brought down by public opinion when backbenchers realised that it could affect their chances of re-election. In due course, Boris Johnson was found guilty of lying and misleading Parliament, forcing him eventually to resign his seat in the House of Commons. After his resignation, he continued to breach the rules. He immediately took a job at the *Daily Mail,* which could provide him with a platform to undermine the Government further, without seeking the required permission.

Johnson reacted in a similar way to Donald Trump when facing an unfavourable result. He attempted to undermine democracy by discrediting the work of the Parliamentary Committee on Privileges, which had investigated 'Partygate'. He described it as a 'kangaroo court' and that he was the victim of a 'witch hunt'. He questioned the integrity of some of its members, claiming that the chairman was not impartial and that another was a hypocrite. The process was a political assassination, he claimed, based on trumped-up charges.

Parliament disagreed and, when it voted on the Report of the Privileges Committee, 354 members voted in its favour, while only seven voted against. Rather than face humiliation and excoriation, Johnson had already resigned his seat without any apology. As he had done all his life, Johnson displayed contempt for the workings of democratic institutions and ignored the rules and norms of parliamentary behaviour. Fortunately, he was not strong enough to ride roughshod over his party. British democracy had been sufficiently robust to withstand a determined effort to undermine it.

Nevertheless, overall, British democracy suffered a setback in the Johnson era. It survived the attacks on the judiciary, Parliament, and the BBC, but, unfortunately, the collateral damage was severe. Voters discovered that the leadership was incompetent and could not be trusted, while the behaviour of individual male politicians was reprehensible and inconsistent with traditional Tory values. The damage done may not be restricted to the party, but can also undermine the respect for political leaders and public confidence in democracy as a form of government. The Johnson era was a bad chapter in the history of British democracy. Nevertheless, a comeback cannot be ruled out if the Tories want a new leader to face Nigel Farage's Reform Party. [11]

The Public Perception of Politicians

In many countries, the electorate has become highly cynical about politicians, whose credibility is comparable to that of a second-hand car salesman. They are often accused of putting their own interest above those of the electorate. This has fuelled the growth of populism, providing an opportunity to be exploited by aspiring and unscrupulous autocrats, as described in Chapter 16. Politicians are remunerated generously by way of pay, perks, and pensions. Often, they are surrounded by well-paid 'spin-doctors', whose primary function is to get them re-elected, even if this involves distorting the truth.

Promises made at election time can soon disappear and bring into question the integrity of those who had peddled them. Voters believe that their traditional representatives are out of touch with their problems. Large regions that have suffered from deindustrialisation, such as the North of England, may feel particularly aggrieved. The elite is blamed, and anyone seen as anti-elitist may receive a good audience, who may be disillusioned subsequently, when the promises are broken.

Voters are attracted to those who offer a fundamental change, often made by parties unaware of the realities of office.

In Ireland, Sinn Féin has filled this vacuum. Fianna Fáil and Fine Gael, the present coalition government, have formed governments for a century, and their centrist economic policies are relatively similar. Sinn Féin offers a more left-wing alternative. It became the largest political party and has built up strong support, especially in poorer city areas and amongst young voters. Internally divided, their rating by opinion polls has fallen, and they performed badly in the 2024 elections, though they recovered shortly afterwards. While they have been involved in power sharing in Northern Ireland, they have never been involved in Government in the Republic of Ireland.

Yet there are many unanswered questions about the past of Sinn Féin and how policy is determined. [12] The party was formed as the political wing of the Irish Republican Army, which led the armed struggle for the Nationalist community in Northern Ireland. The IRA was involved in serious sectarian killings, kidnapping, and carried out numerous bank robberies. There are also disturbing claims that it failed to protect vulnerable young members of its community from serious sexual abuse and discouraged subsequent investigations. It was accused of bullying party members and having an ambivalent view regarding the use of hard drugs by its members. It was claimed that the party was run in a secretive manner, at least initially, with a top-down structure. The leader was then Gerry Adams, who ran it in a way common to modern populists. A journalist, writing a biography of the current party leader, has claimed that the party in the Republic takes its orders from the Army Council, a shadowy military organisation, based in Belfast. [13] No democracy likes its leaders to take their instructions from an outside agency, whether in the USA or Ireland.

Democracies may fall suddenly by way of a coup or more slowly by a surrender to populism. They are open to criticism as never before, and confidence in the system is low. Liberal democracy needs to demonstrate how it can perform better to deal with the complex challenges it faces, if it is to thrive and prosper in the years ahead.

CHAPTER 14

Different Types of Autocracy: A Ski Run Classification

An authoritarian regime favours and reinforces strict obedience to authority at the expense of personal freedom. By its definition, it cannot be compatible with the freedom central to democracy. Sometimes its existence is obvious, but at other times it is subtler, with a populist leader claiming to represent the will of the people while overriding the views of elected representatives.

The fundamental theory underlying democracy is the separation of powers, as set out by an eighteenth-century Frenchman, Montesquieu. He divided French society into three classes: the monarchy, the aristocracy, and the commons. There were two types of governmental power: sovereign and executive. A stable system operates through checks and balances. The three functions are interdependent in a democracy. The Executive should not be allowed to usurp the functions of the legislature, which makes the laws, or the judiciary, which interprets them. It became a foundation stone of many constitutions around the world, including the USA, where the founding fathers were familiar with the writing of Montesquieu.[1]

An authoritarian regime seeks all power for the executive and therefore needs to limit the powers of the legislature and the judiciary. With the growth of autocracies, this is becoming increasingly commonplace. Authoritarian regimes may vary in their degree of strictness over time. It may be helpful to illustrate the differences by considering a mountain with authoritarianism at its summit and democracy at its base.

The Slippery Upward Slope of Democracy

From the top of the mountain, the quickest route downwards is by falling or being pushed over a precipice, as happens in a coup. Normally, these are bloody affairs with enormous damage, the scars of which may last for many years. Examples already discussed in Chapter 13 are Greece, Spain, and Chile. They rarely end peacefully, although in the case of Spain, it came with the death of General Franco. An analogy for classifying democracies is the description of ski runs. Ski runs are classified according to their levels of steepness.

Black runs are the steepest. In terms of authoritarianism, these are the totalitarian dictatorships, such as Russia, its close ally, Belarus, North Korea, and China, all of which are contemptuous of liberal democracy principles, considering them to be part of Western decadence. The executive exercises total control. If elections technically exist, they are farcical. Opponents of the regime are imprisoned, thus drastically curbing freedom of speech. The leaders often entitle themselves to remain in power indefinitely. The independence of the judiciary is non-existent, as Sergei Magnitsky and Bill Browder discovered in Russia. The group includes all dictatorships, such as African and other military dictatorships, together with Muslim dictatorships, such as Iran and formerly Syria.

Iran is a Muslim autocracy. Narges Mohammadi, a prominent Human Rights activist and Women's Rights activist, who was awarded the 2023 Nobel Peace Prize, is serving a ten-year sentence for "Spreading anti-state propaganda". She has been convicted five times, sentenced to 34 years' imprisonment and 154 lashes. [2]

Red runs are the next most challenging ski runs. In these countries, while elections technically exist, in practice, it is virtually impossible to dislodge the governing party. The experience of the Law and Justice party in Poland, described in Chapter 15, illustrates how this can be achieved. Hungary is somewhat similar. Viktor Orban, in his first spell as prime minister from 1998 to 2002, governed democratically through his Fidesz party. But when he returned to power in 2010, he became authoritarian. He simply packed key institutions, such as the Prosecution Service, the State Audit Office, and the Constitutional Court, with allies. Effective opposition became a virtual impossibility. He remains at loggerheads with the EU over the independence of the judiciary and adopts a friendly foreign policy towards Russia, while he exercises considerable influence in Eastern Europe. If his political model were to spread, democracy in the EU could be seriously undermined.

But a politician can also be legitimately elected before turning to autocracy. One such example is Venezuela under the populist Hugo Chavez. Fulminating against corruption in government, he was elected president in 1998. Five years later, he turned quickly towards authoritarianism. He closed a major television station, arrested, or exiled opposition judges and media figures. Finally, he abolished the term limit on the presidency, enabling him to remain in power until his death in 2012. He had many admirers, such as Jeremy Corbyn in England, but the reality was widespread corruption.

At that stage, the presidency passed to Nicolas Maduro, who has ruled in a similar fashion, despite causing economic chaos. The economic mismanagement persisted for more than a decade, resulting in the mass emigration of a quarter of the population, hunger, and poverty. The United Nations has accused him of crimes against humanity, as death squads under his control committed thousands of extrajudicial killings. In 2015, an election was held. While it may have been free, it was not fair to the opposition, who won a crushing victory. Maduro quickly moved to strip the Assembly of its power. The 2018 presidential election was widely condemned as fraudulent. But Maduro has successfully resisted attempts at home and abroad to force him from office, showing increasing authoritarianism.

He managed to prevent a charismatic female leader from standing against him. He has also got the support of the army, many of whom are involved in widespread criminality and drug trading. Heading into the 2024 election, he warned that the country would 'fall into a blood bath in a fratricidal civil war'. The election seemed to be completely fraudulent. Observers were banned from attending the count. Despite a 20/30% deficit in opinion polls, Maduro was announced to be the winner. There is no guarantee that, even if heavily defeated, he will ever peacefully relinquish control. [3]

He seems, like Trump, not to believe in 'loser consent' when he loses an election, but this may not matter. He is a member of the autocrats' club. Russia supplies him with arms, Cuba supplies surveillance equipment, while the Chinese invest in the country. [4] Unsurprisingly, he was quickly congratulated by Putin and Xi on his re-election. There were protests from Opposition leaders, whom he threatened with arrest. It was a complete victory for the forces of autocracy and a total loss of any semblance of democracy.

His discredited regime remained in power by a policy of total oppression, backed up by the army and the Cuban forces brought in shortly before the election. Many of its citizens and others around the world consider that the leader of the Opposition, Edmundo Gonzales, who has taken refuge in Spain, to be the legitimate President. For the ordinary citizens who had experienced a 75% contraction in the economy, the wish to emigrate has only increased. Trump has responded by deporting impoverished Venezuelans back to their country. Venezuela is undoubtedly now a 'Rogue State'. The ski classification has moved from red to black.

A further example is Peru. In 1990, Peru had serious problems with a Maoist guerrilla group called the Shining Path, hyperinflation, and drug trafficking. Alberto Fujimori was a university professor and a candidate, opposed to the Establishment. When elected, he quickly demonstrated his authoritarian tendencies. He attacked uncooperative congressmen and judges. He ruled by decree, bypassing Congress. Less than two years after his election, he dissolved Congress and governed as a dictator.

Authoritarian regimes, which arrive by red runs, are particularly insidious and may be difficult to recognise, because the changes may occur gradually and not attract much publicity. They masquerade as democracies, but operate in a very different manner. For a Machiavellian autocrat, it may be easier to acquire power in this way, rather than by way of a coup.

Niccolò Machiavelli was a diplomat, historian, poet, and political thinker in 16th-century Florence. This was a time of warring city-states, which frequently made alliances with other cities or foreign powers, such as Spain and France. He wrote his most famous book, *The Prince,* as a guide to rulers, while he sought a job in the Florentine court. [5] His advice was designed purely about gaining and retaining power in a world of realpolitik. It has been described as satanic, totally immoral, and a cynical handbook for tyrants. Mankind is fickle, hypocritical, and greedy, so a prince must think only of war, its institutions, and discipline. Those autocracies on a red run, including Trump in America, seem to have naturally put his ideas into practice.

In the first place, the prince must be cruel and ruthless. Take out the existing rulers and crush the powerful. It is better to be feared than loved, because love has obligations. If an injury must be inflicted on a man, it should be so severe that vengeance need not be feared in the face of likely further punishment. Avoid dependence on those people who cannot be trusted, like mercenaries. It seems that Putin was unaware of this advice while copying most of the remainder.

In the second place, it is deeply cynical. Appear to be merciful, faithful, humane, upright, and religious, but act otherwise. Make promises, but break them as necessary. Never win by force what can be won by deception. Delegate unpopular measures, but distribute favours personally. Be a cunning fox and a fierce lion. Occasionally, moderation may suit the prince. Machiavelli cautions against changing laws, raising taxes on conquered people, or widespread confiscation of land to avoid unnecessarily antagonising them. The Prince should avoid contempt and hatred since they may lead to a conspiracy against him.

Autocracies with Elections

Some autocracies still hold what purport to be open elections to persuade the electorate of their legitimacy, which should suit the autocrat in power. The most extreme abuse occurs in Russia, where any semblance of fairness is totally absent. In the presidential election of 2024, an opponent of the Ukraine war was prevented from standing, while opponents or critics of the regime have been imprisoned and murdered. The election was neither free nor fair.

A successful election, even if rigged to favour the Government, conveys a sense of legitimacy and undermines the opposition, who are deemed to have lost. Prime Minister Viktor Orban has described Hungary as an 'illiberal democracy'. In Syria, after years of brutal autocracy and economic hardship, protests throughout the country against the regime of President Assad mounted. For years, the support of Russia had kept Assad in power, but that era finally ended in 2024.

In Thailand, a military coup occurred in 2014. However, the country still holds elections. In 2023, opposition parties won an overwhelming majority of the seats, which was a humiliation for the regime and a big boost for Asian democracy, exerting pressure for change. The military subsequently aligned itself in government with one party, but how much change will happen remains to be seen. They have succeeded by means of 'lawfare' through the courts in dissolving the liberal party, which gained more votes than any other in the last election, and banned its senior members from politics for a decade.

Many autocracies try to retain power by imprisoning, harassing, or detaining political opponents and members of their families. If elections are held in these circumstances, democracy is fundamentally undermined.

Potential Autocracies

Blue runs exist where a moderate authoritarian regime is in power, but there are still some forms of apparently legitimate periodic elections. Many observers would classify them as democracies. Freedom of speech still exists, and the judiciary is largely independent of the executive, but often human rights are violated. They can quickly move to a red or even black classification if their problems are not addressed.

Increasingly, Latin American governments are resorting to an iron fist approach in dealing with violence generated by drug gangs. El Salvador is a poor, dangerous Central American country with a high murder rate. President Nayib Bukele successfully reduced the murder rate by imprisoning 80,000 people, about 3% of the male population, many of whom did not receive a proper trial, but the basic human need for security was satisfied. Bukele was re-elected with a landslide majority and has become one of the most popular leaders in the world. [6] Ecuador, Brazil, and Mexico face similar challenges, but where civil rights are eroded, democracy becomes endangered. [7]

The world's largest democracy, India, has a proud history of religious tolerance, dating back to the time of the Emperor Ashoka the Great in the third century BC, and has embraced democracy since it achieved its independence from Britain. But President Modi persistently attempted to silence any opposition and wants to bring the appointments of senior judges under Government control. He also refused to condemn Russia's invasion of Ukraine and supplied arms to Russia. A visit to Russia in 2024, where he publicly embraced Putin, caused widespread dismay. It was later revealed that India covertly supplied sensitive goods to Russia and had explored building facilities to secure components for the war effort. [8]

If, as has been alleged, his government had a hand in the assassination of a Sikh leader in Canada, then a further move away from democracy has occurred. An opposition leader, who is Delhi's First Minister, has been arrested on alleged corruption charges. When 141 Opposition MPs were suspended for demanding a discussion following a security infringement, there were further charges that Modi wanted to undermine democracy. After ten years in power, he lost his overall majority in the 2024 election. The ending of the 'Modi Raj' promises to prevent a slide into autocracy and buttresses democracy.

The government party, the BJP, reflects a Hindu nationalist ideology or 'Hindutva', where the rights of minority religions are not respected, as they traditionally were in the past. Modi persecuted Muslims, especially in Kashmir. The policy includes expunging references from the school curriculum relating to the great Muslim Mughal Empire. It has been able to remove the leader of the Opposition over a sardonic remark made on the campaign trail about the President. Modi's handling of COVID was poor, but Western criticism of him has been muted, at least in part, because India is regarded as a counterweight to China and is the world's fastest-growing major economy. [9] Freedom House reduced the classification of

Indian democracy from 'free', which it had received in 1997, to 'partly free' in 2021.

Green runs are the gentlest slopes. Democracy still exists, but there are signs that this could change, perhaps quite quickly, thus aligning them with autocracies. Far-right groups have growing support and can be found running demonstrations, which can become violent. In Italy, a right-wing government has been formed, but initially avoided an extremist position. In the Netherlands, the Freedom Party with anti-Islamic and anti-immigrant views has become the largest party. In Austria, the right-wing Freedom Party tops the opinion polls. Elsewhere in Europe, right-wing parties exist in Greece, France, and Germany. Both Marine Le Pen, the leader of the far-right and potentially a future French President, and Gerhart Schroeder, the former socialist German Chancellor, have made speeches supportive of Russia. France and Germany must now fall into green runs with the rise of the Far-Right.

In Latin America, a right-wing libertarian has been elected President of Argentina. It is premature to judge whether he will succeed. He has promised major cuts in government expenditure. Fully fledged democracies, even those with a taint of corruption, are not on the slippery slope, but operate instead on the level of snow. Poland is seeking to re-enter this group if it can recover from the injuries sustained on the red runs in recent years.

In Europe, fully fledged democracies include all other EU countries, except for Hungary and Slovakia, as well as Switzerland, the Scandinavian countries, and Iceland. Asia includes Japan, South Korea, and Taiwan. In the Americas, it includes Canada, the West Indian islands, but no longer the USA. No country is guaranteed to remain a permanent democracy, and its status may be recategorized quickly with a change of government.

In Ireland, there is no alt-right party with representation in politics. But there are groups whose main function is to disrupt the workings of the Government, using social media to spread unrest. An example was the rioting and looting in 2023 following the knifing of a child in Dublin, a new and unwelcome development in the national capital. It seems that hard, far-right parties and movements, opposing refugees and immigrants, are continuing to gain ground. The seeds of authoritarianism may be sown, but have not yet germinated.

Finally, there are the *Nursery Slopes.* Skiers start off learning the basic skills of stopping and turning in both directions on the nursery slopes. If they fail, they cannot advance to the coloured runs. Some countries set out to become democracies, but fail at the early stages, becoming the victims of infant mortality. Some time ago, in 1960, researchers examined 117 young democracies around the globe. [10] Several failed more than once. By 2024, 52 of them could no longer be deemed to be democracies, a failure rate not short of 50%. The highest rate of failure was in sub-Saharan Africa.

While much has changed since then, with ever more democracies failing, their conclusions may prove instructive today. Young democracies usually emerge in very challenging conditions: widespread extreme poverty and inequality, dependence on a small number of basic commodities, and a high level of ethnic fragmentation among other social divisions. Wild promises are frequently made to the electorate, which cannot be fulfilled. Often, the parties are ineffective, and checks on the chief executive are minimal.

Elections should enhance accountability, creating an incentive for opposing parties to compromise. But too often this fails to happen. Struggling leaders may seek out special support from their ethnic group and friends, giving rise to general cynicism. They may even obtain support from other countries in exchange for favours to help them remain in power. Inevitably, then, democracy fails. The conventional reason given for failure is poor economic growth, but the researchers believe that the basic reason is weak institutions. Those who survive birth have a better chance than those who die in early infancy. But all could be assisted with better nursing support.

The Success of Autocracy on Black Runners

Putin and other autocrats are openly contemptuous of Western values. Tolerance and democracy are dismissed as Western imperialism. Yet it is not clear what values they do espouse, other than 'Might is Right', certainly not those of traditional communism. They demand total obedience from their citizens and tolerate no opposition. There is neither freedom of speech nor freedom from fear. To the outsider, such an autocracy has little to commend it. Autocrats, their families, and their friends become extremely wealthy. They usually move their wealth abroad to safeguard it, rather than build up the domestic economy, which could put it at risk of confiscation. They ignore economic growth (with the notable exception of China) and the welfare of their people. In Africa, the people may starve, and minorities, such as other tribes, are routinely attacked. In the Middle East, Muslim States enforce their religious values, causing great hardship, particularly for women.

How, then, can they pose a threat to democracy? Autocracies are resilient because they tend to support each other. With a Machiavellian absence of ethical considerations, there are few boundaries to alliances. In earlier times, there were absolute monarchs who acted as autocrats, but they had always to consider the countervailing power of the Church, which could severely limit their freedom of action. Modern autocrats face no equivalent countervailing power or any other effective opposition. Russia and other autocracies can gain support from unexpected quarters, including many African dictatorships and Iran. In return, they only have to help autocrats remain in power.

If there are no elections, then autocrats can persist in power, however badly they govern. Citizens may not be aware of the democratic alternative either through ignorance or suppression of the media. Fear of offending those in power is understandable. Perhaps citizens are relatively happy with the status quo and are persuaded by anti-Western propaganda. But, where elections do exist, as in Turkey, the name of the autocrat is well known, while opponents may struggle for publicity. Lethargy, an unwillingness to risk any change, and religious beliefs may also be factors. Many voters have never experienced and therefore do not value individual freedom. They may, on the other hand, be attracted by possible strong economic growth, which has been experienced in China. [11]

A factor that seems to be commonplace is the belief that autocracies can deal more effectively with drugs and crime, given that they are unhampered by the rules of justice. They may also believe that they are better protected by the army for defensive or aggressive purposes, but the experience of Russia in Ukraine should cast doubts on this hope. [12]

The intention of the autocrat may be to prioritise party and personal interests over democracy, allow corruption to prevail, destroy their opponents, or infiltrate the body politic without being noticed. They have the advantage of familiarity with voters, who are constantly exposed to official partisan publicity and may believe the propaganda, so fear and ignorance often prevail. Whatever the reason, the result is the same. As truth and reason take a back seat, autocracy becomes entrenched.

Until recently, there was only a vague understanding of the ways autocrats helped develop unlikely alliances. [13] There are plenty of potential members. Members of the World Liberty Congress, all of whose members are opposed to autocracy, first met in 2022. They included founding members, such as Russia, Belarus, China, North Korea, and Cambodia, who represented Asia; Zimbabwe, Uganda, and Rwanda came from Africa; Venezuela, Cuba, and Nicaragua came from South America; the Middle East supplied Syria. All of these autocracies are welcome to join the club, which already includes many of their number. They offer a number of attractions:

The first is military; Russia can supply arms, ammunition, and military training. Occasionally, it will supply soldiers, as it has done in Mali with brutal Russian mercenaries. They can also support each other. North Korea sent troops to Russia to fight in Ukraine after the Russian military was severely depleted by heavy casualties.

The second is finance; This may be in exchange for mineral rights for the country or the oligarch and his cronies personally. China regularly provides loans to African military dictatorships, which can never be repaid, enabling it to exercise its influence.

The third is the provision of friendly news; This can be done directly and openly at a lower cost than other channels. It can also be translated into local languages, and its origin may be hidden. It is devastatingly effective where no other news source is available. For example, most Russians believe that Ukrainians are Nazis. It presents a friendly image of the autocracy and can be used to smear opponents. Soon afterwards, it can be disseminated widely through social media platforms, such as X, by paid or unpaid agents.

Fourthly, it can also provide advice on repressive legislation; Many autocracies now use 'lawfare' through the courts. Legislation is passed that enables opponents of the regime to be imprisoned or banned from politics for long periods. It has been successfully used in Venezuela, the Philippines, Thailand, Pakistan, India, and Zimbabwe. Recep Erdogan in Turkey is trying to go down this route in 2025.

Fifthly, it can provide surveillance advice; America enthusiastically exported human recognition technology to China for help with crime detection, which was developed there to provide spyware that can be used to identify activists, opponents, and unfriendly journalists. Once identified, they can be dealt with by anything from smearing them to threatening them and their families with imprisonment. Meetings, purchases, and contacts can all be traced.

Finally, club members support each other in their hour of need, irrespective of any atrocities they may commit. Despots want the survival of other despots. For example, Putin gave asylum to President Assad of Syria, his ally of many years, who must be considered to be one of the most loathsome, ruthless, and evil tyrants of modern times. Shortly after he was ousted, the world was shocked by the scale of his actions. Many Syrians had been imprisoned over long periods for minor offences or perceived slights by them or their families before being tortured to death. Survivors were often mentally impaired for life. Countless others ended up in the largest mass graves of the century. Yet Putin granted Assad asylum in Russia, a country to which he had made enormous financial donations. [14] It was the moral equivalent of befriending Adolf Hitler in 1945 to protect him from the unfair and unjust criticism of his opponents.

Concern has long been expressed over the power of big tech companies, such as Facebook and Google, to capture, render, and analyse the behaviour of individuals. This gives them incredible influence and can amount to economic oppression, threatening the freedom of the individual and the freedom of markets. It is generally seen as the inevitable, if undesirable, outcome of the digital age. [15] But its abuse by autocrats is much more dangerous, since it can be used for political oppression. Totalitarian autocrats have taken Orwell's description of "Big Brother is watching you" to a frightening new level.

Anticipating the Slippery Slope

The best way to stop authoritarianism from developing in a democracy is to ensure that any party's candidate for the leadership has no such tendencies. America has done this in the past when popular, but undemocratic, national figures have expressed an interest in becoming president. Examples include the antisemitic Henry Ford, Left-wing populist Huey Long, the Governor of Louisiana in the 1930s, Joseph McCarthy, a communist scaremonger in the 1950s, and racist George Wallace in the 1960s. Somehow, in the smoke-filled rooms of party conventions, their names did not appear at the top of the list of candidates and were not named on the ballot sheet. Where any candidate has already been nominated, but not formally confirmed, and does not wish to withdraw, this is immeasurably more difficult, provided he retains adequate financial resources, as Joe Biden showed in 2024.

Most candidates can be expected to follow the traditional norms of political behaviour. Once an authoritarian figure, such as Donald Trump, gets nominated, it is very difficult for the party elders to contain him, however much they may try, if he is determined to disregard these norms. Ultimately, the choice for the party is whether to put the interests of democracy first or, alternatively, to prioritise the interests of the party to gain or retain power. It seems now that democracy comes second and that, consequently, its future is under threat. Democracies are seldom united, while autocracies are more cohesive and therefore are much better positioned to win the argument.

Authoritarianism of whatever hue poses a threat in many countries. Some have existed for many years, while others have the potential to join them. Even in the heartland of traditional democracy of the United Kingdom and the United States, there have been disquieting attempts by populists to overturn the conventional democratic rulers. The defences appear to be weak. Democracy has not been subject to dangers on so many fronts for a long time.

CHAPTER 15

Autocracy by Stealth: The Four-Legged Chair

Autocracies can sometimes develop under the radar. The incumbent government selectively changes the rules of democracy to serve its own purposes and strengthen its position of power in the future. Examples of how this can happen are Turkey, two EU States, Poland and Hungary, together with two shorter regimes in the Philippines and Brazil.

Turkey

Turkey is an interesting case, uninhibited by any EU rules. Recep Erdogan, leader of the AK party, became prime minister in 2003 and president in 2014. His lifestyle resembles that of an Ottoman Sultan more than a modern political leader. His approach to politics has been strongly autocratic, neutralising the judiciary with a tame legal appointments board and muzzling the media. Many journalists were imprisoned on trumped-up charges, which encouraged others to be cautious in their reporting. Erdogan has diminished the role of parliament, ruled by decree, imprisoned opponents, calling them terrorists, and deposed elected officials. He has also purged the military, central bank, civil service, and academia, while attacking the Kurdish Opposition. Turkey is an Islamist, broadly supportive of Russia, and has become a country where many people fear for their livelihood and their freedom. Turkey is the only holiday destination outside the former USSR countries that Russia allows its citizens to visit. It has become a unique combination of an Islamic State and a very illiberal democracy.

In many ways, Erdogan resembles Trump. They both live in great luxury and are very rich. Both are strong nationalists, determined to make their country great again. They have turned the government into a family business and have promoted their sons-in-law. They have drawn their strength from small towns and rural areas. They have accused their bureaucrats of plotting against them and are contemptuous of Western democracy, while adopting aggressive foreign policies. As mayor of Istanbul in his early days, Erdogan explained his view of democracy. It is like a tram: when you reach your destination, you step off, but resemblances go further. They create fake news and attack 'nefarious elites', accuse opponents of lying, demonise the press and the courts, frame opponents as terrorists, curb freedom, and undermine the constitution.

Erdogan's first decade was an economic success, but by 2023, the currency had collapsed, and inflation was rampant, while he was blamed for poor handling of an earthquake, as well as for relaxing building safety regulations. Nevertheless, in 2023, with strong religious and rural backing, together with heavy support from the state-controlled television service, he beat the combined opposition in a run-off election. The election was free, but not fair, since many journalists were still imprisoned. The opposition parties were badly handicapped, since they were limited in their ability to spread their message and were at a disadvantage with unequal media resources. But the loss of support for Erdogan in the 2024 local elections may mean that the tide is turning. However, in 2025, he renewed his attacks on legitimate opponents, such as the mayor of Istanbul.

Poland

Poland has shared many of the same characteristics as Turkey until recently. It is, in theory, bound by EU rules insisting on an independent judiciary, but these rules have been flagrantly flouted. The rise of the Law and Justice party in Poland, which was founded in 2001 by Jaroslaw Kaczynski and had won a slim majority in the 2015 parliamentary elections, is an interesting illustration.[1] It is a right-wing party, which reflects the views of the Polish Catholic Church. It improperly appointed new judges to the constitutional court, packed the Supreme Court, and tried to punish judges who contradicted government policy. It took over the state broadcaster and dismissed critical independent reporters and presenters, replacing them with far-right extremists, who loyally spread government propaganda. They also sacked thousands of civil servants, replacing them with party hacks or their relations. Diplomats and army generals were similarly targeted. Where the media, civil service, and courts are controlled, there is no need for violence or terror police, as was employed by the Nazis. In 2023, the party failed to gain a majority, and a coalition of other parties formed a government, which immediately set about restoring the rule of law.

Poland has become a major European military and economic power. Whether the liberal government remains is heavily dependent on who wins the 2035 election. If the right-wing candidate, favoured by Trump, were to succeed in the run-off, further liberalisation would likely be blocked, [2]

Hungary

Autocrats seem to have taken note of Hungary's control over the judiciary. This path has been set out by Viktor Orban, the current Prime Minister. Orban first rose to fame as a student activist, demanding the withdrawal of Russian troops from Hungary in 1989. He entered politics and became Prime Minister in 1998 and ended his first term in 2002. He was re-elected in 2010, 2014, and 2020, by which time he became the country's longest-serving Prime Minister.

In his first term, he led a conservative party in a multi-party State, tackling economic issues in a conventional manner. In subsequent terms of office, he curtailed press freedom, weakened judicial independence, and undermined multi-party democracy. He is a rabid critic of Brussels and has denounced the country's major benefactor, George Soros, who had provided him with a scholarship as a foreign agent while describing the country as a 'Catholic Illiberal Democracy'. Orban remains friendly with Russia and China. He relaxed visa rules for applicants from Belarus and Russia, which could, in due course, lead to full citizenship.

Control of the media has been key to suppressing opposition views in both Poland and Hungary. The courts were packed with friendly judges. A law was enacted, obliging the Constitutional Tribunal to act with a two-thirds majority, thereby giving the government an effective veto. To institutionalise the system, key positions in the civil service, army, and press are filled by party hacks or 'reliable' friends. Once the judiciary is infiltrated, it is difficult for citizens to resist autocracy. In Britain, there was an outbreak of anger against the judiciary from right-wing sources when they demanded that the law be followed, as politicians sought to 'Get Brexit Done', and attacked the judges who insisted that the law be followed. Fortunately, its legal system stood up to the challenge.

The Philippines

Rodrigo Duterte was elected president of the Philippines in 2016. He quickly identified the drug business as providing a major challenge, although there was no statistical evidence that it was worse than in most other countries. He went to war with the 'Narco State', urging Filipinos to take the law into their own hands and kill addicts. According to Amnesty International, more than 7,000 killings occurred in the first six months. He publicly named suspects, who were sometimes shot by police while 'resisting arrest'. Vigilantes often kidnapped them and murdered them in their homes or on the streets. Nevertheless, Duterte enjoyed a huge popularity rating.

Duterte's actions diverted attention from corruption in government. Like Trump, he was an expert in using the big lie and was adept at using social media to disseminate disinformation widely. Although he castigated the Establishment, he made his appointments on the basis of loyalty, attacking the judiciary and journalists whenever they criticised him. Duterte surprised many people by not changing the Constitution to allow him to stand for a second term in 2022. He wanted his daughter to succeed him, but this did not materialise since she allied herself with the Marcos family. He then retired from politics before being arrested to face international criminal charges in 2025.

Brazil

Jair Bolsonaro was a military captain who entered politics in Brazil as a far-right candidate in 1990. In 2018, with the country in an economic downturn and political chaos after corruption scandals, he emerged as a candidate who was tough on crime in a style reminiscent of Latin American *Caudillos* or military strongmen, supporting better pay for soldiers. At his swearing-in ceremony, his guests of honour were Orban and Netanyahu.

He quickly placed his son in an important political position. Like Trump, he castigated the 'deep state' and 'fake news'. He demonstrated contempt for state institutions and, like other populists, used social media to good effect in spreading conspiracy theories. He gave many friends the right to ranching and forestry, doing major damage to the Amazon rainforests. He supported the powerful gun lobby and appealed to the people with evangelical fervour. In 2023, after rising inflation and high unemployment, Bolsonaro was voted out of office, being defeated by his old rival, Lulu, who was committed to social reform.

The Four-Legged Chair

Strongmen tend to learn from each other and attract admiration from Trump, who stated that the 'tougher and meaner' strongmen were, the better he got along with them. He dubbed Putin's Syrian policy an 'act of genius', an interesting observation in the light of the atrocities revealed after the overthrow of Assad. He described Xi as 'a great leader and a very good guy'. He rang to congratulate Duterte on the great job he was doing in tackling drugs. He befriended Farage and called Johnson 'Britain Trump'. When Erdogan made multiple arrests of journalists and sacked judges, Trump dismissed this as fake news. [3] Journalists are frequently targeted by Israel in Gaza, while more than a hundred journalists are 'detained' in China.

Ultimately, provided that the judiciary and the media are onside, it becomes difficult, if not impossible, to dislodge the populist autocrat. Countries that have attempted this include, with varying degrees of success, Poland, Hungary, Israel, Peru, and India. It also becomes much easier to imprison opponents, especially when countries attempt to undermine the independence of the judiciary. If successful, the damage may be permanent. Even when a democratic government has been reinstalled, as happened in Poland, it is not easy to dismiss the political appointees, party hacks and other cronies of the autocrat, who occupy many key positions in the judiciary, state companies and the state media, even if the President's independence is questionable. [4] Fortunately, however, when there is any semblance of a free press, these moves are difficult to hide. The ultimate step for an autocrat is to dissolve Parliament and rule by decree, which Alberto Fujimori did in Peru. As the British historian Lord Acton remarked, "Power tends to corrupt. Absolute power corrupts absolutely".

Democracy resembles a four-legged chair upon which democracy is precariously seated. If any of the legs of the chair were to break, civic rights, freedom of the press, an independent judiciary, and accountability of the executive, then democracy would break down. Any aspiring autocrat typically will attempt to smash each of the four legs, avoiding publicity wherever possible. But if the autocrat succeeds in breaking only one leg, the chair will probably eventually collapse, and democracy may perish. Successful democracies need an independent legal system to protect the individual rights of citizens. The executive and the police must be held accountable for their actions. There is normally at least one television channel and radio station independent of the Government. The key element of support is the media, which, if completely free, can publicise wrongdoings without fear of reprisals.

A free press is an anathema to aspiring autocrats, and a friendly television network is vital. Fox News, for example, became a friendly and important outlet for Donald Trump. So most of them, with the exception of Duterte, who abolished key individual freedoms of the citizens, started by attacking the media. Any independent medium can be vilified as a tool of America or some other foreign power. In extreme cases, neutral media can be threatened or bought, as happened in Turkey under Recep Erdogan. Finally, State Television may be the only available media outlet, as is the case in Vladimir Putin's Russia. Journalists are frequently detained in China and Gaza. Outside of the media, autocrats may try to stifle free speech at universities by attacking academic freedom and independence.

If the aspiring autocrat is successful, then unpleasant and unwelcome publicity can be avoided while the other legs of the chair are attacked. Belarus, Cambodia, China, Iran, Pakistan, Russia, Saudi Arabia, and Turkey have all been accused of transnational repression against journalists. Physical attacks, unlawful deportation, detentions, renditions, digital harassment, and reprisals against family members are among the tactics used by authoritarian regimes to pursue journalists working in exile. [5] In Israel, when Netanyahu was following a similar plan, he started by attacking the judges and courts since freedom of speech was well entrenched in the country, and he faced strong opposition from both the military and civilian population.

Democracies outperform autocracies in many important aspects of government. Citizens are protected from arbitrary imprisonment. Freedom for individuals is respected. The rule of law is paramount. The Nobel Prize in Economics for 2024 was awarded to three economists evaluating the importance of societal institutions for a country's prosperity. Societies with a poor rule of law that exploit the population do not generate growth or change for the better. They tend to reward their cronies by awarding them with monopolistic contracts, as Russia has done for its oligarchs. Democracies may not have matched the historic economic growth of China, but they have continued with economic prosperity, creating a reasonable standard of living for the least well-off citizens.

Every MBA student studying change management will be familiar with force field analysis, a technique created by social psychologist Kurt Lewin in the 1940s. The forces for change are put on one side, and the forces resisting change on the other. The key force for change for autocrats is a determination to remain in power and accumulate wealth for themselves and their cronies. The forces resisting change are the four legs of the chair. When they are removed, change will occur.

To the surprise of many people, democracy disappeared partly by stealth in the USA, since most Americans take democracy for granted. But, with the exception of a few immigrants, the citizens had not experienced authoritarianism in the same way as citizens of Poland, Hungary, Germany, Venezuela, Turkey, or India had. So, the defenders of democracy cannot afford to be complacent. What democrats can do to stem their declining popularity is examined in Chapter 23.

CHAPTER 16

The Allure of Populism

Demagogues have existed from time immemorial. Plato warned against them, and the American Founding Fathers were acutely aware of their threat. They exploit the desires and prejudices of the common people rather than relying on reasoned argument. The modern populist leader is a demagogue in a slightly different guise, employing the same approach and disdaining reasoned arguments while often claiming to be a democrat. Professing to serve the public interest, generally, populists pander to the special needs of their supporters, who brought them into power and can return them in the future. He (it is usually male) has access to tools that were unknown two thousand years ago. A good starting point to understand populism is to consider the rise to power of arguably the greatest demagogue ever, Adolf Hitler.

Adolf Hitler and the Downfall of the Weimar Republic[1]

Adolf Hitler was born in 1889 near the frontier of Austria and Bavaria. His lower-middle-class family was poor, and he had an unsuccessful schooling, showing little ability or application. He left school early and settled in Vienna, where he stayed in a doss house. He made no effort to find employment but occasionally sold small pictures which he had painted. He learnt to lie with conviction and dissemble with candour. He left Vienna and moved to Munich in 1913, probably to avoid military service.

Early Development

During this difficult, formative period in his life, he developed views that were to stay with him. He read widely but ignored anything that did not fit in with his preconceived views. He became a fanatical right-wing German nationalist, blaming all problems on communists and the Jews, whom he hated and believed were part of a world conspiracy to destroy the German people. He considered the inequality of individuals and races to be a Law of Nature. In particular, he believed in the innate superiority of the Aryan race. He had no respect for any democratic institutions, such as free speech, a free press, or parliament, and was disdainful of politicians in general. Despite his lack of achievement, he believed in his personal superiority. After the outbreak of war, he enlisted in the Company of the 16th Bavarian Reserve Infantry. He acted as a runner and was eventually made a corporal. He was wounded and was awarded the Iron Cross First Class in 1918 for bravery.

Development of the Party

The end of the war in November 1918 came suddenly and was a surprise to many people since there had been important German victories during the year. Blame was ascribed by the military to the civilian government. Hitler and many others considered it to be a stab in the back, adding to his contempt for politicians. In an atmosphere of discontent and chaos following the downfall of the imperial regime, Berlin remained the capital, but the town of Weimar was the seat of the Constituent Assembly, which set up the first government. Individual States had considerable power and were often able to defy the Reich, which was the Central Government.

It was openly claimed that loyalty to the fatherland necessitated disloyalty to the Republic. It was a time of unrest, insecurity, and fear. The army had been humiliated and sought to regain its former status. A campaign of violence against the regime ensued, an atmosphere in which Hitler, then aged thirty, thrived. When the Police President of Munich was asked if he knew of the existence of murder gangs, he replied: "Yes, but not enough of them".

In 1920, Hitler left the army and joined the German Workers Party, shortly after renamed the National Socialist German Workers Party or Nazi Party, in Bavaria as its seventh committee member. He was put in charge of propaganda, in which he had considerable expertise, and started to build up the party. But he was still only a regional politician. He believed that vehemence, passion, and fanaticism, feeding on insecurity and disorder, were the keys to increasing party numbers. Before long, he received the title of Honorary President.

Germany After the First World War: 2023

General discontent was widespread when the National Government was experiencing major problems in meeting punitive reparation terms imposed on Germany, which led to the French occupation of the Ruhr. The currency collapsed, and hyperinflation ensued, wiping out the savings of the people while unemployment grew rapidly. Hitler amassed a crowd of twenty thousand stormtroopers for an attempted coup in May 2023 but had to back down in the face of military pressure. But this was not the end of the matter since he still wanted to overthrow the Republican Government, and in November, he attempted a further putsch. When police blocked his stormtroopers, shots were fired. There were 16 casualties; Hitler was wounded, but only two Nazis were killed, while the remainder fled.

Hitler was arrested and tried in March 1924, which lasted 24 days. He was sentenced to five years' imprisonment but was released less than nine months later. In prison, he was well-treated and started writing his memoirs, *Mein Kampf*. The party then entered democratic politics. Various disputes emerged in the party, which Hitler encouraged so that he could not easily be replaced as leader. As a gesture to the authorities, he resigned his formal leadership in July. When the party was re-founded in February 1925, Hitler had two major objectives: To establish his absolute leadership and build up his membership, which proceeded steadily but unspectacularly. His speeches were fiery, threatening Jews and Marxists, which resulted in him being banned from speaking initially in several States. He cultivated a fierce image of himself, driving a supercharged Mercedes and carrying a rhinoceros whip.

The Weimar Republic had reached an agreement on reparation payments to the victorious allies of the First World War, enabling relative prosperity to be restored, which did not suit the Nazis. The political results of the party were modest, securing only 810,000 votes in the Reichstag election and only 12 of its 491 seats. But that in no way diminished Hitler's appetite for power, using the legal route only when it was convenient.

Hitler's next opportunity arose in 1930 when, following the Great Crash in America, the world fell into a deep slump with massive unemployment, destabilising the Republican Government. He abandoned any semblance of socialism and allied the party with big business, which provided a major source of funding. He responded to any threat to his leadership with a combination of appeals, bribery, and threats. In the deteriorating economic situation and in the absence of any stable government, the Nazi SA paramilitaries resorted to periodic street violence.

He ran unsuccessfully for the presidency against the incumbent in 1932, while his party almost doubled its national vote. In July, the Nazis emerged as the largest party in the Reichstag. In 1933, the President appointed him as Chancellor, but at this stage, he was not yet a dictator. In February, the Reichstag was set on fire, an act blamed on the Communists. Hitler then persuaded the President to pass a decree severely curtailing the rights of German citizens. Under the decree, Hitler began eliminating his opponents, assisted later by an Enabling Act that allowed him to pass laws without parliamentary oversight. He then constructed the first concentration camp at Dachau for communists and other political opponents. In August 1934, following the death of the president, Hitler merged the office of President and Chancellor, becoming Führer and the sole leader of Germany.

His rise to power was now complete. He had waited patiently until the right opportunity appeared. He then acted quickly and decisively, with the threat of violence never far from the surface. He went on for the next ten years until his suicide in 1945 to become a ruthless, tyrannical dictator and warmonger, leading in due course to the enormous damage inflicted on Germany during the Second World War.

Hitler's rise to power features many of the characteristics found in modern populist autocrats. His philosophy was extreme right-wing and fanatically nationalistic, based on a racist belief in the superiority of the German people. He thrived on social and political unrest. He tolerated no opposition in the party and showed little loyalty to his friends. He developed paramilitary support through the SA or Brown Shirts and the SS, broke the law frequently, and often encouraged violence.

Hitler used democracy only when it suited his ends and attacked the Republican State, being contemptuous of conventional politicians. He developed the party and built up a coterie of loyal friends, uniting his followers by drumming up hatred of Jews and Communists. He was a superb orator and master propagandist, cultivating his own image with posters and adopted emblems, such as the swastika and other visual insignia. He used bribery and threats to further his ends, but always persisted after major setbacks. Having risen only to the lowly rank of corporal, he was careful not to alienate the army.

Populism Around the World

While modern populists may not have modelled themselves consciously on Hitler, their core beliefs and features are similar. The populist purports to know the will of the common people and what is best for them. Populists consider that those who oppose their views are part of a corrupt 'elite' or 'establishment', such as big business interests, banks, and other politicians, to be attacked or ignored. Populism is not based on hard data and facts but rather appeals to emotions, usually feeding on national pride. It tends to spread easily during times of economic hardship or a crisis.

In the aftermath of the 2008 financial crisis, left-wing populism grew with the advent of Syriza in Greece and the Podemos party in Spain. Radical populism spread shortly afterwards throughout the Arab world with the rebellions against misgovernment during the Arab Spring. Elsewhere, it developed in Turkey under President Erdogan with strong Muslim support and under Modi in India with the backing of Hindu fundamentalists.

Populism has existed in America for many years. With two long-established political parties, it is difficult for outsiders to make much headway. Starting as a social movement, sometimes it dies a natural death, as is the case with "Occupy Wall Street". At other times, it is absorbed by an existing party, as was the case with the Tea Party Movement, a conservative group seeking tax reductions, which disappeared when its ideas were absorbed by the Republican Party, as that party moved further to the Right. The major exception was the Solidarity Movement in Poland under the leadership of Lech Walesa, which eventually brought down the existing communist regime.

Undoubtedly, the leading exponent of populism has been Donald Trump, who has made considerable headway since he essentially captured the Republican Party in the USA. He identifies the enemy as non-white Americans and seeks to represent those who have felt left behind in the era of globalisation, particularly in the de-industrialised Midwest. His slogans are not original. "Make America Great Again" was based on Mussolini in Italy and later by Ronald Reagan. For his attack on the elite, he coined "Drain the Swamp", which he also borrowed from Mussolini, the Italian fascist populist. Trump's populism, as it developed in his first presidency, will be examined in greater detail in Chapter 18.

Latin America has produced many populists, which is unsurprising given the enormous inequality of wealth. The most famous was General Juan Domingo Peron of Argentina. Others include Evo Morales of Bolivia, David Ortega of Nicaragua, Alberto Fujimori in Peru, Jair Bolsonaro in Brazil, and Hugo Chávez in Venezuela. They depend heavily on the charisma of the leader with minimal supporting infrastructure, identifying the enemy as the rich landowners and industrialists. The military sometimes ends a populist regime by way of a coup d'état.

Incredibly, demagogues may enrich themselves enormously while the wider population remains in poverty. Yet the electorate may not complain, however much the leader enriches himself, as is happening in Russia, even if they are aware of it, which is difficult to establish without a free press. National pride may outweigh personal welfare.

A key to this thinking is the identification of a common enemy. For many smaller countries, such as Cuba and Venezuela, the enemy is usually the USA, while for Britain, it was the EU. In Ireland, the enemy has traditionally been Britain after eight hundred years of occupation, but this has now matured to a less hostile approach in the context of the EU. For Russia, China, and North Korea, it is represented by decadent American and Western values, which they believe are doomed to failure. But, as it is an appeal to emotions rather than reason, facts may become irrelevant. The truth may disappear and be replaced by propaganda.

Different Kinds of Populist Leaders

Populists come in many different shapes and sizes. Typically, they are led by charismatic strongmen. In Latin America, Peron and Chavez both came from a military background. Populist leaders are usually deemed to be strong, while unpopular leaders are considered to be weak, typically portraying themselves as strong, 'macho' men. Less commonly, women like Eva Peron in Argentina and Marie Le Pen in France have succeeded. Sarah Palin in Alaska and Frauke Petry of the extremist AfD in Germany, too, have made their mark on the political landscape of their countries.

Successful entrepreneurs can turn to politics; Ross Perot in America and Silvio Berlusconi in Italy are good examples. Others emphasise their ethnic origins. Evo Morales represented the indigenous people of Bolivia, who historically had faced discrimination. They are not necessarily from the majority racial group. Fujimori in Peru came from the small Japanese minority. Populists may claim to be political novices, though normally they have political connections. Thaksin Shinawatra in Thailand had twice been vice-president before launching his own populist party. Of course, many conventional politicians may profess to be populists at election time. Populism can be thought of as politics for ordinary people by extraordinary leaders who construct ordinary profiles. [2]

The Threat from Right-Wing Populism

Populists tend to be strongly nationalistic and despise experts, whom they claim are on the side of the elite against the people.

Their enduring influence is based on developing a strong party infrastructure, as Hitler did with the Nazis in Germany and, more recently, Marie Le Pen has done in France through the National Front. In Western Europe, they are invariably Eurosceptics. [3]

Although usually, but not always, far-right in substance, they generally exhibit many features of autocracy. [4] In 2023, populist governments developed in Hungary, Italy, Slovakia, and Turkey. But strong right-wing populist parties have also made strong electoral gains in other European democracies, such as Austria, France, Germany, and the Netherlands, while former President Trump retains a strong following in the USA. Typically, they espouse extreme nationalism and racism while opposing immigration, the expansion of the State, and the 'green agenda'. Many of them, in varying degrees, support Russia and can readily adopt violence when it suits their purpose.

These right-wing groups have abandoned the suspicion of rapid change, as advocated by Edmund Burke. Instead, they want to overthrow or undermine existing institutions. Many have a remarkable similarity to the Nazis of the 1930s, sometimes using their slogans and, indeed, often wearing their swastikas and other emblems. Like Mussolini, they do not often have a coherent ideology but may identify their supposed enemies, such as liberals, immigrants, black people, Muslims, Jews, and the LGBT community. Their attacks can become violent and are invariably accompanied by conspiracy theories.

The Essence of Populism

Although Peron formed a populist Government in Argentina in 1946 following a visit to Fascist Italy, the first populist European Government since the Second World War was not formed for forty years in Europe, when Papandreou was elected to power in Greece. An observer painted a vivid description of the victory there and subsequently in Hungary. [5] There were enormous rallies on the streets, speeches from balconies generating widespread enthusiasm in the crowds with seductive slogans, resulting in massive social resentment and polarisation. Their enemy was the establishment, the elite, and people who disagreed with them.

Democratic Governments are dismissed as inefficient, corrupt, shortsighted, irresponsible, dominated by special interest groups, and ignore the public good. A conflict is inevitable with democracy, which stands for overlapping interests, moderate consensus-seeking, together with respect for public institutions and the rule of law. The populist purports to represent the real people: the little people, the wage earners, the forgotten underprivileged, the small property owners, and those who are resentful, believing that they are being victimised.

The Route to Populist Autocracy

It is easy to identify the route to populist autocracy with the advantage of hindsight, but it may not be obvious at the time. Usually, they are right-wing, but left-wing populists are also possible, as Hugo Chavez eventually proved in Venezuela. The process can happen quickly, as with Donald Trump, or more slowly, as occurred with Jaroslaw Kaczynski in Poland and with Viktor Orban in Hungary. The stages may be largely out of sight and not widely reported at the time, making their detection difficult.

The starting point is that the populist represents the real voice of the people. Paranoid nationalism and rabble-rousing inflame the people and strengthen the position of the incumbent populist ruler, diverting attention from misgovernment or corruption. Often, it is accompanied by a chauvinistic, xenophobic, and racist view to identify the true, loyal citizens, reminiscent of Hitler's Aryan cult. The use of this form of extreme nationalism seems to be increasing. Daniel Ortega in Nicaragua brands his enemies as agents of the Yankee empire. Kais Saied in Tunisia blames black people for the country's problems. Putin claims that Ukraine is a NATO puppet. In India, Modi fingers Muslims as seducers of Hindu women. Viktor Orban in Hungary targets immigrants.

The populist leader aims to unite the country against the phantom enemy. Contrary views are dismissed as representing a self-serving elite or perhaps the interests of foreigners. Opposition is derided, vilified, and deemed unworthy of respect. Minorities are often accused of heinous crimes as the country becomes ever more polarised. Social media can be used effectively to spread propaganda, irrespective of its truth.

The populist then assembles an inner cadre of supporters. They may be believers or simply those who see it as a means of personal advancement. For Modi's India and Muslim States, these will be fellow religionists. In any coup, it will be the military. Boris Johnson surrounded himself with a tiny caste of Oxford Tories, who were public school, especially Eton and Oxford-educated males, studying politics, philosophy, and economics. Many hankered for the glories of the British Empire. They included members of the notoriously snobbish Oxford Bullingdon Club, antisocial, which despised the common people or 'plebs' and indulged in periodic bouts of heavy drinking. [6]

Over time, there is a gradual effort to infiltrate the key institutions of the State: the Civil Service, the Military, and the Judiciary. Some individuals may fear the results of dissent, while others can be threatened with tax or corruption investigations, or are offered the prospect of comfortable, well-paid jobs. Once the key institutions of the State are taken over, the populists become very difficult to dislodge.

Populism can have, surprisingly, some useful contributions to democracy. It gives a voice to groups who feel unrepresented by the elite, thus bringing them into politics and also surfacing key concerns. But, while professing to be democratic, they are certainly not liberal democratic since they circumvent minority rights. They erode confidence in the key institutions of the State because populism divides society and prevents reaching an agreement between competing groups.

Populism thrives in harsh economic times or when political scandals are exposed. In the era of austerity following the property crash of 2008, populist leaders in the worst affected countries made significant inroads: Beppe Grillo, co-founder of the Five Star Movement and later Giorgia Meloni of the pro-fascist Brothers Of Italy, now prime minister; Alexis Tsipras of Syriza, along with the Neo-Nazi Golden Dawn in Greece; Gerry Adams and Mary Lou McDonald of Sinn Féin in Ireland; Podemos in Spain.

Populists with Deranged Minds

Ever since the time of Tsar Ivan the Great, whose brutality is legendary, including the murder of his own son, in sixteenth-century Russia, people with deranged minds have made an enormous impact on the history of their people, making them particularly dangerous. [7] A psychologist has explained that, usually, as a result of neglect in early childhood, some people can develop disordered minds. The three most dangerous disorders are psychopathic, narcissistic, and paranoid. They seek unfettered power for themselves while treating others with brutality and disdain.

Their mental health difficulties may not be easily recognised. It was not widely known that Hitler was addicted to a cocktail of powerful drugs, which caused him to experience violent mood swings. [8] But they can thrive, particularly in times of insecurity and unrest. They may attract normal people to join them, although their inner circle is usually composed of like-minded people. Often, they appear to be intelligent but are poor listeners and prone to violence.

Some of the worst examples of tyrants who typically suffered from all three disorders are Stalin, with his use of terror, starvation, Siberian Gulags and random executions; Mao Tse Tung, with his imposed famine and slaughter of opponents, who dared to voice any disagreement to his cultural revolution; Hitler with the Holocaust; Pol Pot with the Killing Fields of Cambodia. Often, they took pleasure in seeing the sufferings of innocent people and could watch or participate in torture.

None of these despots themselves experienced a violent end, but their people were less fortunate, facing a life of hardship and terror. In each country, millions of people were arbitrarily tortured and summarily executed at the whim of the tyrant. It is extremely dangerous to allow people with deranged minds to arrive at positions of power. In each of these cases, the outcomes were crimes against humanity. All that is required is a destructive leader, susceptible followers, and a conducive environment.

Poverty often empowers dangerous personalities. In Africa, normally, the primary goal of a dictator is to amass enormous wealth for himself and his family through crime and corruption, which can become endemic in endless wars.

Democracy cannot thrive in countries such as the 'Democratic' Republic of Congo, Liberia, Sierra Leone, Angola, and Sudan. Kleptocracies are not compatible with democracy, nor can democracy thrive in theocracies. The Taliban in Afghanistan, the Islamic State in Iran, and Boko Haram in Nigeria, as well as several states in the Middle East, are intent on imposing Islamic law on all the people, regardless of their beliefs.

The Success of Populism

The allure of modern populism is obvious. It is easy to understand how populism is attractive to those with little time to consider issues in depth. The simple message that the populist promises to transform the lot of the common people is superficially attractive and readily spread on social media. The populist is their friend, and his opponents are their enemies, responsible for their deprivations. When populism uses social media effectively, it can quickly spread dangerous, distorted, and often racist messages, particularly where immigration is a major concern. Opposition parties are placed at a disadvantage when they seek to rebut the simplistic and often dishonest arguments, which they may not even see or hear directly. Often, people are unwilling to listen and prefer to believe the conspiracy explanations that are circulated.

It is easy to understand how populism now threatens liberal democracy around the world. [9] It plays on genuine fears, worries, and prejudices. Some are soundly based, such as the sense of deprivation arising from an absence of growth in real wages and increasing inequality. It also thrives on the adverse image of politicians, some of whom are corrupt and seem focused more on their own welfare rather than that of their constituents.

Anger was widespread when none of the bankers responsible for the 2008 crash were ever prosecuted. It responds, as well, to a feeling of alienation, where voters believe that the elite is not interested in their well-being. Above all, it flourishes on worries about the sense of national identity, where citizens are wary of immigrants who do not share their tradition, culture, or even language. This leads to a rejection of multiculturalism and often racism, fearing a threat to their jobs, although this belief is rarely supported by factual evidence. Yet without immigrants from countries such as India, the Philippines, and Brazil, the health system in countries such as Ireland would collapse. The system is mutually beneficial. Immigrants provide their services and learn English while upgrading their academic skills.

But most populists promise much and deliver little. They rarely reduce inequality since they tend to reward their cronies and often their families to get re-elected. Frequently, they degenerate into kleptocracies with the never-stated basic rule that theft is good. Providing there is some semblance of genuine elections and limited restrictions on the media, reality can catch up with them and reduce their power. Kaczynski in Poland, Bolsonaro in Brazil, Johnson in Britain, and Trump in 2020 lost their grip on power. Erdogan in Turkey, Orban in Hungary, Netanyahu in Israel, Modi in India, and the military regime in Thailand have all suffered a diminution in their popular support at some considerable cost to themselves. However, the election of Trump in 2024 demonstrates the continuing allure of populism with its beguiling, facile promises.

CHAPTER 17

The Influence and Dangers of Social Media

In the twenty-first century, the media have undergone a far-reaching revolution. The most important new media came with the advent of social media, by which individuals can communicate with their friends or followers directly and quickly, using the internet. It was employed as a tool to good effect in the Arab Spring over a decade ago, leading to discontent spreading quickly over national boundaries. Subsequently, it was widely used in the USA 'Occupy Wall Street' campaign.

However, social media can also be easily abused by both adults and children. It is simple to spread hatred or racism when the initiator can do so anonymously without a face-to-face encounter. It has been used by far-right groups in Dublin to promote rioting and looting. Another growing abuse is the use of the internet for malicious purposes. It may be hacking, illegal extraction of information, fraud, or blackmail, typically aimed at American businesses. 'Bots' are software running automated processes, most of which are good, but some are malicious. A survey found that worldwide, the amount of 'bad bots' amounted to 32% of internet traffic. Ireland, which is a major host of data centres, was the worst at 71%. [1] It appears increasingly likely that the internet will contain ever-increasing levels of disinformation as the world enters the 'post-truth era'.

The use of social media is popular with politicians since it enables them to communicate directly and immediately with their constituents. Governments also take up advertising space to spread their messages. With rapidly growing usage, it is likely to play an increasing role in the future. It has fundamentally changed how people, particularly younger people, relate to one another, being interactive and web-based. Users generate their own content, often by taking digital photos or videos. Users also create service-specific profiles for the website, which is self-managing and can also quickly link to other similar groups.

Messages are typically brief and are seldom carefully reasoned. The information may not be accurate, spreading misinformation, disinformation, and fake news. This is particularly worrying since, for young people around the world, it may be their primary source of news. Digital photographs can be edited to show the desired effect. Anyone can invent 'alternative facts', rumours, or conspiracy theories with impunity and distribute them instantly to their network. In turn, they may be passed on to others and may even become viral, reaching an enormous number of individuals.

Barack Obama used social media to good effect in the 2008 and 2012 American presidential elections. Today, Donald Trump is the best-known user of 'alternative facts', but he has many followers. Bolsonaro in Brazil, Johnson in Britain, Modi in India, and Orban in Hungary have all made statements or claims and maintained their untenable positions when facing questioning by opposition parties. The public today seems more tolerant of untruths than in the past.

The Widespread Dangers of Social Media

Twitter, now rebranded as 'X', is a popular means of communication with more than 500 million followers, which allows users to vent their frustrations and biases without being answerable or facing the consequences. It has an enormous influence since short tweets can reach an audience many times the circulation of the largest newspaper. Worryingly, it permits hatred and lies concerning the war in Gaza, where feelings are very strong on both sides. Social media can also build up 'groupthink' among followers, however outrageous their claims may be. In some respects, it is a return to the inside of Plato's cave. Reality becomes subjective, but it is a powerful influence on others, nevertheless.

A report by the Institute of Strategic Dialogue found some disturbing facts about the operation of X, the most important platform in Ireland, in 2023. Misinformation during the pandemic increased enormously. Right-wing groups regularly target refugees, asylum-seekers, and members of the LGBT community. Posts often reflect disinformation by pro-Kremlin sources, describing the Ukrainians as Nazis and spreading conspiracy theories. In 2022, Elon Musk, the owner of X, secretly ordered his engineers not to turn on the company's Starlink satellite communications network near the Crimean coast to disrupt a Ukrainian attack on the Russian naval fleet. [2]

Another disturbing piece of misinformation made false claims that Irish troops in Lebanon were sympathetic to Hezbollah and had failed to enforce the UNIFIL mandate. [3] This appeared to be an attempt to urge Ireland and UNIFIL to withdraw from Lebanon. Military experts have been unable to trace the source to the Israeli Government, but noted that it resembles a campaign of the Israeli Government to influence US legislators.

Since the takeover of X by Elon Musk, a self-described free speech absolutist, many of the guardrails against misinformation have been abandoned, which has led to a large fall in advertising revenue. [4] Staff have been instructed not to suspend users who post explicitly racist, sexist, and homophobic content. Racism, hatred, and violence now flourish on X. [5] The company is currently the subject of an investigation.

Musk himself posts his own far-right views. X became particularly controversial in Ireland when messages of hatred were posted on the platform immediately preceding the 2023 Dublin riots. Extreme racist and anti-Islamic posts were not removed. Research showed that many right-wing posts originated from the USA or the UK. [6] Disappointingly, Musk declined to give evidence to Irish public representatives investigating the riots regarding his role in the spreading of harmful online posts on the platform. Both the Taoiseach, who described the platform as sewerage, and the Tánaiste, the deputy leader, have expressed their concern.

Not only have many guardrails vanished, but Musk himself posts right-wing opinions that are hard to square with reality. He has stated that former Irish Taoiseach Leo Varadkar hates the Irish people. [7] Bizarrely, he endorsed a former mixed martial arts champion, Conor McGregor, who was subsequently found guilty of rape in a civil case, and later echoed by Donald Trump, to be the next president of Ireland. This would seem to be a worrying attempt by the world's richest man to intervene in Irish domestic politics. He has intervened in the US presidential election, which is disturbing, given his past cooperation with Russia over Ukraine. Reports that he has regular contact with Putin have also aroused concern. [8] Misinformation emerged in the 2024 Irish elections, where far-right groups sought to spread racial hatred, which was widely spread by X.

The nature of social media has changed fundamentally since the launch of Facebook, where users were interested in communicating with their own network of friends. With TikTok, through user names, posts from populists are largely anonymous. Creators or 'influencers' have become more powerful, often distorting the facts and sharing revenue, providing potential for using such media to post political messages. Threads, a platform on Instagram owned by Meta, the Facebook parent, gained a million users in 5 days and has ambitions to eventually reach a billion viewers despite a decline following the initial surge.

China uses technology to crush ideas with which it disagrees. To this end, it has banned both Facebook and Instagram. TikTok may be a Chinese invention, but it has never been permitted to operate in China. [9] There can be no more powerful evidence of the influence of social media. They have been accused of misleading advertising in the 2024 election and also in the 2025 Romanian presidential election, where a far-right candidate who supports Putin was narrowly defeated in the run-off election.

During the 1960s, it became fashionable to state that the medium is the message. [10] Certainly, the nature of the media affects the way the message is formulated, spread, and interpreted. Today, it is difficult to separate the medium from the message. In the hands of the unscrupulous, who disregard traditional professional journalistic standards and values, social media can be very powerful, potentially dangerous, and sometimes deadly weapons.

Conspiracy Theories

In a world where truth and untruth are blurred, it is not surprising that fanciful accounts of events are circulated, however implausible they may be. Problems can be explained by conspiracies, which do not need to be backed by any evidence. The elite can be blamed for all the setbacks. Fundamental to the spread of conspiracy theories circulated by QAnon is the deep distrust of all institutions, together with the belief that they do not tell the truth. [11] Postings can readily gain traction because they excite the suspicions of citizens. Stories can be about the deaths of celebrities, the spread of the COVID pandemic, or any other topic that is in the news.

When conspiracy theories relate to political issues, the dangers are obvious. Populists are often adept at using conspiracy theories to their advantage. The motives of opponents can be called into question, and serious damage can be inflicted on their victims. Hitler was an expert on using conspiracy theories. Any problem could be attributed to the sinister machinations of the Jews or Communists. He was successful with his propaganda without any social media to assist him. Impressionable people existed then, as they do today.

Politicians and Social Media

Social media fundamentally changed the nature of the relationship between politicians and voters. Few people understood this better than Donald Trump, who became a master in its use. In particular, he used it to persuade his followers that the 2020 presidential election had been stolen from him, even though no evidence of this claim was ever substantiated. Examples of its influence on American politics are examined in Chapter 18.

Voters do not always behave rationally. The British cognitive psychologist Peter Wason coined the phrase 'bias confirmation' to explain decision-making. This may lead to 'knowledge resistance' and thinking traps. People prefer views that agree with their own biases, rather than take a logical approach. Tribal reasoning results in groupthink, as users increase, under the 'bandwagon effect'.

If politicians can establish what these biases are, then they can design their campaigns accordingly. This could explain the Tory electoral victory in 2019, as already described. It could also throw light on the unwavering support for Donald Trump despite the serious civil and criminal charges levelled against him. On social media, users decide who and what they follow, meaning they are choosing the information to which they are subjected. As they will likely only follow those with similar ideological standings, they will only be exposed to a relatively narrow scope of information. As exposure to this information increases, the more social media is used, they are subjected to a constant feedback loop, continually reaffirming potentially harmful ideas through an echo chamber.

Social media has an enormous advantage over traditional media and is most attractive to populists. [12] Users can bypass journalists, who usually act as gatekeepers and don't publish blatant falsehoods. They do not need specialist technical knowledge, which could be exposed by a competent interviewer. They can avoid the normal financial costs of broadcasting or have limited exposure due to their small initial size. They can attack the traditional media and the elite with impunity. Their messages can be short and go viral, spreading their messages to thousands or even millions with the click of a button, instantly, however outrageous the content may be. By picking selected audiences, they can bombard them with the same messages and prejudices, which are then repeated by similar groups; the more messages they receive, the more they are believed.

Contemporary social media algorithms also play a role here. Their aim is to keep users engaged for long periods of time, supplying them with personalized content specifically tailored to their interests. Again, this results in extensive exposure to narrow feeds of information. The scale of its influence could increase. BookTok, a platform developed by TikTok, is already making its mark in the world of publishing with its recommendations.

The extent of the misuse of social media is a matter of conjecture, but it may be very significant. The Russians have been using it since 2014, when they spread fake news about their invasion of Crimea. It has been reported that they have been bombarding journalists with emails, fake videos, and various social media messages. [13] Meta has banned Russian State media from its apps, citing foreign interference. In 2024, following his kidnapping in Thailand, a blogger in Vietnam was sentenced to 12 years' imprisonment for blogs criticising the Communist Party government.

In America, where TikTok has 170 million followers, many young people use it as their primary source of news. Given its Chinese ownership, there are fears that it could be used for propaganda and also that it might make information about Americans available to the Chinese authorities. It was banned in the USA at the end of the Biden presidency, but Trump gave an extension of 90 days to allow a deal to be struck with divestment of 50% of the company. It was reported that Musk may take over the American subsidiary to prevent its closure. [14]

Russia uses this platform extensively to spread disinformation for electoral purposes abroad. The decision of Meta to cease fact-checking content on its platforms is likely to increase the spread of widespread misinformation and hate postings on Facebook. This is likely to be particularly insidious on Instagram since their videos are widely circulated amongst younger people. It may, however, have to submit a risk assessment on its implications to the EU, together with large fines.

The French authorities have discovered a vast network of 193 websites, many of which have been dormant but are now being activated for a disinformation campaign in France, Germany, Poland, and other European countries. [15] Shortly afterwards, misinformation, based on a fake video of President Macron, was posted on X by the Russians. Russian disinformation has been widespread in Slovakia and has largely gone unchallenged. It reached a climax during the annexation of Crimea and the invasion of Ukraine. It enormously contributed to the increasing polarisation there and increased again in the 2024 European elections. [16]

Artificial Intelligence

The basic concept of artificial intelligence is not new. One of the pioneers in computing, Alan Turing, was one of the major code breakers, who broke down the German military and especially submarine codes from Bletchley Park in England during the

Second World War. He went on to write a paper entitled "Computing Machinery and Intelligence" in 1950, which was arguably the first major step towards artificial intelligence. Unfortunately, he was persecuted for his homosexuality and eventually committed suicide. His modern-day counterparts are likely to be treated considerably better.

The development of artificial intelligence today is likely not only to affect the workings of the media but also to pose a threat to democracy. It could display only the contacts that the individual is expected to like, curtailing the environment for pluralistic, equally accessible, and inclusive public debate. It absorbs enormous quantities of energy and may also have a major impact on military operations, as drones are programmed either for defence or attack.

Fear of machines is not new. There have always been worries about how machines could replace jobs. The Luddites, a group of British craft workers in the early nineteenth century, systematically destroyed textile machinery, which was displacing their jobs. Having read Darwin's 'On the Origin of the Species', a Victorian satirist thought machines might evolve to replace humans and stated, perhaps facetiously, that they should be abolished. [17] Economists have always dismissed the notion that machines create unemployment. There is no 'lump of labour', so other jobs can be created to replace those lost by mechanisation. Yet, with the advent of artificial intelligence, it seems that there will be a massive disruption to the job market, which will make many occupations and qualifications obsolete.

Artificial intelligence could also create realistic fake videos, audio, and images. One such example is deepfake porn, where the faces of celebrities are attached to plausible-looking bodies and then widely circulated. The misuse of artificial intelligence can present financial risks, harm reputations, and challenge decision-making. If so, this could increasingly lead to separation and polarisation in the political sphere, providing a platform for the manipulation of elections. The EU intends to develop a standard on its use, concerned that it puts citizens into information silos. The Irish Minister for Media considers it a real potential threat to the operation of democracy.[18]

Control over Social Media

There is a widespread dark side to social media. Social media is incredibly powerful but can be abused, often deliberately, for political ends. The Murdoch Group discovered that abuse could result in heavy costs when they questioned the reliability of voting machines to reflect the views of their audience. Fox News settled the court case for $787 million. The damage caused can be immense if the messages go viral, sometimes reaching millions of followers. Doubts have been expressed about the future viability of artificial intelligence. It may never be capable of meeting the 'Turing' test: Can machines ever be capable of imitating human intelligence? The enormous investment required could endanger the financial viability of the industry, though this may change with the emergence of a cheap platform, DeepSeek in China; it is likely to encounter philosophical, ethical, and practical, as well as financial challenges. [19]

Many countries are struggling with the control of social media. The dangers have been known for several years [20] An early Facebook investor, who later became a whistleblower, produced a manifesto, sharply critical of social media companies, especially Facebook. They exploit the social environment, using a massive artificial intelligence base, to maximise advertising revenue and profits, which is based on an ever-growing network of over two billion users. They target groups and frequently prey on their anger and fears, which are reinforced by restricting information to what they like, as triggered by their response of 'like'. When users are concerned about their body weight, this can lead to the encouragement of anorexia. It can also encourage bullying and addiction. It played a distasteful role in Myanmar, spreading hatred of the Rohingya people. It has also been used by right-wing terrorists to encourage terrorism, as happened in Christchurch, New Zealand.

They subvert democracy by secretly manipulating the views of voters, influencing the way they vote, which is often then based on misinformation and far-fetched conspiracy theories reinforced by filter bubbles of like-minded people. It has been described as persuasive technology or 'brain hacking'. They are believed to have played a significant role in the 2016 US Presidential Elections, when it was discovered that voter profiles, collected by Cambridge Analytica, were made available, and also later in the Brexit referendum. The data set may have been used in the 2024 Presidential Election. Information collected by facial recognition can be passed on to favoured parties, who can misuse it. The company's motto, 'Move Fast and Break Things, ' ignores the inevitable collateral damage it causes, abusing public trust in its platform.

Facebook argued that it is a media company and will take no responsibility for what its users do with the information. Unfortunately, the warnings from his former mentor that Facebook was harming innocent individuals were ignored by Mark Zuckerberg, and attempts at regulation are opposed by his strong team of lawyers. Any attempt by foreign countries to control US tech companies is vehemently opposed by Trump and Musk. It seems that Facebook will continue to undermine democracy unless it is somehow checked.

A Harvard professor has highlighted how personal autonomy can be undermined. By the aggregation of user data to control human behaviour in a way similar to what can happen in a totalitarian state. [21] Technology companies are gathering ever more data about individuals without their knowledge or consent to predict their behaviour. This is a gross invasion of personal privacy and a dangerous, obtrusive practice, particularly when the information can then be made available to third parties, such as marketing organisations or even subversive bodies, for financial gain. Facebook, Instagram, YouTube, Google, Amazon, Microsoft, and Twitter are the major culprits, but not Apple, which is more conscious of its public obligations.

The EU is taking the lead in regulation with the Digital Services Act of 2024. It aims to make social media companies more transparent, with a particular focus on banning or limiting targeting practices and introducing tighter control on content. An obligation is placed on search engines to report and remove illegal content. Very hefty fines can be levied on offenders. The possibility of controlling social media in the US has received a setback, given the influence of Elon Musk over Trump and his campaign for minimal regulation. Washington resists any regulation of social media with libertarian fervour. Giant tech companies are often monopolies in their sector and are generous donors to political parties.

The French took the lead when they arrested 2024, the chief executive of Telegram, as part of an investigation into cyber criminality. Telegram, sometimes described as the 'dark web in your pocket', is a messaging platform that has almost a million users and has minimal regulation of content. Founded by a Russian, it is based in Dubai and is widely used by the Russian military and far-right groups. Brazil, too, had acted when its supreme court banned X for refusing to block accounts suspected of spreading hate mail or disinformation, much to the dismay of its 20 million users, [22]

How should they be controlled in a society that values freedom of speech? It has been claimed that they can be used dangerously. The longer users stay online, the more revenue the platform makes. TikTok has been accused of promoting self-harm and suicide to vulnerable children without verifying their age. [23] Similarly, it has been reported that young boys are bombarded with misogynistic material. [24] In Albania, where it is widely used by school children, the government announced a one-year ban on its use after a school child was murdered following widespread circulation of hostile coverage. A universal problem is the control of smartphones in school. While they can be a useful learning tool, they can also be used for cyberbullying. Some countries have banned their use in schools, while others are exploring less extreme measures.

Should regulators intervene in cases of propaganda? Hitler spread his message through his oratory, but with social media, it could have spread far more widely. The Syrian regime used TikTok to normalise relations with the Western world, downplaying the horrific cruelty of the government and producing one-sided reports to attract tourism. The extent and causes of its power are not always clear. [25]

What is clear is that the existence of social media has transformed the way democracy functions. An example in the

2024 Irish local elections: a one-minute video of police escorting school children was made into a fake news story by an anti-immigrant candidate, purporting to highlight the dangers posed by immigrants. With the assistance of a few overseas conservative platforms, the story went viral on X, which has a large Irish following. [26]

When a young boy was killed in Springfield by a Haitian driving a minibus, Vance, the Republican vice-presidential candidate, denounced it as murder, but the victim's father stated that it was a normal road accident. Vance went on to spread racial hatred by claiming that immigrants were eating the pets of local residents, an untrue and ridiculous claim repeated by Trump in the presidential debate.

TikTok, which claims to have over two million followers in Ireland, has a policy of banning political advertising. But in practice, such rules may not be enforced, which is both a breach of the company's rules and the EU code of practice. [27] There were formal complaints that the rules were not observed in the 2024 elections. Another concern is its abuse by young children. Mobile phones are effectively banned in public schools across Australia. The fear of being separated from your phone has been called 'nomophobia'.

The USA takes an extreme libertarian approach, which benefits the owners of the platforms financially. It does not accept the need for fact-checking and resents the EU's regulation of its platforms. When META announced that it would no longer fact-check postings, one of their lawyers struck them off his client list, describing it as a descent into masculinity and Neo-Nazism [28] Under the Trump presidency, a major conflict is inevitable.

The full ramifications of social media should become better understood in the future. One prominent commentator on democracy has warned that we have handed over control to Corporations, States, and AIs, which could eventually destroy us. [29] Certainly, social media have been used to good effect by the enemies of democracy. For twenty-five years, platforms in the US and the EU have been protected by laws that limit their liability for serious inaccuracies. Most platforms have adopted a voluntary code to counter disinformation, with the exception of X, where hate speech has been reported to have increased by 50% under the ownership of Elon Musk. [30] These laws are now seen as not fit for purpose, and the era of light regulation is drawing to a close, particularly because of the disinformation widely spread in the Gaza war.

Social media tends to be one-dimensional and extremely time-absorbing. Some people claim that it dehumanises politics and absolves people from the guilt of inertia in the face of major economic and social crises. It can generate hatred readily through a simple process. First, it identifies an enemy who is perceived as a threat. The information can then be distorted and passed on to those who share the bias. Finally, it is reinforced by regular messages, which are often anonymous. It has become a dangerous weapon, spreading disinformation by unscrupulous individuals to further their aims.

It is easy to understand how Putin can use it to garner support. An insidious aspect is that it can occur without being noticed. Individuals do not have to declare their allegiance and may appear to be independent right-wingers. This was considered a reality in the 2024 European Parliamentary elections. How many Moscow 'moles' exist is a matter of conjecture.

As Aldous Huxley remarked, technology has provided us with more efficient ways of going backwards. How has it fared in its traditional home, America?

CHAPTER 18

American Democracy During the First Trump Presidency

The USA has often been considered a democratic role model for the rest of the world, but this has not always been plain sailing. People called its economic model into question, following the banking crash of 2008. The Vietnam War also left a bitter legacy. Confidence was shaken when the West invaded Iraq, based on false information about weapons of mass destruction. It also suffered damage to its reputation as a democracy when it was discovered that it had maltreated and tortured prisoners suspected of being terrorists at Abu Ghraib prison in Iraq. Similarly, the military detention centre at Guantanamo Bay in Cuba, set up during the War on Terror in 2003, permits indefinite detention without trial of suspects and still remains in operation. A further setback came with the war in Afghanistan when the Americans were forced to withdraw in 2021. They had sought to persuade the rival warlords to provide education for women and introduce other democratic values. This all disappeared with the return of the Taliban and Sharia law.

The US has a particular sphere of influence in the continent of America. However, some of its interventions in Central America and Chile have generated considerable scepticism about its real attachment to democracy internationally. Its unbalanced policy towards Israel over the Gaza war could erode confidence further. Unfortunately, when America sneezes, the rest of the world can catch a cold.

The model was to receive critical examination when Donald Trump became president. The nature of the office of the president was to change fundamentally when he was elected the forty-fifth president of the USA in 2016.

Donald Trump, the son of German and Scottish immigrants, joined the family property business. In the past, he managed to dodge military service due to a mysterious bone spur diagnosis, which earned him five deferments. He regularly scorns US military heroes. Questions have been raised about the way his business has operated. More than 20% of his sales over the last four decades, totalling over 1300 properties, have been made to anonymously owned shell companies for cash without a mortgage.

Some of these properties sold again on the same day for much higher or lower amounts, which could indicate the presence of money launderers. There is, of course, no implication that Trump was complicit in money laundering. A *Financial Times* investigation in 2008 found that Russian oligarchs were laundering money through Trump-licensed properties. [1]

His major hobby is golf. Although he claimed that he would have little time for golf as president, he played more than most presidents during and after his presidency. He likes to see himself as a 'winner' and, to this end, proclaimed that he frequently won competitions. On one occasion, he did this despite the fact that he had not played on the first day. He simply used an old card to submit his score [2] and has often been accused of cheating. [3]

Donald Trump's Presidential Appeal

The Republican Party had moved to the right when Trump announced his candidacy. A few years earlier, it had absorbed the thinking of the Tea Party Movement, which advocated reducing the public sector and taxes under the influence of some wealthy libertarians, opposed to any attempt at regulation. The views of their members were pro-life, pro-gun, and pro-prayer. Trump added a touch of racist anti-immigrant rhetoric.

Voters saw him as a successful businessman who could use his skills to make 'America Great Again'. His appeal to voters was that he wanted to disrupt the system. Disaffected voters seemed to believe that any change could only be for the better. The fact that he broke with conventional rules and norms worked to his advantage. What gelled was that he was taking on the hated Washington elite and establishment. He understood well what his supporters, particularly those based in the impoverished Midwest, wanted. They had suffered from the outsourcing of industry abroad. Traditional manufacturing had almost vanished, unemployment was high, and living standards were low. Many were struggling to make ends meet. Their interest was focused on domestic issues, rather than the intricacies of foreign policy. They did not welcome outsiders or diversity and wanted to see a return to their long-held values, which were English-speaking, evangelical Christian, socially conservative, and white. This adherence to a particular religious sect is at variance with the freedom of conscience, so cherished by President James Madison, one of the American Founding Fathers.

Their views were commonly found on Fox News. Tucker Carlson summed it up: "Happy countries don't elect Donald

Trump. Only desperate ones do". [4] People yearned nostalgically for the former culture. Only in this way could 'America Become Great Again'. They believed that immigrants, many of whom were illegal, were stealing their jobs. Trump tweeted short messages designed to play on voter fears and prejudices, referring to immigrants from the third world as coming from 'shithole countries'. He promised to build a wall on the Mexican border to stop illegal immigrants, whom he described as rapists, and ban Muslims from entering the country. His rejection of multiculturalism is a profound break with traditional American values.

Trump's Presidential Style

Trump despised experts, as did the Johnson Tory party government in the UK. He tended to lose concentration at long meetings and seemed to be strongly influenced by the views of the last speaker. Ill-disciplined and virtually innumerate, he was impulsive and often made decisions relying on his hunches, rather than any argument. He thrives on both conflict and flattery. While he reads little, he is a TV addict, often watching programmes for up to eight hours a day and not starting work until 11 am. His mind wanders during lengthy briefings, as he prefers long telephone conversations with his friends.

His main medium of communication is tweeting. His messages tend to be confused and self-centred, with little regard for the truth. He demeans and insults opponents. He comes over as bombastic, authoritarian, and increasingly neo-fascist. While purporting to appeal to ordinary Americans, his policies most often benefit the rich.

He is disrespectful of women and has been regularly accused of sexual assault. He believes that he is smarter than anyone and brags that, if he gunned down someone on Fifth Avenue, he would get away with it. He perceives himself as a global peace-maker, due to his close relationship with other authoritarian leaders, such as Putin and Xi. He also sees himself as a skilful negotiator, though this is contested by those who notice his inability to grasp details.

He seemed to take to heart Machiavellianism instinctively. 'Fear', he explained in his bid for the Republican nomination, was 'real power. [5] Rage was his way of getting things done, as he later boasted. [6] When fear and rage are combined, democracy loses out, as Adolf Hitler had demonstrated almost a century ago. Bearers of unwelcome bad news are regularly attacked, and those who disagree with them are subjected to scorn and humiliation. In a comparative emotional study of different presidents, his dominant emotions were stated to be anger, sadness, scepticism, and disgust. [7] This was far removed from the idea of Plato's philosopher king. In many ways, his style resembled that of a reality TV show, of which he had considerable experience. He must be a 'winner'. Any suggestion to the contrary could infuriate him. There was a high turnover of staff, some being fired for providing unwelcome advice and others resigning of their own accord.

Donald Trump could not have been expected to follow the norms of behaviour, given that he had no relevant political experience. Many people in such a situation might rely on expert advice. But this is not the style of Donald Trump. He wants to be seen as smarter than anyone, while he acts impulsively. His wish to reward loyalty and show that he is the decision maker could lead to difficult situations, which his staff could not control. It has also resulted in seats lost in Congress, due to his insistence on choosing candidates based on loyalty rather than competence.

Donald Trump's Health

Trump has claimed that he is the healthiest president in American history. It is hard to accept this assertion unless all their medical records exist and he had access to them. Certainly not everyone would agree, particularly when he wrote his own medical report.

In 2015, a wealthy New York doctor and Republican Party donor was reported to have called the Republican Speaker, Paul Ryan, who was second in line to succeed the President after the Vice President. He stated that Ryan needed "to understand what a narcissistic person is". Ryan studied the evidence and concluded that the description fitted Trump. He had an antisocial personality disorder. The advice was not to humiliate him in public, because narcissists can lash out frantically if they feel threatened or criticised. [8] Certainly, Trump often reacted in a rage when faced with disagreement or perceived criticism. In this respect, he resembles another narcissist, Adolf Hitler, who vowed to make 'Germany Great Again', following its defeat in the First World War. [9] More recently, Putin has promised to make Russia Great Again.

Many people describe Trump as narcissistic, but there are also worries over his mental health. [10] A Psychiatry professor at Harvard Medical School wrote to President Obama, questioning Trump's mental health. A Yale professor wrote about Trump's mental health, questioning his grandiosity, impulsivity, hypersensitivity to slights or criticisms, and an apparent inability to distinguish between fantasy and reality. Some of his senior advisors worried that he might not be fit to remain in office. Trump responded to such doubts by describing himself as a 'stable genius'.

Impeachment proceedings were brought against Trump over his involvement with Russia in the 2016 election. He attacked those 'disloyal' Republicans who had voted for his first impeachment and targeted them for revenge, which remains a strong motivation for Donald Trump. So too, he is reluctant to condemn illegal acts by those he considers to be his friends. His relationship with the 'Proud Boys' and other far-right groups is at best ambiguous. He described the rioters who attacked Capitol Hill as 'peaceful people' and 'great people'. Given his strong reaction to criticism, his reactions can be erratic, and the outcome unpredictable. Volatility became part and parcel of his presidency.

Russian Interference in the 2016 US Election

A disturbing revelation was the interference by Russia in the 2016 Presidential Election, designed to harm Hillary Clinton, promote Donald Trump, and increase political and social discord in America. It was known that a Russian team had visited Trump Tower, where they had a meeting with Trump's son and son-in-law. [11]

From the early days, Russians invested heavily in Trump properties, thereby providing him with valuable financial support. He, in turn, praised Russian policies and had destroyed important evidence of Putin's war crimes.[12] An unsubstantiated rumour was circulating that Trump was being blackmailed over his involvement with Russian prostitutes on a past business visit to Moscow in 2013, some years before he stood for the presidency.[13] He appears to enjoy a close relationship with Putin, often shrouded in secrecy. It seems bizarre to outsiders that Russian policy was designed to favour a right-wing American candidate over a moderately left-wing candidate, but the traditional communism that existed in Russia a hundred years ago no longer exists.

The US Intelligence stated that the operation of interference was ordered by Putin himself. A 'troll farm' in St Petersburg created thousands of social media accounts that purported to be Americans supporting radical groups and promoting Trump events. They reached millions of social media users. Hackers also infiltrated Democratic sites and released stolen data. The Special Counsel appointed to investigate the facts examined numerous contacts between the Trump campaign and Russian officials, but concluded that there was insufficient evidence to bring any conspiracy charges against Trump or his associates. It is, nevertheless, a serious concern that any country, particularly an enemy of America, should be able to spread disinformation to US voters, seeking to influence the outcome of the election.

Trump and Authoritarianism

If authoritarianism poses a threat to democracy, it is helpful to recognise it, where it exists. Angela Merkel, in her recent memoir, claimed that Trump was enthralled by autocrats. [14] Two Harvard academics have researched authoritarianism and believe that there are four warning signs. [15] Authoritarians tend to:

1. Reject the democratic rules of the games or, at best, have a weak commitment to them.
2. Deny the legitimacy of political opponents.
3. Tolerating or encouraging violence.
4. Be willing to curtail the civil rights of political opponents and the media.

They have assessed the election of Donald Trump and his first year in office for these symptoms. They found that he had broken virtually all the norms of presidential behaviour in a single year. Presidential private and public interests should be kept separate, while appointing family members to the cabinet is prohibited by law. Donald Trump appointed his daughter and son-in-law to high-level advisory posts. He declined to divest himself of his business interests, thereby facing inevitable conflicts of interest. His authoritarian style was very quickly established early in his presidency.

He challenged the legitimacy of the election with an unsubstantiated claim that millions of illegal votes had been cast in the 2016 election, thereby undermining public confidence in democracy. He attacked both his defeated rival and his presidential predecessor. He also lied continuously, even though his claims could readily be disproved. He claimed the largest Electoral College victory since Ronald Reagan, which was false. He also claimed that he had signed more bills than any other president in his first six months, which did not correspond with the facts.

He failed to show respect for the media, unlike his predecessors, who never did so publicly. He described them as "the most dishonest human beings on earth". He tweeted that they were 'the enemy of the American people'. He even mimicked a disabled reporter on the campaign trail. Criticism was simply branded 'fake news'. Hostile journalists from major papers were banned from press briefings, while handpicked sympathetic reporters from lesser-known papers were warmly welcomed. He threatened to change the libel laws, which could limit freedom of speech and help prevent unfavourable comments.

President Trump targeted any institution that might impede him, including law enforcement, intelligence, ethics agencies, and the courts. He expected personal loyalty to him from the key office holders, as he sought to undermine their impartiality. He dismissed the head of the FBI, which had happened only once before in American history. He also tried to get the Justice Department to investigate his defeated rival, Hillary Clinton.

He abused the system of presidential pardons. While there is no limit to this power, previous presidents exercised it with restraint by consulting the Justice Department first and not issuing them for self-protection or political gain. Efforts were made in Republican controlled States to disenfranchise poor voters, who would be likely to support the Democrats. This was achieved by demanding voter identification, such as a driving licence or Government-issued photographic identification, at polling booths. Many poorer voters simply had no such ID available to show.

The Trump presidency started and continued in the same destructive, erratic manner, with little consideration for the longer-term implications. In the interests of short-term financial gain, he decided to withdraw the USA from the Paris Climate Change Agreement. He sought to renegotiate the treaty made with Iran, even though that country had not violated the agreement. As part of 'Making America Great Again,' he embarked on protectionism by imposing tariffs, since the president thought that international trade was bad. He also scrapped numerous regulations designed to protect citizens. America's allies fared little better, as he threatened to tear up the trade agreement with South Korea. The only significant legislation in 2017, his first year in office, was tax reform, which largely benefited the wealthy.

The second year was dominated by the threat from North Korea. Kim Yong Un launched missile tests, which demonstrated that North America was within range. Having repeatedly insulted him, Trump threatened him with "Fire and Fury, the like of which the world has never seen before". The crisis was resolved by a meeting, instigated by Kim Yong Un, that cancelled further missile tests, but no new treaty ever emerged.

The other main event was a private meeting with Putin in Helsinki. Trump shocked many Americans when he made a craven speech in which he seemed to be beholden to Russia.[16] This was followed by the midterm elections. After an erratic and disastrous campaign, the Republicans lost control of the House of Representatives, thereby weakening the remainder of the presidency. The year ended in economic shutdown after Trump failed to obtain his funding for the wall on the Mexican border.

Trump had always had close Russian connections. In 2013, he visited Moscow on business. One of his sons told a reporter that "Russians make a pretty disproportionate cross-section of our assets". [17] In 2016, he appealed to Russians to find emails written by Hillary Clinton. The visit of Russians to Trump Tower, offering damaging information on Hillary Clinton, raised further concerns.[18] The year 2019 opened with the publication of the long-awaited Mueller report into Russian involvement in the election. It reported that the investigation did not establish that members of the Trump campaign had conspired or coordinated with the Russian Government in its election interference activities, but it specifically did not exonerate him.

Trump withdrew the USA from the World Trade Organization. He also tried to force Ukraine to investigate his political rival, Joe Biden, and his son for what he alleged was corruption, backed up with a threat to cease all aid to Ukraine. Impeachment proceedings were commenced, but while many senators were highly critical of the president, only one Republican supported it. So, Trump dodged the bullet.

The election year 2012 has been overshadowed by the COVID pandemic. Trump regularly overruled the medical advice and frequently declined to wear a face mask. Unsurprisingly, he and many of his White House staff contracted the disease. Bizarrely, he advised the public to drink bleach to protect themselves. Vaccines were brought out and distributed in 2021, before it was finally brought under control. In America, the number of reported cases eventually exceeded 100 million and deaths over a million, which was high by international standards. The chief medical advisor to the President believed that implementation of the program had been poor, and lives could have been saved. The country was handicapped by an underfunded health system. Re-election considerations took priority over COVID management.

In May, a Minneapolis policeman was caught on video torturing and killing a Black man. This led to widespread protests and started a movement, 'Black Lives Matter'. The President took a strong, divisive law-and-order approach. Riot police were used to disperse a peaceful protest in Washington, depriving citizens of their traditional right to free assembly.

The result of the presidential election was not a Republican 'landslide', as claimed by the President, but a narrow victory for the Democrats, once the numerous recounts and unsuccessful legal challenges were over. One particularly disturbing allegation is that he requested the Secretary of State of Georgia to 'find' extra votes, a matter which should eventually be resolved by the Courts. He and his supporters still maintain that the election was stolen from them, despite the lack of any evidence. This 'Big Lie' still poisons American politics.

He lost a civil case when a jury in New York found that he had sexually assaulted the plaintiff and awarded her damages of $5 million. He faced potential criminal charges relating to his role in the 2021 insurrection for the attack on the Capitol, and charges over his attempt to overturn the 2020 election in Georgia. He dismisses the charges as 'persecution' and 'Nazism', stating that he would discontinue them when he becomes President or pardon himself, if found guilty. In effect, he tried to place himself above the law, as he issued threats to his opponents on social media. If he were to pardon himself, this would present a real challenge to the operation of democracy in the USA. One of the most serious charges that Trump faced is that he mishandled highly confidential documents, including nuclear material, by transferring them to his house shortly before the end of his presidency. This has not adversely affected his popularity among the party faithful and prominent Republicans. He threatened 'death and destruction' if he were charged.[19]

One nomination candidate hopeful, with a cavalier disrespect for the law, before the evidence was heard, announced that he would pardon Trump if he were elected president and challenged other candidates to do the same. Subsequently, with one exception, all the other candidates stated that they would still endorse Trump, even if he were jailed. In 2024, a convicted felon, a man found guilty of fraud, became president of America. While they might decide to forgive him for federal offences, this might prove more problematic for a State conviction in Georgia.

The March on the Capitol

Donald Trump's most notorious disregard for democracy was his refusal to accept that Joe Biden had won the 2020 Presidential Election. He could not admit to being a 'loser' and claimed repeatedly that the election had been stolen from him, a view that he has maintained ever since, despite the lack of evidence then or subsequently. He was unable to persuade Vice President Mike Pence to declare the election result invalid. Refusing to accept the result, Donald Trump tweeted to his followers on 6 January 2021 to march on the Capitol and, in a speech at a "Save America" rally, urged them to "fight like hell". A mob of over two thousand rioters forced their way into the building, vandalising and looting, trying to find lawmakers, particularly Mike Pence, to capture and harm them. This became the first successful assault on the Capitol since 1814, over 200 years earlier.

Molotov cocktails were found in a vehicle nearby, and pipe bombs were in the headquarters of both the Democratic and Republican National Committees. Five people died and many people were injured, including 138 police officers. Following the riot, Trump gave out his final swathe of pardons before facing an impeachment charge after the end of his presidency. Seven Republican senators, of whom only one was seeking re-election, voted for impeachment, but the outcome was short of the required two-thirds majority. So, Trump survived the second impeachment of his presidency and became free to stand for the Republican nomination in the 2024 election. Instigating an insurrection is an unprecedented charge to lay at the door of an American president. The day 6 January 2021 was a bad ending of the presidency and a bad day for American democracy, but it may not be the only threat to face America today.

The Supreme Court

Another worrying aspect of American democracy today is a loss of confidence in the Supreme Court. According to a Gallup poll in 2022, only 40% of Americans approved of the way the Supreme Court does its job, compared with 58% three years earlier. [20] One issue is how vacancies are filled. In 2016, the Senate kept the vacancy under the Democratic Presidency vacant for ten months, insisting that the position be filled by the next president, allowing Donald Trump to select a conservative judge. On the other hand, when a liberal judge died six weeks before the 2020 election, the position was immediately filled by a conservative candidate. The result is that conservatives now have a 6-3 majority. It seems that the system has become politicised.

The Supreme Court has now overruled the 1973 Roe versus Wade decision, which enshrined the right to abortion. A Gallup Poll shortly afterwards showed that American confidence in the Supreme Court declined from 36% to 25%. They have also ruled that gun owners can carry concealed weapons in public. Subsequently, they have undermined two further cornerstones of social policy by preventing affirmative action by universities in student selection and preventing student debt forgiveness.

There is also concern that the judges are not bound by any code of ethics. In 2023, an investigative journalistic group revealed that the most conservative judge, Clarence Thomas, had taken millions of dollars in hospitality from a Texan billionaire with right-wing views. It included numerous luxury holidays, a house for his mother, and the private education of his children. [21] It also emerged that his wife, a political activist with alt-right views, had received substantial donations in one of her businesses from a group that had business before the Supreme Court.[22] The judge claims that he was not obliged to disclose the gifts and has done nothing wrong. The scandal is that he cannot be sanctioned or even held to account. As in the clerical abuse scandals, the worry is not so much the behaviour of a single individual, but the inability of the system to deal with it effectively. Technically, a judge could face impeachment in the Senate, but this is most unlikely to happen.

The courts must be seen to be independent and not biased in favour of any political party. This was perhaps not understood by Donald Trump when he described his three nominations to the Supreme Court as "my judges". One commentator stated that two judges were partisan and that the court was corrupt. [23] Too many American judges are not impartial, but are, in practice, Republicans in disguise. The rise of partisan judge appointments is eroding Americans' trust in the law. There is also concern about 'judge-mandering', the practice of appointing judges with strong party political affinities to make judgements in line with the Republican Party agenda. [24] Between 2000 and 2023, the number of Americans who stated that they trusted judges fell from 75% to 49%. It seems likely that this disclosure will further erode confidence in the working of the court, which has the support of less than half the population.

It is unlikely to be enhanced by the decision of the Supreme Court to exempt Trump from prosecution for previous acts as president. "My judges" have delivered a remarkable and surprising judgement, which has astonished many Americans, but pleased the former president. Many are likely to agree with the dissenting judge who criticised her conservative colleagues. She feared that it would place the president above the law and damage democracy in America.

It seems that America has now travelled far along the road to autocracy under Trump. The Supreme Court decision makes him no longer accountable for crimes. It also calls into question the independence of the judiciary and, therefore, its ability to act as an effective check on the exercise of presidential power. The Founding Fathers must be turning in their graves. Trump has expressed contempt for the press and unfriendly journalists while dealing harshly with public protests during his presidency. Bizarrely, it seems now that Trump could indeed shoot someone on Fifth Avenue and avoid any penalty!

Three legs of the four-legged chair are now badly damaged, if not already broken. This placed America on a red ski run during his first presidency. To make matters worse, Trump is an admirer of Putin's black ski run. Worryingly, on social media, he has pledged to prosecute political opponents, calling for the jailing of Joe Biden and Kamala Harris, Republican senators Mitch McConnell and Liz Cheney, together with his former vice-president, Mike Pence.

Declining Confidence in Liberal Democracy

Pride in American democracy has fallen dramatically in recent years. A 2023 Gallup Poll showed that only 36% of Americans were proud of their country, compared with over 70% two decades earlier. Amongst 18 to 30-year-olds, it was a mere 18%. [25] Congress seems to have a disconnect with the wider population. Perhaps this is unsurprising in the light of its composition in 2023: 82% are male, 83% white, and 50% millionaires. Women, coloured people of colour, the poor, and important minority groups are seriously underrepresented. Often, politicians are seen as self-serving or corrupt. Americans increasingly distrust their politicians. In 1964, 77% of Americans generally trusted their government, but fifty years later, in 2024, only 7% had confidence in Congress.

If citizens no longer trust their governments, it is hard to see how democracy can operate effectively. Something must fill the void. It seems that some, at least, have adopted a new view of reality, and alternative facts are widely accepted. The people have retreated to Plato's cave and do not want their view of reality challenged. Slogans become more powerful than reason. If these slogans address emotional fears, they can become very persuasive, particularly when they are widely disseminated by social media.

In 2024, democracy in America is in a parlous state and facing a real challenge, following the 2024 presidential election. There are allegations of serious electoral impropriety by the past incumbent president. Some Republican Governors have effectively tried to disenfranchise poor voters. The name-calling of political opponents has reached an unpleasant level in a seriously polarised country. Donald Trump has attacked the referees of democracy and damaged its guardrails, demonstrating a strong authoritarian record before seeking his second term of office. [26]

Confidence in the system has fallen dramatically, not just because of the behaviour of its president, but because democracy appears to be secondary to party political advantage. By abusing the use of presidential pardons, Trump put himself and his cronies virtually beyond the criminal law. Ethical considerations, other than a narrow puritanical sexual morality, seem to be ignored in 'Putting America First'. And 'Making America Great Again'. If a Republican Executive can control both the Legislature and the Judiciary, a very different democracy may emerge with implications both for America and the rest of the world.

Trump accuses anyone who opposes him of being "RINOS", Republicans in name only, but he seems to be the person who disregards the traditional Republican principles of stating the truth and upholding the Constitution. Critics claim that he does not care about American values and sometimes acts as if he prefers America's enemies to the United States. He respected Putin, even though he was a killer.[27] A traditional Republican Congresswoman, Liz Cheney, stated over the attack on Capitol Hill that Trump summoned the mob, assembled the mob, and lit the flame of the attack. The Proud Boys, leaders of the attack, received lengthy prison sentences, but Trump subsequently pardoned them. It has been argued that he breached his presidential oath to uphold the Constitution and therefore should not have been permitted to stand again.[28] The State of Colorado banned his name from the ballot paper, but this decision was reversed by the Supreme Court shortly before he was confirmed as the Republican candidate.

This case was heard more quickly than cases prosecuting Trump, the dates of which allowed them to be postponed until after the election. This has provoked further criticism of the system. It must be unlikely that these serious charges will ever reach the courts, and if they did and he were found guilty, he would simply pardon himself. He cannot, of course, pardon himself in the Stormy Daniels hush money conviction, since this was a State, not a Federal case.

Trump has made clear his intention to take on the 'Deep State', which he believes is a conspiracy designed to thwart him. To this end, he wants to create a 'unitary executive presidency', centred on destroying the independence of the judiciary. He may weaponize the judiciary to deal with opponents in a similar way to most autocrats. It also intends to bring scores of independent agencies under White House control, while stripping job protection from tens of thousands of career civil servants, making it easier to replace them with acolytes if they are deemed obstacles to his agenda.[29] If he acts in this manner, he may violate his presidential oath of office to defend and uphold the Constitution, since it fundamentally undermines the separation of powers, but this is unlikely to concern him. A prominent commentator and historian has warned that America has faced many challenges to its belief in equality and has replaced it with some form of hierarchy over the last two centuries. It is facing this challenge once more.[30]

As stated in the preface, Senator Bernie Sanders has argued that America is no longer a democracy, but rather an oligarchy.[31] Wealth is predominantly in the hands of billionaires, who effectively control the media and can dictate to both major parties, who rely on their donations to fund elections. There is widespread dissatisfaction amongst voters and distrust in politicians. For most poorer people, there has been no real increase in wages for 50 years. The inequality that exists is undermining the operation of the political system. A former member of staff claims that Trump has some unusual heroes. He admires Hitler and is infatuated with Putin. He also likes Kim Jong Un and Xi Jinping, all enemies of the USA. [32]

The American Republican Party has evolved dramatically in recent years. [33] It is now a far cry from the party of Abraham Lincoln, who cherished human and civil rights. He wanted a society that operates with malice to none and charity for all. The tradition of progressiveness, which was upheld by Teddy Roosevelt and others, including Ronald Reagan, has vanished. It is also very different from the time of Frederick Douglass, the slave who campaigned against racism and slavery. One popular journalist warned that the Republican Party has moved so far to the Right that this may prove to be the end of democracy in America if Trump were to win the 2024 presidential election. [34]

Trump's son boasted that the Republican Party was now Trump's Republican Party, which seems correct in light of the election results. Those wishing to further their political careers and avoid his revenge would be wise to accept that the 2020 election was stolen.

America has experienced populism over the years. In the post-war period, Senator McCarthy launched an attack on suspected communists, although the evidence was flimsy. Later, Governor George Wallace of Alabama promoted segregation with the slogan "segregation, segregation tomorrow and segregation forever", and gained a significant following in the South. But until the arrival of Donald Trump, no populist rose to the top of the party.

If Trump succeeds in creating a unitary executive presidency, he will undermine one of the cornerstones of the Constitution, the separation of powers, deriving from Montesquieu and highly valued by the Founding Fathers. It could herald a new cynical world of extreme Realpolitik, devoid of any underlying principles or ethical considerations. At that stage, the battle for the survival of American democracy will be well and truly lost. [35]

A dictator could still emerge in America at some stage in the future. Trump shared a video on social media that included a reference to a 'unified Reich' if the Republican candidate were to win a second term in the White House. [36] The office of the President holds wide powers under the Insurrection Act. If the holder were to be granted immunity for actions during his presidency, as Trump has argued, an unscrupulous office holder might attempt it.

A film released during the election campaign portrayed Trump in a very unfavourable light. [37] From an early age, he practised, under the tutelage of his ruthless lawyer, Ray Cohn, raw ambition, a determination for success, and the willingness to do whatever it takes to win. This translates into endless attacks, denying everything, and always claiming victory. Vulgar ostentation and endless publicity seeking are tools of the trade, while threats and dirty tricks are used when necessary. Mendacity, violence, and amorality are never barriers, but neither his mentor nor his family could expect any special favours. True to form, Trump denounced the producers as 'human scum', a phrase frequently used by many of the greatest tyrants to describe their critics. Trump has proudly claimed in the past that he is always right, a claim consistent with autocracy. [38]

Considering Trump's misogyny, xenophobia, psychological instability, incitement of his supporters to violence, together with the fact that he is a convicted criminal found guilty of sexual misconduct, who has shown a total disregard for the fundamental values of democracy, many countries outside of the United States would find him to be an unsuitable leader. He did serious damage to democracy in his first term as president.[39] The functioning of government suffered from ignorance, lack of preparedness, inappropriate appointments of people without the necessary skills or experience, and unwise cost-cutting for short-term gains. Inconvenient facts, such as the existence of climate change, were ignored and therefore not managed. Education, science, and energy management all suffered. His rambunctious style essentially undermined effective democracy. Nevertheless, the Republican Party was prepared to nominate Trump as their US presidential candidate. Now that he has been re-elected President, it would seem that America no longer attaches to the preservation of democracy.

The dangers to liberal democracy were evident at the outset of Trump's first presidency. [40] There had been strong economic growth around the world, particularly from China. But the benefits were not evenly spread, with the middle class being hard hit, particularly in America, and enormous resentment had spread, as basic liberal values were ignored. Without any improvement in the meantime, there are few grounds for optimism and change in Trump's second presidency.

CHAPTER 19

The Scourge of Polarisation

Extreme polarisation, where two opposing groups can find no common ground, is a relatively new phenomenon, usually associated with the growth of populism, which can easily result in an increase in violence.

The Impending Cataclysm or even Apocalypse

Many commentators consider that the present situation is more dangerous for humanity than it has been for many years. The wars in Ukraine, Gaza, and Lebanon could easily escalate, particularly if they expand into a wider conflict and fall out of any country's control.

In these circumstances, it is unsurprising that some people have turned back to read the writing of a famous Irish poet, William Butler Yeats. This poem, written in the aftermath of the 1917 Bolshevik revolution in Russia, contains dire warnings. [1]

"Turning and turning in the widening gyre

The falcon cannot hear the falconer.

Things fall apart; the centre cannot hold;

Mere anarchy is released on the world.

The blood-dimmed tide is loosed and everywhere

The ceremony of innocence is drowned;

The best lack all conviction, while the worst

They are full of passionate intensity".

Could this be relevant today? Can the centre still hold? Certainly, the poet Yeats' ominous wartime warning has often been quoted, most recently to describe France in 2024. [2] The centre did not hold in the 2024 US Presidential Election. Will mere anarchy be released upon the world?

Solidarity

A recent commentator has pointed out that there is enormous income inequality in England. [3] The Southwest is wealthy, but the Midlands, typified by the former shipbuilding city of Sunderland, lag far behind, raising complaints of neglect and injustice. Talk of a universal basic income has receded on the grounds of costs, the impact on other public services, and the effect on personal motivation. The NHS used to be a source of national pride, providing the same medical service to all citizens without any charge. But now, controversial charges have crept in, the service has declined, and the rich seem to get quicker treatment than ordinary citizens. International solidarity is also diminishing, as governments cut their overseas aid budgets.

The Dangers of Polarisation

Just as the North Pole and the South Pole are as far apart as is possible, polarisation divides countries into two groups. The centre, as described by the poet Yeats, does not exist, and therefore cannot hold, which obviously occurs widely with populism. Without moderation and compromise, traditional liberal democracy becomes unworkable.

It happened in Britain over Brexit, where some families banned the issue as a topic of conversation, due to the strident hostility it generated from opposing sides. In America, it was even worse, where Democrats could not tolerate the behaviour of Trump, whether it was his attitude to women, his contempt for the law, his removal of highly confidential documents, nonpayment of creditors, or his encouragement of insurrection. The Republicans were contemptuous of the corrupt elite, which they associated with the Democrats. Serious dialogue between the two sides became impossible, resulting in devastating consequences. The losing side feels alienated from the political system, as they can never expect a share in Government. Democracy works best when Governments rotate over time and minority groups cannot be ignored, if coalitions are to be formed. They have seen deep social changes, but what has brought about extreme polarisation?

Some degree of polarisation is inevitable in any two-party system. Both sides compete for votes. The degree to which whips enforce party members to follow party policy is critical. Periodically, some latitude may be allowed for serious matters of conscience, particularly in legislation of minor importance. The extreme case occurs in populist regimes where leaders do not want to see the elite as being in any way accommodating. In America, this was taken to extremes under Trump, as vengeance was threatened on any dissenter. But lines are not only drawn in politics. A journalist traveling around America found polarisation practically everywhere. [4]

Two writers describe the situation as a cultural backlash. [5] They found that older citizens born before the end of the Second World War and, to some extent, baby boomers born in the next twenty years tend to be socially conservative, while younger people, whether members of Generation X and 'Millennials', have lived with major social changes, which leads them to be less socially conservative. The older generation has fears over immigration and increasing multiculturalism. Their base of supporters includes non-college graduates, the working class, white Europeans, and the more religious men, and is strongest in rural areas, whose people fear for their security, their jobs, and look nostalgically on bygone days. They want conformity from their members and are happy to be led by a decisive and strong leader. The younger generation has grown up in a liberal society, tending to be more highly educated, urbanised, while being comfortable with multiculturalism, LGBTQ rights, and are interested in environmental issues, especially climate change. The two sides have little in common, and there is no serious communication between them. They regard each other with a mixture of contempt and dislike, sometimes verging on hatred, poisoning politics as a result.

Values and a Question of Ethics

As mentioned in the introduction, I first came across the values underpinning American democracy in 1963. These were honesty, tolerance, respect for others, unselfishness, compassion, generosity, and the resolution of differences by peaceful means. These principles were not new to me because they were the values I always espoused in childhood, both at home and at school. It is not surprising that they should exist in democracies, since the three main countries, which developed the practice of democracy, Britain, America, and France, were all Christian countries, and these are fundamental Christian values. The ethic can be encapsulated in the simple humanitarian advice: 'Treat others as you wish them to treat you', encapsulated in the parable of the Good Samaritan. This, of course, is not uniquely Christian, and similar advice can be found in most other major religions.

It is interesting to establish if these liberal values still exist today and, if so, how they are interpreted in practice. I shall do this by reviewing the conduct of the political leader, Donald Trump, in his first presidency: He was not honest, he lied repeatedly and blatantly in the presidential debate with Joe Biden, but this did not damage his reputation. The biggest lie of all was his assertion that the election had been stolen from him, which justified the attack on the Capitol. Elsewhere in business, he avoided paying his creditors, which led to repeated bankruptcies. He has been convicted of 34 felonies, and he stands accused of tax fraud.

Nor is he a tolerant man. He surrounded himself with family members and many sycophants while demanding blind loyalty from all advisors. He attacked anyone who happened to disagree with him and has threatened vengeance against those people who would not support him on particular issues. He sought to get rid of public servants who provided him with unwelcome advice. He was disrespectful, particularly in his treatment of women. He abused journalists and political opponents, giving them offensive nicknames, even mimicking a disabled reporter. He does not respect immigrants, especially those who come from 'shithole countries', as he abuses them with racist taunts. The individuals he appeared to respect most are autocrats, Putin and Xi, both of whose countries are enemies of America.

He even has little respect for the law, refusing to obey judge rulings, as he did repeatedly in the 2024 criminal case taken against him over the Stormy Daniels hush money affair. He followed this up on his conviction, when he denounced the trial as a disgrace, that it was 'rigged' and a 'scam', while he claimed that the judge was corrupt and crooked. Yet the convicted felon was rewarded by receiving the Republican nomination for the presidency, and will avoid a custodial term in prison. His court appeal may have broadened his political appeal, but his conduct throughout has done nothing to enhance respect for the law.

His respect for human life, too, is questionable with his support for gun laws, even after repeated atrocities committed by gunmen at schools and public places. He claimed to be the best friend that gun owners have ever had in the White House. This support does not appear to have diminished after an assassination attempt on him during the 2024 election campaign. He has not accepted the need to avoid violence. His obsession and professed expertise about nuclear warfare are not reassuring. His attitude to human life was demonstrated at the attack on the Capitol, where he openly incited his followers to use violence. In the presidential election, he suggested that a Republican opponent could face a firing squad.

The question must be asked, in view of the widespread support for Trump, with the full knowledge that he disregards the fundamental values of democracy: do these traditional values matter anymore in America? It has been argued that anti-liberalism or illiberalism has spread widely in America in some kind of revolution. Certainly, anti-liberalism, in the guise of support for slavery, featured during the Civil War, has emerged periodically since then, although it did not gain widespread support. The ideas promulgated by John Locke in England, by Rousseau and the Enlightenment in France, and also by the Founding Fathers in America are no longer valued or considered relevant now in much of America. Trump is merely a vessel for the expression of these views [6] If so, the outlook for liberal democracy in America is extremely worrying. Certainly, many Republicans support him with blind, unquestioning loyalty.

The Republican Party has always been the party of law and order and family values. They may choose to ignore the seedy revelations in the Stormy Daniels hush money affair and have no problem with nominating a convicted felon, who was facing charges of fraud. Other Republican candidates stated that they would pardon him if they became President without hearing any evidence. Judging by the reaction of many Republicans to Trump's guilty verdict, they share his contempt for the law, thereby undermining the rule of law in America.

Lying and repeated disrespect to others do not bring any rebukes. Surprisingly, he has had the support of millions of women, numerous devout evangelicals, and Roman Catholics coming from Latin America. All of which would suggest that voters no longer place much weight on traditional values. Kamala Harris, the Democratic candidate, believes strongly in the freedom of the individual, but this carried little weight in the end.

What guides individuals in this new world? The answer would seem to be naked self-interest or total selfishness with no shred of generosity, unconstrained by any effect it may have on others, which is at odds with the teaching of most religions. For politicians, it centres on gaining or retaining power in the short term, even if this entails opposing sensible government proposals. In the American case, the result can be the abandonment of international cooperation on defence or attempting to address major questions, such as climate change.

It could even take seriously the request from Putin to surrender Bill Browder.

At an international level, this may result in abandoning commitments to assist with the defence of Ukraine and suggesting that there is no problem if Putin wants to attack NATO allies. The test is purely pragmatic: does the proposal make America better off or not? Objections can be met with 'spin', usually with the assistance of social media. So, Putin, adopting a traditional policy of territorial expansion, can claim that he is trying to eliminate Nazis. Netanyahu, with a similar Zionist goal in Palestine, claims that the Gaza war is purely about self-defence, and opposition is attributed to antisemitism. The suffering of many innocent civilians is irrelevant.

The belief of Donald Trump that such an approach will 'Make America Great Again' is controversial. It is essentially a retreat into a type of quasi-isolationism, which is more like 'Make America Little Again'. But, if America abandons its role as a world leader, will it make the country great again? Unlike Hitler in Germany, he proposes to reduce international commitments. Certainly, many minority groups would disagree. Is it really necessary to abandon the American dream, as epitomised by the iconic Statue of Liberty?

Attempting to resolve world issues between a would-be dictator, Trump, and two absolute dictators, Putin and XI, who have already formed an alliance, each acting on mutual self-interest, is a frightening prospect. It demonstrates a strange, dysfunctional version of Realpolitik and is a very dubious proposition, which bears no resemblance to traditional liberal democracy. Perhaps the greatest split in the polarised world of America today is between those who uphold the traditional values supporting liberal democracy and those who do not. If the latter groups now comprises the majority, the foundation of democracy in America is already under grave threat, and Bernie Sanders' pessimism may be well justified. Where the two sides operate with a different set of values, it is difficult to see how any agreement can be reached.

Immigration

One major difference that polarises many countries is their attitude to immigrants and, especially, asylum seekers. With the large numbers entering Europe from the Middle East and Africa, as well as the many Mexicans and other Latin American countries entering America, attitudes have changed. It is particularly difficult in Greece and Cyprus, both of which have experienced a large number of asylum seekers. The traditional liberal approach has always been to welcome them from the country of their persecution.

The same has been the case all over Europe, but as numbers grow, so does the opposition. The EU has rules that it should follow, but with the growth of right-wing parties throughout Europe, the problem is becoming more difficult to resolve. Many countries refuse to allow them entry. In England, immigrants, most of whom cross the English Channel in small overcrowded boats, who were refused admission, were then threatened with extradition to Rwanda, though this decision was rescinded by the Labour Government. In America, where Trump wanted to build a wall on the Mexican border and deport millions of them to El Salvador or elsewhere, the issue has grown in importance.

Fears have grown with the large, unprecedented volume of immigrants seeking asylum. In Britain, there are cities with a majority of minority groups, and in primary education, there can be up to 70% of pupils comprising immigrants. Opposition may be simply racist or may be concerned over job competition, education facilities, and pressure on the health system, but reactions can be very strong. Scare-mongering and name-calling are not new. In 1968, a British Tory Minister, Enoch Powell, predicted that 'rivers of blood' would result from immigration. Now, some scaremongers are suggesting that Europe might morph into 'Eurabia', with an influx of Muslims who want to introduce Sharia Law. Trump has denigrated Mexicans as rapists.

Even in Ireland, with its own long history of emigration and whose motto has always been 'Cead Mile Failte' or 'A Hundred Thousand Welcomes' in the Irish language, there is now some opposition. It appears that the traditional 'Ireland of the Welcomes' has at least partly vanished. While many Ukrainians have settled here, attitudes are now hardening with the growth of numbers. Ireland has proportionately the highest rate of asylum seekers of any EU country. Arsonists have attacked hotels designated to house refugees. Worryingly, it was reported that a former senior Ku Klux Klan leader was assisting small Irish far-right groups opposed to immigration. [7]

Disturbingly, there now seems to be an international network of anti-immigration extremists, who are prepared to assist similarly minded people abroad. This would indicate that it is not about local inconvenience but more of an attempt to undermine democracy internationally. Riots broke out all over the UK when misinformation was spread that three young girls were stabbed by a Muslim immigrant. Rioters in Belfast were assisted by people from the South of Ireland and unionist paramilitaries. Whether these agitators are paid by other far-right groups or by members of the autocrats' club is unclear. They seem to believe in a form of anarchy when opposed by the State. Sadly, some of them, such as American Republican vice-presidential candidate Vance, are prepared to use disinformation to stir up racial hatred.

A national television documentary shocked many Irish viewers. Immigrants, reporters, construction workers, security guards, and politicians were all subjected to horrific intimidation with threats of violence, lawlessness, arson, assault, and racist hatred. [8] Some of the protesters were masked, and others earned money from circulating their films on social media, through which they circulated misinformation. This small but very vociferous minority was able to recruit like-minded people from outside the area who were opposed to housing immigrants. An opinion poll showed that a significant majority of Irish people saw that immigration was beneficial, but wanted tighter controls. [9] It has been reported that right-wing extremists in Ireland are getting ready for violence.

In the existing state of polarisation, it is virtually impossible to conduct a reasonable debate. Unfortunately, groups often disseminate misinformation and spurious statistics, which aggravate the problem. [10] As a former British prime minister, George Canning, remarked You can prove anything by statistics, except the truth. In 2024, some progress was made in exposing misinformation in the EU, Taiwan, and South Africa, but, in general, reactions have proved to be too little and too late, especially where misinformation has gone viral. Neo-Nazi networks with cells in the USA and Europe hold virtual meetings to attract members, describing themselves as 'White

Nationalists', who advocate violence against immigrants. Although their membership is small, it is a fact of life. [11]

Attitudes to immigration vary in different countries and cultures. The latest country to discourage immigration is the UK under Starmer. Only Spain, which has set a target of 300,000 migrants a year to combat a declining population, encourages it. It would appear that many Christians do not put into practice the biblical teaching of helping people in trouble, as illustrated by the parable of the Good Samaritan. Like the Pharisee, they choose to pass by on the other side and even try to take advantage of victims. Muslims, with their tradition of assisting travellers, may be more accommodating. The proposed mass deportation advocated by Trump signals a swing to the right in the USA.

CHAPTER 20

The Perils of Complacency

Why Democracy Has Lost Ground

Fukuyama was naïve to believe that, because liberal democracy has both theoretical and practical advantages over autocracy, it would automatically prevail. After all, liberal democracies in their present format have basically existed in most countries only since 1945. Before that, there were many twists and turns as democracy developed, with many ebbs and flows of its spread. It is naive to expect liberal democracy to thrive and prosper indefinitely into the future, since it has many strong and powerful enemies. Putin in Russia and Xi in China are both contemptuous of Western values. There are also many self-serving autocrats, willing to undermine democracy whenever possible, as are also enemies from within.

It was assumed that after the fall of the Berlin Wall, democracy would be automatically accepted as the means of governance. But even in its traditional bastion, the UK, the mother of parliaments, it was coming under pressure over the issue of Brexit. Where democracy is newly and suddenly introduced, acceptance may not be universal.

One major problem is that many countries were unused to the important separation of powers, outlined in Chapter 14. Existing politicians wanted to retain power as long as possible, ideally indefinitely. This could be possible if they disregarded the freedom of the media, the rights of the legislature, and the independence of the judiciary. Opponents could sometimes be coerced into acceptance, bribed, or threatened. Would-be supporters could be enticed by financial inducements and offers of permanent, paid jobs.

Loser Consent and the Democratic Trap

A basic problem is that voters look to their own interests first, although what is good for an individual may not be in the best interests of society as a whole. Arguably, there may be no such thing as 'the will of the people'. A former UK Chief Justice has claimed that for democracy to succeed, it must have the capacity to identify common practices, common bonds, and common priorities, which override individual differences. This capacity is under widespread attack today with the demand for firm government. [1] Libertarianism, with its disregard for regulation, might be an equally powerful, destructive force.

A problem can arise when the loser refuses to accept the result. At its worst, it can lead to a civil war, as happened in Spain in 1936, when the left-wing Popular Front narrowly defeated the conservative opposition. The time when losers graciously accept defeat is now rarer in America. In the presidential election of 2000, the result hinged on the votes in the State of Florida, but Al Gore conceded defeat after several recounts in the best interests of the country, despite the fact that he had received a majority of the popular vote. Donald Trump reacted otherwise after losing the 2020 election, which resulted in an attack on the Capitol, which certainly did not represent the will of the people.

Perversely, democracy under some models of two-party systems can produce results that do not reflect the will of most of its citizens. American Presidents can be elected, even when they do not obtain a majority of the popular vote. Conservative Governments can be formed in the UK when they have a minority of the popular vote, since the votes for the Liberal Party are not equitably reflected in the final result. Hilary Clinton had the majority vote in the 2016 US Presidential Election, but lost out to Donald Trump. It can also result in an election where many voters do not wish to vote for either of the two major parties, as may be the case for many in America for the 2024 Presidential election.

Proportional representation can better reflect the views of minority interests, but can lead to chaos. In Belgium, the largest political party has 17% of the vote, while the French-speaking Walloons had slightly less, disregarding five other existing parties. In 2011, a Government was eventually formed eighteen months after the election. In Ireland, where members of the same party are competing with each other in the same constituency, it leads to prominent GAA sportsmen and other celebrities being selected as candidates, irrespective of their political abilities.

The two-party system in the US and the UK is leading to increased polarisation, as the extreme wings take over control of the party. This makes it difficult to obtain an overall consensus, but coalitions are better able to reflect the views of the Centre.

The Essence of Democracy: Freedom

The French Revolution of 1789 centred on "Liberty, equality, and fraternity". These remain the focal points of democracy, two and a quarter centuries later. The world's shortcomings on equality have already been addressed, but freedom and fraternity are also under attack today.

The word 'freedom' is a popular word, but not always used in its literal sense. These aspects have been succinctly set out at the start of a book, recently by a Yale Professor of Political Science.[2]

"Freedom is not just the absence of evil, but the presence of good. No country is free; only people can be free. The moment you believe freedom is given, it is gone. Freedom for you means freedom for me. Freedom is neither the lack nor the acceptance of constraints, but the use of them. Freedom is not about being right, but trying to do right. Freedom of speech means nothing without free speakers. There is no freedom without solidarity. Markets cannot be free, only people can be free".

Freedom and solidarity are now under attack from tyranny, dictatorship, despotism, self-serving populism, autocracy, and polarisation, as never before in history. These people claim to be supporters of freedom, but few others would accept this assertion. The growth of illiberalism was explained over twenty years ago. The strongest and most enduring Western democracies already had the rule of law supported by the privileged classes and preferably with some capitalist tradition before they sought democracy. If democracy is imposed on people not used to freedom, it can be fragile and perverted by autocrats. Polarisation and institutionalised corruption exacerbate the problem. It, therefore, should not be surprising that many democracies emerging after the fall of the Berlin Wall were doomed to failure. It is easier for a truly liberalising autocracy to introduce a longer-lasting democracy, as happened in South Korea, which was once an unstable military state, before it embraced economic growth and subsequently overcame an attempted coup in 2024. [3]

No better example of real freedom can be given than the heroic resistance of the Ukrainian people in defending their country against the Russian invasion, despite the overwhelming odds against them and the enormous casualties that they suffered. Unsurprisingly, the Russians claimed that they were liberating Ukraine. Ukrainians must wonder how bombing, torture, rape, arson, dishonesty, and the forcible kidnapping of their children for indoctrination constitutes any kind of freedom. Freedom and its defence, however, were shown by President Zelensky, who remained at the helm.

Similarly, the citizens of Russia must question if the absence of a free press, judges who do the bidding of their political masters, the absence of consumer goods at affordable prices, a collapsing rouble, endless surveillance, arbitrary imprisonment, torture and banishment to the gulags of Siberia, not to mention the heavy military casualties suffered in Ukraine, constitutes freedom.

Sovereignty, the right of a country to rule itself, free from foreign domination, is also fundamental to freedom. The Ukrainians have embraced it, while the Baltic States and others are preparing to defend it. It obliges countries, conversely, not to attack other countries, allowing freedom of speech, the right to peaceful protest, and a fair trial. It does not equate to selfishness, but expects individuals to treat others as they wish to be treated themselves, which requires a degree of empathy, as exists in personal dignity. It also obliges individuals to accept decisions, which they may not like, if they are the decision of the majority.

Freedom should not suppress individuality, because only individuals can evaluate, transform, and take responsibility. In many former communist countries, there is a drab uniformity, banning aspects of Western culture such as rock music. Increasingly, they resemble *Brave New World,* a novel written by Aldous Huxley almost a century ago [4]. In it, the author portrayed a society that sacrificed individuality for the sake of stability and superficial happiness. It was considered fanciful at the time, but it exists in many undemocratic countries today, where citizens are expected to live as obedient zombies.

Other important freedoms include the freedom to travel and choose one's own job. Importantly, in true democracies, freedom entails the absence of racial discrimination and the possibility of upward mobility, which enables poorer people to join the middle class by their own efforts. Sadly, these two elements are absent or very limited in many democracies. Freedom of speech cannot exist when journalists and other purveyors of free speech are oppressed or even murdered, as happens in many tyrannies. Whether the USA can still be called the 'Land of the Free' under the 2025 Trump presidency is highly questionable.

The Performance of Modern Democracies

Liberal democracy is inextricably linked to capitalism. A historian reminds readers that Darwinian capitalism may not survive forever. It has already suffered setbacks in the form of protectionism and also faces a formidable opponent in Putin. But it has been argued that inherent features of modern-day capitalism have sown the seeds of the growth of autocracy. [5]

Capitalism's light shines most brightly when it is shown to benefit those at the bottom level of the economic ladder. Its reputation was enhanced in the aftermath of the Second World War with the creation of the welfare state and consumerism after the deprivations of wartime rationing. Another wave of popularity followed years later when income tax rates were significantly reduced, but the present system does not have the same attractions. [6] The welfare state is struggling with underfunding, a shortage of hospital beds, and the increasing costs of new drugs. Homelessness has become more widespread in practically every country. There have been many benefits from the spread of third-level education, but in some countries, students have been left with crippling levels of debt. Young people, faced with rapidly rising rents and high costs of buying a house for themselves, are obliged to live with their parents and see little prospect of ever achieving the same standard of living as their parents. They have now become the new poor.

Cutbacks in public services in order to finance tax cuts, which disproportionately affect the poorer citizens, have been commonplace since the era of Margaret Thatcher and Ronald Reagan. Their views were given an academic backing from a Harvard professor, a libertarian, who advocated a 'minimal state'. [7] There is a growing sense of inequality, where the super-rich can often avoid completely paying their tax contribution to society by changing their residence or domicile, which does not seem remotely fair to those who are struggling to make ends meet.

In general, there is a disenchantment in the way democracy functions in a capitalist economy, with growing numbers believing that they are being left behind. Although autocracies have performed worse than democracies in reducing inequality, as shown in Chapter 9, some voters feel naively that they might fare better under an autocracy. This may be backed up by a dubious selective nostalgia, typified by "Make America Great Again", despite the enormous improvement in living standards. Nevertheless, unfettered laissez-faire capitalism needs to be re-examined, as does the trend towards protectionism.

Finally, in times of political instability, citizens may become increasingly worried about their security. [8] Since safety is a major basic need, some people hope and naively believe that any change will be an improvement, believing that autocrats might move more swiftly and decisively to tackle the problem. It seems that the reputation of capitalism has suffered a sharp reversal in recent years on many different fronts. Democratic leaders have done little to persuade the doubters and promote the superiority of democracy over autocracy on the lines put forward by Fukuyama.

A recent memoir of a former British minister highlighted how dysfunctional and unrepresentative political systems may become. [9] It is hard to attract good party candidates with wide relevant experience. Rory Stewart himself was a widely travelled, multilingual individual who eventually went on to become a deputy governor of a province in Iraq, where he recounted that his challenging tasks were not typical. [10] It is hard to believe that many candidates would start with or eventually develop their breadth of experience, and certainly not manage the enormous challenges that they faced in Iraq. The selection process is archaic, and if the candidate is elected, he or she faces years of mind-numbing boredom as a backbencher. They have limited ability to offer dissenting views and too often must vote as instructed if they wish to further their careers. In Ireland, there is a preponderance of teachers who have always been permitted to retain their teachers' pension, due to a historical anomaly, despite the fact that they may not have taught for many years, a dubious qualification.

In effect, prior to Brexit, the country was run as an elected dictatorship. In Britain, cabinet ministers are too often chosen on grounds of loyalty, rather than ability. Policy decisions can be reached on the basis of popular publicity, rather than proper evaluation of alternatives. The views of people with relevant expertise are routinely ignored. Communication between key individuals and departments can be weak. A complex and lengthy party leadership selection process is centred on a small number of elderly party members and produced one leader who only survived a few weeks.

Two Major Challenges: Inequality and Short-Termism

The popularity of liberal democracy has declined because two major issues have not yet been seriously addressed: Inequality and Short-termism.

Inequality, as discussed in Chapter 9, is less extreme in Western democracies than in autocracies. But, nevertheless, the situation has been deteriorating over the last few decades. In America in the 1970s, the wealthiest 1% of the population owned 10% of the wealth. By 2014, their share had increased to 20%. The poorest 50% of the population in the same period shared 20% of the wealth, but this share has dropped to 12%. In 2018, 0.1% (one in a thousand people) held almost 20% of the social wealth of America. [11] Jeff Bezos' gratitude to the staff of Amazon sounds rather hollow, given that he earns three million times that of the typical employee. The poor can only blame the system, but no party has attempted to radically reform the system with a significant wealth tax. Maybe this is related to the fact that wealthy people tend to be major providers of funding for political parties.

Short-termism has always been a problem for politicians who fail to look beyond the next election, which is typically a maximum of five years in Europe and four years in America. The difficulty is that, when dealing with longer-term problems, such as climate change and expanded infrastructure, major investment is required immediately, while the benefits will be felt over the long term. So, some group must bear the costs of the investment and be worse off in the short run. Politicians usually have difficulty persuading the electorate that this is a good idea. But if issues, such as global warming, are not addressed quickly, there may be no planet left to support human life.

There is no evidence that autocrats have been successful in providing answers. Russia, China, and the Gulf States have made little progress. So the hope that a strongman, not dependent on votes, can change things radically seems to be illusory. But it does mean that many people in democracies are frustrated by the current outcome and will not defend the system as they have done in the past. Critically, short-termism has been offered as a major explanation for the decline in the popularity of democracy. [12] The world is experiencing a constant emergency, as people are worried by unstable geopolitical instability, rising inequality, and climate change without any sense of a shared future. The long-term issues need urgent attention, instead of the exclusive focus on short-term considerations. Democracy is frequently blamed, even though most autocracies have fared worse.

The New Toxic Culture

Democracy has traditionally thrived in a harmonious, tolerant atmosphere, a system respected by almost everyone, while only the communists sought revolution. In a two-party system, it was most effective if the two parties periodically formed the Government. In a multi-party system, the Government was formed following lengthy negotiations. In both cases, there was a tendency to take some central ground and avoid extreme positions. The traditional virtues were cooperation, stoicism, civic responsibility, and tolerance. The culture has fundamentally changed in the USA and to varying extents in many other countries. Those who advocate radical change come mainly from right-wing elements, rather than those of the left. [11] The problems of drugs and crime remain unresolved. Citizens feel that they have been left behind, blaming the operation of the democratic system, as practised by the elite. A central feature of the new culture is epitomised by Donald Trump. Narcissists have an excessive love for themselves, believing that life centres on them, with no tolerance of any criticism. The surprising fact is that they can appeal to voters, as self-interest has replaced civic responsibility. The mood has changed to anger, rage, resentment, envy, and even hatred. Such attitudes are not easily compatible with the values of traditional liberal democracy.

It can be difficult to separate the political system of democracy from the underlying economic system of capitalism, which forms the foundation of democratic capitalism. The chief economics commentator of *the Financial Times* has addressed the challenges currently facing democratic capitalism. Fundamentally, he believes that democracy and capitalism are interdependent. He discusses his thesis with a number of experts and tries to understand why democracy is being undermined by populism. [13] The first expert, a leading professor, specialising in democracy, at Stanford University in the USA, considered that free and fair elections were rare in populist regimes and that there was too little accountability. [14] Too many people do a poor job of upholding the rule of law and protecting both human and property rights. They then demonise the Opposition, restrict their access to the media, and before attacking the State Institutions. It sounds like a continuous attack on the four-legged chair.

The next contribution by a journalist, who describes the breakdown of liberal democracy in Poland, was already described in Chapter 15.[15] She believes that liberal democracy was not long-established in either Poland or Hungary, leaving them particularly vulnerable. There was, amongst right-wing elements, a sense of disappointment with progress when comparison was made with China, where progress had been very rapid under an unchanged Government. A better civic education was necessary. There had been a period of massive change, bringing with it confusion and a nostalgia for stability. The hope was that a strong leader might be able to find a path through the overwhelming sources of new information, while replacing the polarisation with a greater sense of unity.

A further interview was with Hillary Clinton, the US failed Presidential candidate in 2016. [16] She explains the tremendous pressure derived from a feeling of anti-pluralism, anti-multiculturalism, and globalisation. An alternative version of reality was attractive, however absurd it might seem, during the pandemic. Finally, it was hard to overcome deep-rooted misogyny. Whether democracy and capitalism can remain interdependent under a Trump presidency remains to be seen, since the democratic side is likely to come under serious attack.

The Impact of Social Media on the New Culture

As explained in Chapter 14, social media are rapidly increasing their influence on society, because postings can be made anonymously and are not checked for accuracy. They can contain blatant lies, outlandish conspiracy theories, and too often pure garbage. But appealing to the emotions, rather than reason, they can strongly influence people's views, which may then go viral, a fact not unknown to the Russians.

The enormous scale of the connection for many people with the virtual world and the speed of the transmission of data has created a new and dangerous problem. Many humans are both too connected and too isolated at the same time. Heavy users can become addicted and have little time to do much else. Connectivity is changing the fabric of society in its habits and its culture. Sometimes they feel that others, who are their peers, are more successful than they are without good reason, which leads to envy, verging on hatred. It is making people angrier, more narcissistic, more selfish, more isolated, more withdrawn, and less civic-minded. Information overload results in depressed, anxiety-ridden wrecks. Too many people have less time to pause, consider, and reflect. If the uses and abuses of social media continue to expand, these problems are likely to be exacerbated.

The Need for Liberal Democracy to Evolve

In view of the unpopularity of the workings of liberal democracy today, several critics have looked for ways by which it might change. The current system has its origins in the Reagan-Thatcher revolution, when the system of social democracy, which had existed since the Second World War, was dismantled. The results of the removal of democratic control over capitalist planning have been damaging.

The freedom of individuals is curtailed in practice due to planning in the corporate and government sectors, whose interests frequently coincide. Powerful players, combining together, now determine the distribution of wealth. It seems that 'free markets' are not all that they may seem to be. These are the multinational corporations, which often control the media, banks, and, now recovered from the 2008 crisis, that determine where investment goes and which technologies are developed, giving rise to empires and the State systems that they control. [17] The author points out the generous treatment of Boeing and Ford, which were both given enormous State support, while paying large dividends and engaging in massive share buyback programmes.

Equally, the State resolved the 2008 banking crisis at enormous cost to the public, while not holding those responsible to account. The old empires, whether of the European powers in Africa and Asia or the USA in the Philippines, may have gone, so they cannot exercise their traditional control over their colonies. But they have been replaced by equally powerful multinationals, who are not averse to interfering in the working of overseas democracies to further their interests. Influencing elections overseas is not restricted to Russia. The USA can attempt to influence the formation of governments abroad. It did so openly in the case of Allende's Chile, but also more discreetly through the CIA, particularly through its backdoor in Latin America.

The State is in thrall to capitalist interests, often providing them with generous bailouts to both manufacturers and financial institutions along with subsidies, even when they pay no tax in the jurisdiction, prioritising them over the interests of the national workers. In practice, senior figures in financial industries are rarely prosecuted after major collapses. It gives some doubtful credence to Trump's son-in-law, who considers that the Government should be run like a business in maximising its profits and reducing regulation. While all parties advance their own interests, there has been a serious increase in inequality and transfer of resources to the wealthy in a system of vulture capitalism. The alienation of citizens, as outlined by Bernie Sanders at the start of this book, is the inevitable outcome. [18] The focus on the super-wealthy does not stop at national boundaries. The West is complicit in perpetuating the injustices of capitalism in the third world. A German sociologist explains how the Global North exploits the Global South by developing their resources, passing on heavy costs to them, and appropriating vast profits. The damage to the environment through the extraction of resources, dumping of waste, the use of toxic chemicals in food production, deforestation, and land grabbing is substantial. It has always existed, since there has always been unequal exchange, as the terms of trade are biased in favour of the wealthy countries, but it has increased in an era of outsourcing and globalisation. [19]

For some years, there have been calls for a more humane form of capitalism from a prominent feminist, rather than one based on selfishness and greed. Liberal democracy should reinvent itself as a 'Caring Democracy', based on love, friendship, and solidarity in place of unbridled individualism, tinged with growing libertarianism and the absence of any social conscience. If people are concerned about these issues, they should be prepared to provide care. A lack of care can have heavy social costs, such as rising crime. But for the most part, the appeals have fallen on deaf ears, as populism spreads, with a drift to oligarchy. It would be difficult to achieve without some restoration of the social contract.[20] A lack of care highlights a related issue, the underrepresentation of women in politics. With the exception of Scandinavia, the imbalance is chronic in most countries.[21]

Neoliberalism in Trouble

Neoliberalism owes its origin to the writing of Friedrich Hayek, who wrote at a time of totalitarianism in Germany and Russia, as described in Chapter 2. He believed that the interference of the State in running the country should be minimised and left to market forces. The traditional role of providing social justice should be abandoned. The State should have no role in establishing 'the common good', while adequate conditions of existence, such as income, housing, and health care, should be beyond its remit. [22] This provided a radical break with the past, where voters were protected from inequality and desperation. It was encapsulated by Margaret Thatcher's claim that there is no such thing as 'society', only individuals, who should be free to choose what they want. It led to the privatisation of many industries and the undermining of the welfare system. Nevertheless, many of its supporters emphasised the importance of the family, tradition, and Christianity.

This neo-conservatism has little semblance of traditional liberalism or democracy, as it operated in the past.[23] Particularly in America, it has led to legislation which runs counter to traditional ideas of liberal freedom, such as anti-discrimination against individuals, including protection of the LGBT community and also gender, without abortion restrictions. The downgrading of equality and social justice with the support of conservative judges has fundamentally changed with the prioritisation of evangelical Christianity views and limitations on freedom of speech and worship. These economic views were advanced many years ago by Milton Friedman, who advocated minimal interference in the economy. [24] His Chicago monetary school of economics advocated balancing the books by draconian cutting back of public expenditure. It caused great hardship when applied to Pinochet's Chile and in IMF rescues of countries after the 2008 financial crisis.

Rise of the Far-Right

One disturbing feature resulting from the declining popularity of neo-liberalism is the rise of the far right. [25] There is a growing number of people who feel ignored in the era of globalisation. Most of them dislike feminism, gay and transgender rights. They behave nihilistically with resentment and rage, feeling that the role of the male has been devalued by 'woke' thinking. Looking for someone to blame, they target migrants, who, they feel, have stolen their jobs. What unites hard-right parties is their hatred of immigration, Islam, climate change regulation, and loss of control to a central body. Enthralled by images of disaster and doom, they resort to chaos and despair. Their discontent may spread like a plague with the assistance of social media.

Such right-wing groups, with their collective hatred, may resort to insurrection and violence through their army of vigilantes, as they attack the establishment. They admire strongmen, are opposed to parliamentary bargaining, and often have links with Russian interests. Due to their numerical strength, they can sometimes topple centrist liberal democratic governments or force themselves, as unwelcome allies, into unstable coalitions.

Nietzsche and Far-Right Parties

Friedrich Nietzsche was a renowned German philosopher in the nineteenth century. After a period of obscurity, he returned to prominence in the two World Wars. He explained German aggression and cruelty, although he himself was not antisemitic or strongly nationalistic. However, he had come up with the concept of the 'Übermensch' or Superman, which appealed to the Nazis. With their downfall, he returned to obscurity. As a nihilist, he believed that nothing could be known with certainty, while as an atheist, his starting point was that ' God is Dead. [26] He rejected the concept of good and evil, even to the point of admiring cruelty. There are no absolute values, and his philosophy is totally amoral; nor is there any free will, while quality, fairness, or justice are irrelevant. The exemplary human being pursues a path of self-realisation. He sees the world by what men try to do. Central to this is 'the will to power'. The strong are to be admired and the weak despised. It is the ultimate justification of 'Might is Right.

It is easy to see how such a philosophy has been embraced by far-right groups. Inequality is acceptable, and justice is irrelevant. It has reappeared in the light of Trump's approach to traditional relationships. Most autocrats implicitly behave in this manner, although they may not admit it. Strongmen can reject the immigration of weak people from other countries, claiming that democracy is misguided.

The growth of far-right groups is a serious threat, and they have an effective outlet in the social media platform X, owned by Elon Musk. He personally posts extreme right-wing views and believes that civil war is inevitable in the UK. Subscribers are permitted to post disinformation and messages of hatred with minimal restrictions, which are then widely disseminated. The only conclusion to emerge is that traditional neo-liberalism and democracy itself are in serious trouble and disarray in a new world of neo-fascism.[27]

Very often, far-right parties are dubbed 'extremist', which may or may not be true, as the term is too often used to label anyone who disagrees with the speaker. Not all members subscribe to violence, though many of them do. What they normally thrive on is conspiracy theories. The present difficulties are caused by some implausible, but unprovable, explanation. The right-wing response will usually include an attack on the elite, which is inevitably seen as hostile. When the conspiracy theory is rejected and the views of the citizens are ignored, this may often give rise to an appeal to violence without any consideration of traditional democratic values.

A British television documentary outlines some of the workings of far-right groups. [28] In some ways, they resemble the Fascist movement in Britain under Oswald Mosley almost a century ago. In those days, the target was usually the Jews, but sometimes the communists. Communism is no longer a threat, but Jews can sometimes remain a target. However, the main perceived enemy is now coloured people of colour and the LGBT community. They exploit fears of ordinary people, portraying themselves as the protectors of women and children, while spreading information purporting to show that white people are intellectually superior to coloured people of colour. Ireland has always had a fascist presence, since Italians took up the teaching of Mussolini after the First World War, with its membership reaching 47,000 at its peak. Fascism has re-emerged in recent years with an anti-immigrant platform, but it has failed to make significant inroads in the 2024 elections.[29]

The operation of their organisation is largely clandestine, and they are suspicious of investigating journalists, whom they try to intimidate. They operate across national boundaries and participate in mass demonstrations, which can easily distribute misinformation and encourage rioting through social media. They can have access to substantial donors, who usually prefer to remain anonymous. They have taken great encouragement from the election of Trump in the USA, believing that history is turning their way, assisting nationalism and opposing globalism. They tend to support Israel and are anti-Islamic.[30] The Far-Right has further gained momentum, as the leader of the far-right FPO in Austria, Herbert Kickl, is attempting to form a Government with the support of a centre-right party, even though his party received only 29% of the votes.[31] The political pendulum in Europe continues to swing to the Right. Pessimists see it as the start of the demise of the liberal elite.[32] Certainly, the growing influence of the Radical Right, fundamentally opposed to democracy, threatens the future of democracy in many countries. It had been suggested that democracy in America was in good hands with voters, provided politicians did not abuse their powers, although they might not wish to become directly involved. Now it seems that democracy by stealth has given way to autocracy by stealth.[33]

This factor, along with the rising influence of libertarianism, poses a serious threat to democracy in the years ahead.[3]

CHAPTER 21

Conclusions

Democracy has fallen from grace and has been enormously reduced as a system of government, as already discussed in Chapter 1. Given that it has significant advantages in terms of the freedoms of its citizens and economic growth, this is astonishing. The purpose of the book is to explain this strange enigma. Here are the major conclusions:

Decline in Real Democracies

Many countries, including America, described as 'democracies' are, in reality, populist oligarchies, where the poor get poorer and the rich get richer.[1] It is epitomised by the rise of illiberalism and the swing of the Republican Party to the Right. This inequity is little publicised, especially when oligarchs control the media. Dissatisfaction of the neglected citizens and right-wing parties takes advantage of this problem, attributing the cause to 'democracy'. However, quasi-democracies are still attractive to many people and preferable to autocracies, as evidenced by asylum seekers, who wish to live in them.

Reasons for the Decline in the Popularity of Democracy

First, democracies have been guilty of some fundamental mistakes. Some democracies have done too little to deal with poverty and have alienated many voters, often degenerating into oligarchy. Equality has normally been a vital traditional plank of democracy. John Stuart Mill wrote more than a century and a half ago that the true virtue of human beings is the fitness to live together as equals.[2]

Young people and women, as well as various minorities, particularly the less wealthy, are chronically underrepresented in politics.

The reputation of the USA as a standard-bearer for democracy internationally has been badly tarnished by its continued sale of arms to Israel for its war against Hamas. The continued killing of civilians has provoked ISIS to respond with terrorism abroad and threatens peace in the Middle East. The earlier withdrawal from Iraq and Afghanistan further damaged its global reputation.

Secondly, democracies have ignored important changes.

1. Dissatisfaction with democracy spreads in times of economic or social upheaval. Voters naively believe that a strongman may produce better leadership.
2. Democracy can disappear unnoticed through a process of stealth. Populist governments can break the critical foundations of democracy surreptitiously by controlling the media, disallowing the independence of the judiciary, controlling the appointment of judges, being in practice accountable to nobody, and suppressing individual freedoms. They reward their friends and introduce a form of oligarchy.
3. Populistic leaders, who claim to be democratic, behave like traditional demagogues. They purport to represent the views of the people,

attack the existing democratically appointed 'elites', and attempt to bypass the democratic process. In practice, they usually advance their own interests and those of their cronies. Putin has undermined Western democracy for many years, in the EU from 2013 onwards, then by interference in the US 2016 election and war against Ukraine.[3] Non-democratic leaders, especially in countries like Russia, can use social media successfully, which includes surreptitious interference in democracies around the world.

4. Sometimes, the availability of substantial assistance from Russia or China can assist non-democratic leaders, while their opponents are starved of financial support. Major autocracies are willing to commit substantial resources and recruit spies to undermine liberal democracies. Russia and China use selective sabotage, such as cutting cables in the Baltic Sea.
5. Autocracies have formed a loose alliance under the leadership of Putin and Xi. The membership includes, in varying degrees of loyalty, North Korea, India, and Turkey. With the addition of various military dictatorships in Africa and the Middle East, a few fifth columnists in the EU, along with Venezuela in Latin America, this represents a large amount of the world's population.
6. In the past, Karl Marx urged: "Workers of the World Unite! You have nothing to lose, except your chains". In Russia, this has been perverted

into: "Autocrats of the World Unite! Keep the workers in chains! You have nothing to lose, except your power and wealth"!

7. The 2024 Venezuelan elections demonstrated how far Russia and its allies can go to undermine democracy around the world. Yet the response was little more than a wringing of hands and the threat of imposing economic sanctions, which can be readily defeated by members of the autocrats' club. The parties of the Right in the EU parliament combined to recognise Edmundo Gonzales as the legitimate president, but unfortunately, while eventually the USA recognised the government in exile under Gonzales, this has had little impact. Democracies need to cooperate more effectively amongst themselves and remain vigilant and proactive when they are being challenged.

Thirdly, the Performance of Democracy in Promoting Welfare has Gone Unnoticed.

1. Democracies have dealt with the challenges facing the world better than autocracies, especially producing greater equality for their citizens, although more needs to be done. Many autocrats, such as Putin in Russia, Assad in Syria, and military dictatorships in Africa and elsewhere, have accumulated enormous personal riches, often by dubious means, but the benefits are not felt by their people. Instead, they are reserved for the leaders and oligarchs who support them. The accumulated wealth is

not retained in the country but is usually moved abroad, often to Swiss bank accounts or spent on extravagant yachts.

2. Democracies are more successful than autocracies and military dictatorships at satisfying the needs of their people. When countries have adopted democracy as their means of government, living standards have improved dramatically.
3. Unlike autocracies, real democracies rarely seek to expand their geographical borders by force. Nevertheless, both democracies and autocracies have been guilty of starting or supporting wars. With the USA and Russia holding seats on the UN Security Council, attempts by the UN to bring about peace have been severely impaired when the veto is employed by either country.
4. The problems facing the future of the planet cannot be resolved by either democracies or autocracies acting independently, since they are not confined by national borders. Unfortunately, many countries seek to protect their own interests at the expense of others. The process can only be satisfactorily resolved by negotiation between all parties.

My Personal Viewpoint

I am sometimes asked about my politics. I would not dream of siding with any political party in another country. Outsiders, Russians, or others should not try to influence local voters. I therefore do not support the Tories, Labour, or the Liberals in the UK. If I had a vote there, my allegiance would have shifted over the years. Neither do I support Democrats or Republicans in the US. In Ireland, at various elections, I have never given a vote to either party of the Far-Left or Far-Right, but my allegiance to centrist parties has shifted over the years. I have given my first preference to a centre party, a right of centre party, and three different left of centre parties, while I have also canvassed for an independent candidate. But I do have a bias.

I will digress briefly. When I was a teenager, I started to fish for salmon on the River Slaney. My ghillie was a superb teacher. In common with many of his era in Ireland, he had very limited schooling and was illiterate. He was excellent company and full of immense common sense, which was not always apparent in many people who had benefited from a higher level of education. At that time, there was a dispute about a weir on the river. One side thought it should be removed, while the other side supported the status quo. When Tom was asked which side he supported, he replied, with profound wisdom, that he was on the side of the salmon.

In the same vein, I admit to being on the side of democracy. It seems to be the only way that the weak can be protected from the strong, a worthy goal in any society. But democracy has lost some of its support and popularity in recent years. Its benefits need to be better understood and sold to the electorate.

In Defence of Democracy

Democracy is the translation from Greek as the strength of the people. It would seem laudable that this strength should be allowed to flourish and protected from those who would prefer the people to be weak. Autocrats attempt to degrade this right and attempt to control the people in whatever ways may serve their purposes.

Most importantly, true democracies respect all citizens. I can put forward my views, whether they are well-founded or not, knowing that I will not suffer for doing so. Tolerance is a fundamental value. I tolerate others, and they tolerate me. If I were to live in an autocracy, I could be imprisoned for speaking my mind. Perhaps paradoxically, I am intolerant of the intolerance found in autocracies.

Liberal democracies do not impoverish their people to pursue an aggressive military strategy, as both Russia and North Korea do. They have some imperfections, such as an inadequate focus on longer-term problems, and inevitably are slow in arriving at decisions. There are also legitimate concerns about inequality and the influence of big political donors, particularly in America.[4]

As social media evolves, it will be important to have checks to ensure that they are not used to deliberately mislead voters. But overall, liberal democracy has a record in which people may take pride, since it protects their fundamental values. It is not obvious that any alternative system can address the issues facing their citizens and deal with the problems more effectively.

Democracies may not deal perfectly with all national issues, but they allow the electorate to create a new government when they are dissatisfied with the performance of the current one. This inhibits a tyrannical dictator or autocrat from assuming power and running the country in his personal interest and that of his friends. While many people today are disappointed with the working of democracy in their country, this does not mean that they want to discard democracy as a means of government.

The Future of Liberal Democracy

Winston Churchill famously stated that Democracy was the worst form of government, except for all the others, which was frequently dismissed as merely a witticism. The remark was made in a speech in the House of Commons in 1947.[5] Critically, he described it as insurance. The voter at the ballot box was the means of ensuring that the country could be saved from autocracy and tyranny, as had been evident during the Second World War. He was in a good position to know. He had successfully led Britain to victory over Nazi Germany, but was then soundly defeated in the post-war general election.

While the current tide is running against liberal democracy, autocrats can be defeated. The Salazar regime in Portugal, which had been in power since 1932, was overthrown in 1974, a few years after the death of the dictator, restoring democracy and civil rights by a carefully prepared coup. The military received enormous popular support in the 'Carnation Revolution' and successfully defeated two attempted coups. Where the political will exists, it has been shown that a strongly entrenched autocrat could be deposed.[6]

Recent developments around the world provide some worries for the future. The escalating threats to democracy in Taiwan, the Philippines, and South Korea from China, with their dubious territorial claims to territorial rights in the South China Sea, while North Korea remains unpredictable, are obvious. China, North Korea, and Iran assisted Russia in its

Ukraine war. It is quite possible they will form an anti-democratic and anti-Western bloc after the Ukraine war has ended.[7] The loss of America to democracy under Trump constitutes a major setback.

Some smaller countries have suffered setbacks to their democratic systems in 2024. Juntas in Burkina Faso and Mali have indefinitely postponed elections and transitioned back to civilian rule. Sham elections were held, not just in Russia. Paul Kagame, who has ruled Rwanda for thirty years, claimed to have received 99% of the vote. In Algeria, the incumbent president was supposed to have received 95% of the vote. El Salvador's president has turned to autocratic ways to stay in power.[8]

Defence of Democracy: An Irish Backstop

There is a strong case for allocating a chamber specifically to defend democracy. There are many models with different supporters, some of which are complex and costly to implement. They need to be free from outside interference or manipulation.[9] Ireland, Israel, Germany, and Italy have broadly similar models.

Ireland has a President, elected every seven years, whose functions are mainly ceremonial, but also acts as the guardian of the Constitution in one important respect. The President can refer proposed legislation to a body of independent people to decide whether or not it breaches the Constitution. Where the legislation is deemed questionable, it can be referred to the Supreme Court for advice. While it is a rarely used power, nevertheless, it performs a useful role as a barrier to autocracy and has served the country well. The key to success is that the

Presidency is seen as politically neutral. This backstop may not transfer easily to countries with different types of constitutions. But if they had similar protection, the drift to populist autocracy might have been stopped before it had time to take control over events.

Optimism for the Future

A decade ago, although the general mood was downbeat, there were some good reasons for overall optimism. There had been fifty years of expanded human freedoms, rising incomes, and improved healthcare. Poverty, malnutrition, illiteracy, child labour, and infant mortality were falling rapidly. [10] But the trend to greater equality, especially of income and wealth, has been slow, due to the intervention of strong vested interests. Many former democracies, too, have curtailed civic rights, while immigration is an increasing problem. The picture now for democracy is more pessimistic, especially due to the war in Ukraine and Gaza, but in several countries, there are still grounds for optimism.

Strong leadership in the EU may be restored under a centrist government in Germany. The 2023 Polish election shows that it is still possible to reject an autocracy at the ballot box, just as it had succeeded with its Solidarity Movement in the 1980s. A coalition of centrist pro-EU parties is paving the way to rebuilding Poland's democracy by reinstating freedom of the press, the independence of the judiciary, and the rights of individuals, although it is facing strong opposition from those adversely affected and further Russian interference. There have also been large and long-lasting demonstrations in Romania and

Georgia against Russian interference in their elections, as well as in the 2025 presidential election in Poland.

Turkey has not been able to shake off the burden of autocracy, but has moderated its support for Recep Erdogan. An attempt by the unpopular, struggling president of South Korea seemed to be an attempted coup when he sought to introduce martial law in 2024, creating international alarm, but it was quickly reversed by a united parliament. He has been subsequently impeached, but has resisted arrest.

The regime of Bashar al-Assad, which had been in existence since 2000 and had the backing of Russia, came suddenly to an end in 2024 with minimal resistance from the rebels. Assad fled to Moscow, and the military declared that his era had finished, calling for a peaceful transfer of power. How democratic the replacement government will be remains to be seen. Other countries with signs of improvement were Bhutan and Sri Lanka. Senegal had a genuine presidential election, despite opposition from the incumbent.

Mexico has elected its first female president with a large majority in a high-turnout election, arguably making her one of the most powerful women in the world. She is an advocate of the green agenda, improving social welfare, and reducing inequality. Of course, she faces formidable challenges, ranging from the economy, the war against drugs and crime, security, and relations with America, with the added threat of tariffs after Trump was elected in the USA.[11]

Also, it has been shown that the populist Bolsonaro in Brazil, who rewarded his supporters with valuable farming rights, could be defeated in a general election, and the damage to the Amazon rainforests slowed down. Peru has found a former president guilty of money laundering. Support for Viktor Orban in Hungary has fallen following allegations about his involvement in the cover-up of a paedophilia scandal. Similarly, in India, Modi lost considerable backing. Support for the corrupt ANC in South Africa has also been enormously eroded.

In Bangladesh, Sheikh Hasina, the prime minister who had been in power for fifteen years, acting as an autocrat and had been responsible for many deaths of her opponents, was forced to resign following widespread unrest on the streets led by students. While mass protests have failed in Russia and Hong Kong in the past, they have brought about major changes, such as the Solidarity Movement in Poland, the opposition to the Berlin Wall, and the Arab Spring. Bangladesh showed that there is still hope for change if protests are well supported and organised. Demonstrations in Senegal and Guatemala prevented incumbent governments from illegally remaining in power.

Tunisia became a democracy in the Arab Spring of 2014 and, for the next six years, was regarded as the only democracy in the Arab world. Since then, the President has strengthened his powers and now rules by decree, seriously weakening democracy. In the 2024 election, the first since President Kais Saied's internal coup in 2021, Saied won 91% of the votes in a turnout of only 29% due to mass boycotting after opponents were jailed. So autocracy has returned, and optimism there proved to have been misguided.

Britain has reverted to a more normal democracy after the departure of Boris Johnson, both as prime minister and as a member of parliament. But there remains a concern that it may face another challenge from Farage and the populist Reform

Party. The Tory Government introduced voter identification requirements, like those brought in by some Republican Governors in the US, which can discriminate against the young and the poor. Thousands of voters were turned away when they failed to produce the required proof of identity at the local elections. The backsliding on climate change is also disquieting, but the Labour Party Government has made some overdue changes.

Most important of all remains the iron fist of Putin, who has ruled Russia as a tyrant for over two decades. His authority in Russia and his reputation internationally were damaged by his initial weak response to the army mutiny during the Ukraine war, but he has since restored his control. Now he is struggling with a collapsing currency and a ballooning public sector deficit. His failure to support Assad in Syria indicated a growing weakness in his influence. US diplomacy in 2024 succeeded in gaining the release of some political prisoners in both Russia and Belarus.

Undoubtedly, the greatest recent setback for democracy has been the victory of Trump in the 2024 Presidential Election. Politicians had been warned that he was a fascist and intended to rule as a dictator, but there have subsequently been swings against right-wing parties in countries such as Canada and Australia. The world has lost a country that has always promoted democracy around the globe. It is hard to see it now as a truly democratic country, while it arms its ally, Israel, which shows contempt for international law, assisting it with the genocide of Palestinians, as well as urging another democracy to cede territory in Ukraine to a hostile, invading autocracy.

There is always hope. Populist regimes could implode. Charismatic leaders do not live forever, and their successors may not be as persuasive to their people. Often, they spend heavily to maintain support. If the currency collapses from the resulting financial crisis and savers lose out, their support could be heavily eroded. Optimism is always preferable to self-defeating pessimism.

Those who believe in democracy need to make their views known, wherever they live. Politicians who imprison opponents, as has happened in many countries purporting to be democracies, need to be exposed, as well as those supporting terrorism. Democratic civil rights must be vigorously championed. One prominent commentator and historian disturbingly believes that there has been a return to acceptance of hierarchy, rather than equality. This leaves the country exposed to autocrats, who can exploit the public with their fears and rhetoric. [12] It would be tragic if democracy in the USA were to finally die due to indifference and neglect under the Trump presidency.

The neap tide for democracy is showing some small signs of turning, but it is far from becoming a flood tide yet, especially after the 2024 US setback. What is certainly required is eternal vigilance, as urged by the late President Kennedy. Without vigilance, autocracies can readily grasp power.

The Required Debate

There is little doubt that autocracy is winning the debate with democracy by default. They are increasing their numbers each year, as democracy loses them. The reason does not depend on the respective merits of the two systems of government, but rather their approach to voters and the general public. Autocrats frequently are dishonest, expressing untrue or exaggerated claims, designed to appeal to their particular audience, typically those dissatisfied people, who feel neglected and are struggling with their limited finances. They feed on the fears of voters and their sense of insecurity. Their diverse members include ruthless autocrats, trying to further their own interests, together with their oligarch supporters, as well as vicious military dictators. What they share in common is a determination to retain power and their fear of real democracy.

A central task is to emphasise the merits of fairness and justice. A starting point is the freedom of the individual, as outlined in Chapter 1. Freedom of speech and freedom of the press enormously enhance the welfare of the individual. It is important to be allowed to express one's views without the fear of imprisonment. Western democracy also strives to create equality of opportunity, so that discrimination can be minimised. Critically, it should attempt to provide assistance for the least well-off in society.

The right to choose is valuable and preferable to being forced to do unpleasant things. It should enable individuals to enjoy the good life and pursue their chosen path without undue interference, which in aggregate should lead to the common good of the people. Democracy enables citizens to maximise their opportunities and minimise their risks. Autocrats, by contrast, maximise their wealth and security at the expense of everyone else. [13]

Democracy provides greater welfare for its citizens than does any other system of government, but it cannot claim to have created a utopia. If, nevertheless, the aim of government is to create 'the greatest happiness for the greatest numbers', set out in the 'social contract', as utilitarians have traditionally argued, [14] then democracy has a better chance of achieving it than autocracy. But that is not the aim of government, as interpreted by autocrats.

Fairness and justice are under attack, even in America. Consider a 2024 reported speech by Donald Trump. He stated that America is not free, nor is its press. He is their voice, their warrior, and their justice. For those who have been wronged or betrayed, he is their retribution. [15] He has also complimented Putin for his attack on Ukraine, which he considered to have been 'smart'. Populists indulge themselves in mutual adulation. On an official visit to London, Trump was quick to endorse Johnson as the next prime minister, an inappropriate remark from a foreign leader. He has also been quick to congratulate the libertarian Javier Milei on his election as President of Argentina.

Other points to be stressed are how democracies are more egalitarian than autocracies and perform better at satisfying the basic needs of their citizens. It has been argued that America's faith in democracy started to decline since the early 1980s, when Reagan mauled the social security net, leaving the median family worse off at the end of the decade than it had been at the beginning. Confidence in democracy can only be restored if the central issue of equality is addressed. [16]

The debate should include and needs to highlight the values traditionally underpinning democracy: the importance of tolerating views which are not shared by everybody, freedom of speech, honesty in speech and behaviour, together with respect for the individual, the law, and human life. If no debate is attempted, autocracy will almost certainly prevail.

CHAPTER 22

A Wish List for the Future

In my 2015 book on banking, I set out my views by way of a manifesto with recommendations for reform. It is inappropriate to attempt a similar manifesto in this book, since it is the responsibility of politicians to propose solutions for the problems. The most that I can do is come up with a wish list for change, alongside my personal opinions, by posing the customary questions:

Who Should be Involved?

Politicians, national and local, have a key role to play, along with Governments and transnational groups, such as the United Nations and the European Union. Alarmingly, overall engagement has been reduced, as membership of political parties has declined in most countries over the last fifty years, despite modest membership costs. People can see a few benefits and are disinclined to make the effort involved.

There is also a key group who could help, namely the younger generation. When I was a student in the 1960s, students made their views known to Governments, initially on the Vietnam War, but later in 1967 on wider issues, in many countries, particularly Germany and France. Some student leaders went on to political careers, and certainly, Governments were made aware of what students wanted.

Internationally, until recently, there has been relatively little student interest in politics. Change has come with the war in Gaza, the 2024 rioting in Bangladesh, demonstrations in France and Serbia, as well as support for Ukraine. Maybe inactivity has been due to the pressure of exams or possibly to cynicism with the politics of today. Many young people feel alienated from the system of democracy as it now operates, often becoming totally disillusioned. But, with the notable exceptions of two schoolgirls, Greta Thunberg, the Swedish climate change activist, and Malala Yousafzai, the Pakistani women's rights activist, who was awarded the Nobel Peace Prize, there have been few prominent student leaders campaigning for major changes in the democratic system.

Perhaps the legal case taken by a group of students against the EU in the European Court of Human Rights against Ireland in 2023 for failing to protect them from climate change heralds a change. The action was dismissed in 2024, but a similar case against Switzerland was successful. It has taken the war in Gaza to reignite a spirit of student protest.

Elsewhere, protesting can be dangerous. When Chinese students tried to express their views in 1989 in Tiananmen Square, their action ended with a massacre. Subsequent protests in Hong Kong were also suppressed harshly. Protesting in an autocracy carries a high personal risk, but elsewhere, students in democracies have remained surprisingly inactive. This is regrettable because the young of today will have to live with the consequences of decisions currently being made or deferred on issues such as climate change.

In Ireland, where young people do become involved in national politics, they are normally members of existing political dynasties, hoping to inherit a seat in the Dáil, the National Parliament, after spending an apprenticeship in local politics. Since they tend to be members of the traditional parties, they are unlikely to bring any fresh radical thinking. My first wish is to see the younger generation more involved in politics and challenge the status quo.

The other major absence is women participating in politics. A better gender balance should assist in finding solutions. Female equality was advocated in the French Revolution and received a boost with the spread of universal suffrage. Over seventy years ago, the case for female emancipation was forcibly argued,[1] which became the precursor to the modern feminist movement. It has been advanced around most of the globe by feminist writers and campaigners, such as Catharine MacKinnon in America. Although matters have improved somewhat in recent years, until the cause went into reverse under Trump, women have been generally underrepresented in politics, especially in senior positions. They are conspicuously underrepresented in Congress in the USA, and, until recently, there was no female presidential candidate. In European Parliaments, women are also significantly underrepresented in varying degrees, with the exception of Scandinavia.

The EU has tried to rectify the balance of its commissioners, when all members were asked to nominate at least one female candidate, but only a third of members complied. The gender balance on the 2024 nominees remains unchanged, with 14 men and 12 women. However, four of the six executive vice presidents are women. Hungary, which faces charges of corruption over claiming EU grants, has been given the minor health and animal welfare portfolio. The right-wing Italian candidate has been given cohesion and reforms and is also one of the two male executive vice-presidents, reflecting the growing influence of both Italy and the far right.

Progress has been disappointingly slow and varies in different trades and businesses. The professions are well mixed, but investment banking remains mainly a male preserve. Maybe it can be partially explained by the antisocial working hours inherent in politics, which can prove difficult for some people to reconcile with family life. When Trump abolished diversity plans in the USA, the cause suffered another setback.

What Needs to be Done?

Democracies need to be protected from authoritarian regimes, which is difficult where there is no relationship with the offending country showing autocratic tendencies, but where democracies are members of a group, it is easier to influence the outcome. The EU has brought pressure to bear on both Poland and Hungary to ensure independence for their judiciaries. This has been successful in the case of Poland, but Hungary, along with Slovakia, remains problematic. Democracies should support each other and should not invade neighbouring lands, as Israel has done. It is disappointing to see that three traditional major democracies, India, Brazil, and Indonesia, have not provided support for Ukraine, as it fights against Russia to preserve its democracy.

Solutions will not readily be found, and vested interests may impede solutions. The political systems outlined in Chapter 4 do not help, but the problems must be addressed if democracy and, indeed, the future of the planet are to survive. Hopefully, a start will be made by the most relevant transnational agency, the United Nations, but failing that, it might come from the European Union. Here are some suggestions for politicians to restore confidence in the electorate and repair the damaged image:

1. On an individual basis, politicians could and should change their behaviour, leading by example. It would be welcome if they could eradicate any sign, however small, of corruption, sleaze, or undeclared conflicts of interest. They should cease employing members of their families at the taxpayers' expense as political advisors, as happens in Ireland and some other countries. They should also concentrate on reality, rather than 'spin', while accepting accountability for their actions. Too many of them seem to reside in Plato's cave. It would be desirable if all politicians followed again the accepted traditional norms of behaviour, in particular, they should be honest in all their dealings and never lie. They should show respect, especially for women and minorities, such as the LGBT community, and should condemn all violence or any hint of racism.

2. Politicians, by their actions, should try to tackle growing polarisation. Mutual tolerance is required. Governments should respect the Opposition, while the Opposition should not abuse due process to prevent the implementation of government decisions.

3. Politicians need to address the major issue of inequality of wealth and income, both between individuals and sexes. It has been shown that,

while everyone pays lip service to equality, in practice it is largely ignored. In the Pericles era of ancient Athens, all free men were deemed to be equal. Slavery has now become a rarity, and women are accepted as equal to men. If citizens are to be persuaded that democracy is the best way to protect their interests, it must be accepted that greater equality is critical. The reality is that in many countries, the situation is still deteriorating.

4. Politicians should seriously promote equality, as it once existed in Athens, suitably modified for the present. The intrusion of oligarchy is unwelcome, since self-serving groups should not be able to subvert democracy. There is concern over the influence of large donors on political parties and their influence over policy.[1] In particular, the super-rich should not be allowed to determine policy while avoiding the payment of their share of tax. A deliberate move towards some form of democratic socialism, although it may be abhorrent to laissez-faire capitalists, could do much to change the cynical attitude of many people towards politicians. It may not necessitate a full adoption of the Swedish model, but a significant move in that direction could help restore the balance and reassure voters that the politicians are there not just to serve the interests of the rich and powerful.

5. Politicians must promote freedom, which remains the best protection against tyranny. Nations should promote individual freedom, ensure that the media stay free from political interference, and that nobody tries to undermine the independence of the judiciary. Without this, unscrupulous individuals can become entrenched as rulers, controlling the government and eventually depriving the citizens of their freedom. To assist this goal, national politicians should assist exiled journalists, who are plying their trade to the best of their ability and furthering the cause of freedom.[2]

6. Politicians should accept a longer-term perspective and not be afraid to ask the electorate to accept short-term costs for long-term gains. There needs to be a sharper focus on sustainability, even if this is at the expense of economic growth. Excessive concentration on retaining seats at the next election has resulted in insufficient time being spent on longer-term issues, such as climate change. Depressingly, few governments can resist the temptation of introducing a populist budget ahead of a general election, irrespective of the long-term damage it may cause.

Where Should It Happen?

Changes need to be addressed in all remaining democracies, particularly those threatened by populists or autocrats· Democracy faces many challenges around the globe and is battling for survival globally. Continents under threat include Western Europe, which is seeing the growth of neo-fascist parties; Africa, where the threats from military coups and corruption are commonplace; Asia, where Taiwan and South Korea are threatened by totalitarian neighbours; and Latin America, where extremes of wealth inequality are the norm. Now, more than ever, inspiration needs to come from Lincoln's support for human rights and profound belief that democracy will continue to prosper.

When Should It Take Place?

There is a pressing need for change. Ignoring important issues, such as climate change and sustainability, comes at a high price. Satisfactory solutions to problems may not be easy to find, but that does not justify any delay in starting the process.

How Can It Be Done?

How radical change can happen depends on those in power at the national and local levels. Politicians must find ways to change and seek popular support for change while setting up the appropriate structures. The electorate, particularly the younger generation, should urge them to act as swiftly as possible.

An authority on Plato has urged that his approach should be used to tackle the problems of today.[3] If the massive challenges are to be addressed, whether they are climate change, economic growth, or training citizens for democracy, it will require real dialogue and the generation of new ideas. It means accepting that disagreements are normal, exemplified by the Greek thinker of the sixth century, Heraclitus, who argued: "Strife is the father of all".

Regulatory change is necessary. It has been shown how social media and artificial intelligence can both undermine democracy when they are abused. Exposure, regulation, and control are critical to stop abuses. An effective system should help to prevent the increasing polarisation of the electorate, which has been increasing in many countries through social media. A debate on the merits of democracy should be undertaken with the disaffected through appropriate media, using key influencers as may be appropriate.

Final Thought

It is perhaps fitting to conclude with the hopes of a great United States democrat, President Abraham Lincoln.[4] During his Gettysburg address at the end of the American Civil War 160 years ago, he stated, "That those dead shall not have died in vain – that this nation, under God, shall have a new birth of freedom – and that government of the people, for the people, by the people, shall not perish from the earth".

There is no quick-fix universal solution, and no one country or ideology has all the answers. But time is running out, and the dialogue must start without further delay.

CHAPTER 23

A Plea and a Plan for Action

If no action is taken, the situation will almost certainly deteriorate, and democracies will further decline in number. Already, there are more autocracies than democracies in the world. [1] A fresh approach is now required, fully realising that inaction will only lead to the further growth of unfree countries, as outlined in Chapter 1. The defenders of democracy should realise that this necessitates persuading the public that they will fare much better under democracy than any populist alternative.

The task is made more difficult in a deeply polarised world where cynicism and fear are all too common. Anti-politics, often spread by conspiracy theories, is widespread, leading to suspicion about politics and politicians, seriously undermining the operation of democracy. Faith in democracy must be restored, a task rendered more difficult after the 2024 US Presidential Election. [2]

A Plea for Action

Democratic leaders rarely find unity on any issues. They now need to show a united front if they are not to be picked off one by one, which should be possible in the light of the inherent merits of democracy. However, it is critical to choose the appropriate medium to address the target audience. It must also be conducted in a truly open and understanding style on an equal level with the target audience, not as a lecture from the elite. Liberal democracy can enormously improve general welfare and create economic growth with the system of capitalism based on property rights. Civic rights, the dangers of abuses of power, and the importance of human rights need to be emphasised.

The holding of free and fair elections is critical. The key to success is to locate the target audience and enter the discussion without a sense of superiority while exposing the scandal of Russian interference in elections around the world. This will not be easy in a world flooded by dishonest, autocratic, self-serving propaganda, which must be exposed for what it is, but if it is well explained, the case should be persuasive.

What Must Change to Save Democracy

Democracy must change its ways as soon as possible. A critical starting point is addressing current levels of inequality, justice, and peace, as advocated by Pope Leo XIV. Supporters of MAGA, however, may disagree. A determined and sustained effort to date has been sadly absent to bring about a lasting and just peace in Gaza and Ukraine. Success would do much to restore the tarnished reputation of the West as peacemakers and upholders of justice. Unfortunately, as explained by Bernie Sanders, given the influence of oligarchs and improvements in other major issues, equality is unlikely to significantly improve in the immediate future for America. Without radical change, the number of democracies is likely to diminish further, possibly quite quickly.

The present practice of people engaged directly in democracy has too narrow a base, with a preponderance of aging, wealthy males, particularly in America. Young people and more women should be encouraged to participate, especially those of modest means. Too often, political parties ignore the feedback about voter concerns from their backbenchers, who can be whipped into line, irrespective of their views. This suppression of worries and concerns only serves to increase the feeling of alienation among voters and contempt for the system. An open approach to the issues and their underlying causes is vital.

Russia Has Outwitted the Western Powers to Destroy World Peace

1. The West was caught by surprise by the resurgence of Russia and the invasion of Ukraine. They ignored the Russian invasion of Crimea and Georgia, only realising the danger when Ukraine was invaded, and their people resisted strongly. The aims of Russia today are frightening. [3]
2. The Ukraine war has currently stalled in a deadlock, but Russia has recruited North Korean troops, giving them a significant temporary advantage. However many casualties Russia suffers, it is unlikely to seek peace since this could damage Putin's future.
3. To further their war aims, the Russians have access to powerful, inexpensive weapons, such as drones, sourced from North Korea, Iran, and other friendly countries. Many Western countries, for fear of escalating the war, will not

supply the appropriate weapons to Ukraine and have placed obstacles to drones and other key weapons despite shortages of ammunition and exhaustion of front-line troops, thereby inhibiting their effective deployment.

4. The Russians have stated clearly that they will continue until their war aims have been achieved. Enormous losses of mercenaries and former convicts have had minimal impact on the continued conduct of their war. Western support of Ukraine is diminishing due partly to its cost and partly due to the outbreak of war in Gaza, which has diverted attention from Ukraine.
5. Western economic sanctions have not been as effective as had been hoped. Russian oil can be accessed through third countries, while governments are under pressure from both right-wing and left-wing groups to appease Russia.
6. In a further step to restore the USSR, Russia might invade one of the Balkan States, ostensibly to protect Russians there, a ruse that Hitler used in the Sudetenland and that Putin has employed successfully in Georgia and Ukraine. If NATO is fundamentally weakened by permanent withdrawal or reduction of support from the USA, this would pose a major problem for Europe, especially given the existence of the German and French budgetary deficits, while Russia and North Korea can afford to sustain heavy casualties.

7. German intelligence has stated that it cannot rule out an attack on NATO later in the decade. The threat of Russian dominance is growing.
8. The Russians can always use their veto in the Security Council to prevent a cessation of war in Ukraine.

Russian Aims to Destroy Western Democracy on All Fronts

1. Putin is attacking Western countries on a scale never experienced before. It seems to be an 'everything, everywhere, all at once strategy. He employs assassination, arson, sabotage, misinformation, and computer hacking as the basis of his foreign policy. It is as though he wishes to preserve nothing of the postwar international order, just as Leon Trotsky attempted a century ago. [4]
2. Putin ruthlessly suppresses any opposition at home or abroad. At home, opponents and even disaffected oligarchs are imprisoned under inhuman conditions, while abroad, enemies can be tracked down and murdered.
3. Russia damages democracies anywhere in any way possible, with the strong backing of China and North Korea. They have successfully interfered in elections in Venezuela and Georgia and nearly did so in Moldova. Their influence in Europe is growing with the assistance of various right-wing groups. They enjoy close

relationships with Iran and several African dictatorships. They have attempted to influence American and European elections while also demonstrating their ability to hack Western computer systems effectively.

4. In Slovenia, Russian disinformation has sought to undermine membership in the EU and NATO. They succeeded in having their preferred candidate elected as President of the USA in 2016 and again in 2024. There can be no reason to doubt that they will continue to interfere in democracies all over the world.
5. Many countries have been disillusioned by America supplying arms to Israel, which have been used in Gaza. Nevertheless, Russia has managed to assemble a strong alliance with numerous countries with different types of governments operating under different ideologies. These include ruthless African dictatorships and Middle Eastern Muslim theocracies. They also have periodically close links with China and can use economic pressures on many countries, such as India, using the threat of ceasing to provide oil if they do not become allies.
6. They have exploited the declining influence of the USA after the wars in Iraq and Afghanistan. Potential allies of the USA have been alarmed by the abandonment of the Kurds, who fought courageously on their behalf in the Middle East.
7. Russian influence and interference abroad are widespread. Even in Ireland, it has been

reported that there is an unidentified spy in the Senate or Dáil, the national parliament. The disclosure that Trump made numerous contacts with Putin in recent years after his presidency is disturbing. The combination of far-right groups with Russia provides a very formidable opponent to democracy.

8. The current Russian ideology is no longer related to communism. The population is declining rapidly despite Putin's urging of Russian women to have eight children. Their people are subjected to enormous hardship and gross poverty, living with a low life expectancy, as resources are diverted to the military.

Russia Has Many Significant Advantages Over the West

1. Russia has a new weapon, which has proved to be very effective in damaging the West and promoting anti-American populist regimes, namely social media.
2. Russia, in practice, is above international law. There may be an international arrest warrant for Putin, but this is unlikely to concern him. He has travelled to friendly countries, such as Mongolia and Hungary, without fear of arrest.
3. The response from the West to the Russian threat has been slow and uncoordinated, always reactive rather than proactive. Western Governments do not seem to have a clear idea of

who their allies are in terms of countries and powerful individuals. For example, few people expected the world's richest man, Elon Musk of Tesla and X, to favour Russia against the Ukrainians.

4. All of these problems can only increase under a Trump presidency. If they are ignored, autocracy will continue to stifle democracy.

To halt the progress of autocracies, the West needs to operate on several different fronts:

First, They Must Better Protect Existing Democracies.

1. Greater efforts should be made to protect the citizens of Gaza and bring their suffering to an end without further delay. They should demand a lasting ceasefire and rule out a settlement based on Zionist goals.
2. More should be done to support fledgling democracies, many of which perish in infancy due to weak institutions and poor economic growth, as well as Ukraine.

Secondly, the West Must Go on a Counter Offensive.

1. The West must expose the true nature of Russia today, including the enrichment of Putin and the oligarchs at the expense of the Russian people, the lies they spread, the interference overseas, and the inhumane brutality shown to their opponents.
2. The confiscation of the wealth of oligarchs, started by the passage of the Magnitsky Act in

the USA, needs to be rigorously enforced in all democracies worldwide.

3. They must make greater efforts to curtail the growth of far-right parties in Europe and elsewhere, which, in varying degrees, support Russia.

Thirdly, the West Must Improve its Communications.

1. It is clear that populists have misled their people about democracy and its benefits, which requires correction. The better standard of living available under democracy needs to be explained and emphasised.
2. Traditional forms of media communication are likely to prove ineffective. Learned textbooks or even pamphlets are unlikely to be read. National newspapers rarely have a wide readership since many people only read local newspapers if they read any newspaper. Western presidential debates are designed for domestic audiences and are unlikely to reach the wider international audience of struggling democracies through traditional media.
3. The targeted audience must be defined, and efforts must be made to reach them, particularly in Russia and democracies threatened by populists, through social media.
4. Some far-right parties profess to be democratic. A way must be found to engage with those who genuinely accept democratic principles and reject violence.

5. The task is made much more difficult since the USA will no longer lead the defence of democracy around the world, but it must be addressed nevertheless.

Fourthly, Governments Should Lead by Example.

1. All democracies should endeavour to ensure that the basic principles of honesty, tolerance, unselfishness, generosity, and respect for all individuals are upheld.
2. The issues around lobbying need attention. Second jobs for parliamentarians can give rise to conflicts of interest and diversion of time from their primary responsibilities. Various industries offer generous payments to politicians for their support, with many politicians receiving enormous payments. All payments, direct or indirect, should be fully disclosed. A cap could be put on the total amount received by any politician, say 100% or less of their political salary, an issue currently being addressed in the UK.
3. Democracy must be defended everywhere. The Trump Government's policy of supporting Zionism does not do that, increasing international cynicism. Similarly, prosecuting or deporting protesters is another lunge towards autocracy. It seems that the support for democracy for the Palestinians is little more than lip service. Protecting alliances with Israel, a questionable democracy, takes priority.

4. America should never interfere in overseas democracies, through the CIA or otherwise, as happened historically in Chile and elsewhere, to further its interests.
5. Democracies should stand up to strong lobby groups, such as the military-industrial complex, the fossil fuels industry, or social media platforms, never allowing them to dictate government policy.
6. Governments should take action against social platforms that spread disinformation and regulate them strictly, and, however much the USA opposes any intervention, so that they cannot be used to spread hatred. There can be no compromise on this fundamental principle. There needs to be wider consultation with key interest groups, such as farmers, over climate change and agricultural reform.
7. Democracies must tackle the thorny problem of offshore tax havens, which have flourished in a secretive, murky climate of weak regulation and lax enforcement. They have been used by kleptocrats and money launderers to hide their ill-gotten gains while undermining the fundamental operation of democracy, supporting autocrats who help their cause.
8. Above all, greater attempts must be made to address inequality of income, wealth, and gender.

This is the essence of democracy, which cannot survive if these issues are ignored.

Fifthly, Social Media Must be Used More Effectively.

1. Social media should be the primary medium to gain more support for democracy globally. In 2025, Saudi Arabia used it effectively to campaign against Netanyahu in Gaza and could provide useful ideas.
2. A good starting point to tackle abuse of social media is the identification of friendly influencers in various countries and using them and their platforms, rewarding them appropriately. Misinformation, disinformation, and outright lies spread by autocracies should be repeatedly exposed.
3. The operation of the autocrats' club should be widely publicised, along with the dangers of breaking any of the four legs of the chair, supporting democracy.
4. The campaign should be led by the EU and carefully coordinated amongst democracies, rather than the present haphazard approach. Given its importance, the necessary resources need to be found to ensure the success of the messages to be spread.

Could Democracy Perish?

Democracy perished in Athens over two thousand years ago following the military invasion from Sparta, which could be repeated by Putin on Western democracies. The response to the war in Gaza has also diminished democracy, as did the 'March on the Capitol' in America, but the biggest threat lies elsewhere.

The greatest setback ever is the loss of America as the leader of democracies and the free world around the globe.

Liberal democracy could disappear in many major countries. The three great bastions of democracy - Britain, France, and America- have all faced populist challenges. Britain has survived so far, but the jury is still out in France. America has made its choice, and it has not been on the side of democracy.

Confidence in American democracy has been seriously eroded by the US Supreme Court's decision to grant Trump immunity for acts that he performed as president. It appears that this has badly damaged at least one leg of the four-legged chair. In many countries, several of the legs are already severely damaged, and the process of autocracy by stealth is currently well underway.

While Joe Biden was still the Democratic candidate, the election was described as a choice between the 'unspeakable' and the 'incapable'. [6] But once the 'incapable' had withdrawn, the result became more open. The debate between Trump and Harris was followed by at least 83 million viewers in America, excluding social media. [7] But ultimately, the Republican candidate emerged victorious despite the strong television performance of Harris.

Democracy, sadly, could disappear through a combination of incompetence, negligence, and inaction. Failure to recognise the threat is foolish, as is inaction when the danger is understood. If ailing democracies are to survive, their defence must be mounted by fearless champions. Without strong support for democracy, it can vanish, as happened with the rise of Hitler and the failure of the Weimar Republic in 1933. [6]

Jean-Jacques Rousseau, the eighteenth-century Enlightenment Philosopher and the father of modern democracy, famously proclaimed that man is born free, but is everywhere in chains. Until recently, it was commonly thought that liberal democracy had solved that problem. But if action is not taken now, many countries could return to the chains of autocracy and dictatorship. The omens are disquieting.

In 2019, the OECD reported that in most OECD countries, there had been a decline in electoral participation. Subsequently, in 2020, it was claimed that confidence in democracy was at a low point. [8] In 2020, Freedom House said that democracy was 'under siege', but this fell on deaf ears and did not lead to any response. [9] Since then, the situation has further deteriorated. An immediate reaction must not be delayed to avoid a return to chains. 2024 was not a good year for democracy. Incumbent governments in 12 Western countries all lost a major share of votes for the first time in 180 years. Young males were particularly disillusioned. [10]

Another worrying development has been the freedom of the internet, which has declined globally for the fourteenth successive year. [11] China is the worst culprit, but many other countries are following suit. In many countries, free expression online has been diminished by the threat of draconian prison sentences. Censorship and content manipulation were combined to sway elections, undermining voters' ability to make informed decisions, fully participate in the electoral process, and make their voices heard. Governments interfered and reduced the transparency mechanism on major social media platforms.

There are many countries that pay lip service to democracy, but fewer that genuinely believe in it and are prepared to act to save it as a vital part of life. People must really prefer democracy to oligarchy. Trump, as his second presidency clearly demonstrates, does not. If democracy is to be saved, lethargy must be replaced quickly by a focused, coordinated plan.

CHAPTER 24

The Future of Democracy after the 2024 American Presidential Election

In a deeply polarised country, the 2024 campaign was unsurprisingly conducted in an acrimonious manner throughout its course. It was, arguably, the wildest and dirtiest presidential campaign ever. Perhaps mindful of the advice of his mentor, Roy Coen, to attack persistently, Trump used extremist language, tinged sometimes with racism and xenophobia. He denounced the Democrats as 'evil, dangerous, and the enemy from within'. Political opponents he deemed 'vermin'. [1] Kamala Harris responded by describing him as 'unhinged and increasingly unstable'.[2] During the latter end of the campaign, Trump increased his dark rhetoric and fear mongering, denouncing Kamala Harris as a traitor. [3] A Trump supporter at a New York rally described Puerta Rica as a 'floating island of garbage', another called Harris a 'devil and antichrist', while another compared her to a prostitute. [4]

Trump continued his campaign in an aggressive manner. He informed Americans that he would protect their women, whether they liked it or not, and opposed abortion. He threatened to have Liz Cheney shot, denouncing her as a 'radical war hawk'. His running mate, Vance, insulted Democrats when he referred to them as 'childless cat ladies'. Trump's approach was to stir up hatred and fear, particularly over immigration. He also exploited the cost-of-living increases during Biden's presidency, when the president was obliged to tackle the oil crisis. Kamala Harris, known as 'the joyful warrior', adopted a more positive, upbeat, and conciliatory stance.

Vote counters and administrators became increasingly worried about their personal safety, even though they were sheltered behind bulletproof glass. An assassination attempt was made on Trump, causing him a minor injury. Ballot boxes were reported to have been burned in Portland, Oregon, and Washington State. The traditional American values around tolerance, respecting opponents, and non-violence were little in evidence. Washington, DC, was prepared for trouble if Trump lost.

Deliberate misinformation was employed from the moment Vance accused foreigners of eating pet cats and dogs, which Trump duly repeated. Elon Musk, a strong supporter of Trump and deregulation, spread misinformation about voter fraud and hurricane relief, while he described his opponents as ill-intentioned idiots. [5] Climate change concerns were dismissed. Allegations of voter registration fraud in Pennsylvania also proved to be untrue. Numerous unfounded and inaccurate allegations were made by Republicans against the record of the Democrats in power. An untrue posting that Walz was a sex abuser went viral. Much misinformation was believed to have originated in Russia during the election, but China and Iran were also rumoured to have tried to interfere in the election. Methods have become more subtle and targeted, using artificial intelligence, as tech companies have done little to identify and prevent the spread of misinformation.

The Outcome

Polling closed on 5th November and the results, which were keenly awaited around the world, were announced on 7th November. The turnout was 63.7 % of the electorate, compared with 65.8% in 2020 and 54.8% in 2016. The marginal decline in 2024 could be partly attributed to the number of young liberals and Muslims who could vote for neither candidate, due to the US policy over Gaza. Basically, all fifty States moved rightwards.

Kamala Harris received 74.3 million votes and Donald Trump 76.8 million votes, compared with 81 million votes cast for Joe Biden and 74 million votes cast for Donald Trump in 2020. The Democrats lost more votes than the Republicans gained, as Trump became the forty-seventh president of the United States. The gap in the popular vote was the narrowest since 2000, and the scale of victory was much higher than most commentators expected. The Republicans regained control of both the Senate and the House of Representatives. Given that he will be surrounded by handpicked loyalists and has the full support of Congress, Trump can be expected to be totally dominant, unless some courageous senators restrain him.

The electoral college voting system, favouring small States, was intended to stop a demagogue from becoming president. Trump won by 295 votes to 226, emerging triumphant in every 'swing state'. Since Trump won both the popular vote and the electoral college vote, the biases in the system did not affect the result.

The outcome can be seen as a massive protest vote against the status quo. It seems that the Latino, Afro-American, and young white non-college males voted swung towards Trump, while the expected large increase in women supporting Kamala Harris failed to materialise. She did not set out a clear vision, seeming to ignore the views of dissatisfied people by talking down to them, especially young males. There also could have been opposition to making a woman president in the US, with Trump making the sexist claim that she would be trampled on the international stage. Around the world, there have been prominent women leaders in history, from Catherine the Great in Russia, Maria Theresa in Austria, Indira Gandhi in India, Margaret Thatcher in the UK, and more recently, Angela Merkel in Germany, but none at the highest level in the US.

Racist remarks were ignored, while meaningless slogans carried more weight than discussion of Trump's track record, criminality, or future policy on issues like the minimum wage. The oligarchs and plutocrats had made their influence felt through the skilful use of social media. Explanations of Trump's success emphasised his ability to communicate with poorer Americans, dissatisfied with their lot over recent years, for which they blamed the elite in Washington. In a deeply polarised world, he may have been bombastic, frequently lied and spoke nonsense, but he was considered to be entertaining, outspoken and forthright, while he used social media and podcasting to great effect.

Democracy in America

The signs that America had a dubious commitment to true democracy have long been evident, ever since their treatment of prisoners and detention in Guantanamo Bay in Cuba and retention and torture of detainees in Abu Ghraib in Iraq, where they were detained indefinitely without trial. More recently, the world has been shocked by their willingness to support Israel's policy of genocide and ethnic cleansing in Palestine, providing them with the arms needed to execute this policy. They have sought allies to defend democracy, while abandoning them, if necessary, as the Kurds and Afghans can testify. But, whatever might be its reputation on the international stage, domestically, its form of democracy was always considered to be a role model for other countries to copy. Now they have elected a convicted felon as their president, which inevitably damages their image as a role model.

Trump's respect for fundamental democratic values has already been examined, but it is relevant to discuss them in the wider context of democracy in America. He has threatened to sack dissenting or 'disloyal' advisors in the public sector and has stated his intention to seek revenge against people whom he considers have failed to support him. Generosity to others is usually non-existent, and differences with opponents are rarely resolved by peaceful means.

He has no respect for the individual, as shown by his notorious attitude to women. He has also shown contempt for journalists and political opponents. Above all, he targets asylum seekers, whom he has repeatedly attacked with racist vitriol. His disrespect for the law is obvious. He has called into question the integrity of judges and denounced the trials against him as scams and rigged. He does not seem willing to condemn breaches of international humanitarian law by Israel or the continued illegal settlement of the West Bank.

His attachment to respect for human life and the avoidance of violence is doubtful, as was demonstrated by his encouragement of violence during the 2021 attack on the Capitol, urging the mob to hang his vice-president, Mike Pence. As an ardent upholder of gun laws, he has boasted that he could gun down anyone on Fifth Avenue without suffering any adverse consequences. He befriends politicians who share his low regard for humanitarian issues, such as Putin, Netanyahu, and Xi, who was invited to his inauguration.

Above all, he has no respect for the truth and lies repeatedly. Astonishingly, this is accepted by many Americans today, including numerous evangelical Christians. Traditionally, truth and honesty have been fundamental values throughout American history. Lying has led to the end of political careers, as evidenced by President Nixon over Watergate. Philanthropy and foreign aid also have always been cornerstones of US policy, but have now been abandoned.

For a non-American, it is hard to avoid the conclusion that support for democratic values there has already been severely eroded, long before the outcome of the 2024 election was known. Many people, both men and women, admire Trump's populist rhetoric of 'Making America Great Again' and were willing to overlook democratic shortcomings to achieve this goal.

Disrespect for international law, of course, is not confined to Trump. The Democrats have not condemned the settlements on the West Bank and have been unwilling to take strong action against Israel for its breaches of humanitarian law in Gaza and Lebanon, continuing to assist Israel with the provision of arms. Further afield, Putin can ignore an international arrest warrant, providing him with an important propaganda victory.

The Fascist Precedent

Trump indicated his wish to rule as a dictator on the first day. His former chief of staff, John Kelly, a four-star general, has stated that he is a fascist and confirmed that he would govern as a dictator.[6] Opinion polls confirmed that almost half of US voters agree.

Fascism originated in Italy with Benito Mussolini. Despite a lack of coherent policies, Mussolini was a journalist, drifter, misfit, but skilful orator, who spoke for the renegades and outcasts. Yet he persuaded the Italian people in the turmoil following the First World War that he could solve the economic and social problems of the country and 'Make Italy Great Again'. Although his fascist party won no seats in the 1919 election, it was followed by a period of anarchic violence. The fascists, led by Mussolini's private militia of disillusioned war veterans, the thuggish Blackshirts, were assisted by landowners and business interests, who opposed socialism and trade unionists.

In the 1921 election, despite not receiving a majority of the seats, Mussolini came into power, when socialists were divided between communists and moderates. In an atmosphere of social unrest, periodic murders, and insurrection, he marched on Rome and was made prime minister by the king. In 1924, the fascists won a massive electoral majority with the assistance of recruits from other parties and violence against opponents. As part of a plan to obtain more living space in 1935, 'Il Duce' invaded Abyssinia and then allied Italy with the Nazis in the Second World War. He ruled as an absolute dictator until he was removed by the king as Head of Government in 1943, before his murder in 1945.[7]

There are also similarities to the rise of Adolf Hitler to power in 1933 with the collapse of the Weimar Republic.[8] Hitler was an advocate of violence, vehemently denouncing political opponents in his extremist rhetoric, as was Trump, but perhaps to a lesser degree. Trump may be different, but they saw the challenge in a similar way: to restore greatness to their country. One important difference is that the US did not face an economic crisis, as the Weimar Republic had done. The US economy is envied around the world [9] with low unemployment and falling inflation, although this was not accepted by voters, who focused on their own immediate cost of living. The US, when it voted for Trump, was fully aware of his intentions. Voters went into the election with their eyes wide open. In 2024, the American electorate peered into the abyss and, nevertheless, decided to jump.[10]

Fascists may come into power by different routes, but then behave in a similar manner. They set out to make the country great again and demand blind obedience from all citizens. Hitler had a policy of military aggression and territorial expansion. Trump wishes to reduce US military commitments, withdraw from alliances, and become more isolationist outside of the American Continent, while encouraging aggression by allies, such as Israel, which he arms for the purpose. Some, such as Putin, a crypto fascist, accuse their enemies of being fascists. Trump is a far-right authoritarian with an ultranationalist political ideology, advocating a centralised autocracy, which he leads as a military-style dictator. He suppresses all opposition and believes in a natural social hierarchy. Senior party members have been photographed giving Nazi salutes.

It seems that many people were prepared to ignore the implications of this murky world for civic freedom and freedom to disagree. Perhaps this should not be surprising. America entered the Second World War because the Japanese attacked Pearl Harbour, not because of ideological differences with Fascism or Nazism. What little understanding of fascism existed in America eighty years ago has diminished over time, with many people just regarding it as a pejorative term to describe political opponents. It says little for the attachment of many

Americans to democracy.[11] By definition, dictatorship and fascism cannot co-exist with democracy.

Trump's Second Presidency

Given his influence over the Republican Party, it is unlikely that Congress will be able to ensure that he is answerable to the legislature. In view of his immunity from prosecution for acts committed as president, his judges are also likely to provide him with serious protection. His judicial appointments during his presidency should assure a conservative Republican majority in the Supreme Court for the foreseeable future. The Press and other media might remain apparently free, but he has considerable influence there, even if not all television channels are as supportive of him as Fox News. He has frequently expressed his wish to muzzle the press and now prevents journalists deemed unfriendly from accessing the White House. He has threatened to revoke the licences of TV stations that displease him, to imprison journalists who refuse to disclose their sources, and promise a violent attack on 'radical left lunatics'.

The situation of any opponents to Trump is deeply worrying. He intends to pursue his opponents with dire consequences. If he were to order their assassination in his capacity as president, he may not be subject to prosecution under criminal law. The perpetrators could be pardoned by the president and, therefore, would not be exposed to significant risk. This may only be a technical possibility, but it might act as a serious deterrent to potential critics who wish to voice their dissent in public.

An ominous sign was the pressure by Jeff Bezos, owner of the Washington Post and a Trump ally, for the newspaper not to endorse any candidate in the presidential election, as had been its practice in past years. [12] Its explanation of the dangers of a Trump presidency was less forthright initially than some of its peers, but it later asserted its editorial independence by warning that tariff policy could damage trade and diminish America's influence around the world. As Bernie Sanders has claimed, many media groups are controlled by oligarchs, who may well favour Trump.

Whether or not basic human freedoms, such as the right to peaceful protest, will continue remains to be seen. Large demonstrations could disappear, given his past approach to the 'Black Lives Matter' campaign, in which he took an extreme law-and-order approach, including the use of the military against civilians. The far-right Heritage Foundation Project 2025 has advocated a crackdown against peaceful protesters and journalists, together with greater censorship of the media, although this appears to be unconstitutional, fundamentally undermining civic rights. Trump himself has referred to journalists as 'the enemy camp'. The right of women to make their own choice about abortion has already come under attack. Each leg of the four-legged chair is likely to be severely damaged. The ski run classification may very well be changing from red to black.

The outcome is a major political watershed. The changes to American values and civilisation are profound. Domestically, immigration will be the key issue, and the country will probably swing towards the far right. There will be no serious attempt to address inequality, which could have been significantly improved if the Democratic policy of doubling the national minimum wage had been adopted. His cabinet consists of very wealthy individuals, which should ensure that the interests of plutocrats are well-protected. Musk has been given the task of slashing the size of the State, which, in practice, is likely to reduce the benefits and protection of the less well-off citizens. It is ironic that the world's richest man is to slash the benefits to be received by the poor. The voters were most concerned about inflation, housing problems, health bills, avoidance of war, and immigration, rather than equality. [13]

Responses in America and around the World

The atmosphere before the election was a mixture of hope and fear. Later, leading newspapers expressed concern over increasing uncertainties. [14] America was deeply divided, but Trump supporters were exultant. [15] Nigel Farage of the Reform UK Party had openly canvassed for him. One American newspaper claimed that, due to the narrowness of his popular majority, he has not received a mandate for radical change, [16] but this is unlikely to worry him. The excuse that many incumbent parties around the world, such as the Tories in Britain, Macron in France, the SPD in Germany, and the LDP in Japan, have received setbacks is true, but it does not provide an adequate explanation for the poor performance of the Democrats.

Polite congratulations were offered by European leaders, but they are gloomy and fearful of the 'Brave New World" being forecast. [17] The EU is worried about the competitive advantage gained by the tearing up of regulations, the likelihood of a trade war setting back economic growth, together with the threat to security by his hostility to NATO. It is feared that the past US world order will be thrown into disarray. Global allies are filled with foreboding over the future of multinational policy-making. [18] Trump is likely to attempt to open bilateral talks with EU States in an attempt to divide and conquer. [19] The worry is that beggar-my-neighbour will be the determining principle in world politics in a manner not known for very many years.

The proposed tariff increases are draconian and selective, even if some were subsequently deferred and reduced with many loose ends, as was shown in the case of the UK. China, Mexico, and the EU, especially Ireland with its large number of US multinationals, have the most to lose from higher tariffs, [20] as America reverts to another era of mercantilism, an ideology which fell out of favour in the nineteenth century. They seem to be a repetition of the Smoot-Hawley tariffs of 1930, which deepened the Great Depression, resulting in disastrous consequences for both America and the rest of the world.

Opinion polls have shown that the vast majority of Americans believe that they will be worse off with high tariffs, which many people consider to be fundamentally flawed and in breach of international trade agreements. Trump's support may drop with the opposition of Elon Musk and other senior Republican figures, concerned with the initially rapidly falling stock markets, but quite possibly, the Republican Party may not hold together. China quickly responded with a retaliatory tariff, and others will probably follow their example, leading to a trade war, where all parties are losers. Canada has already responded with a boycott of American products, and other countries are likely to respond in a similar, coordinated manner. Whether these factors, deep divisions in the Republican Party, falling stock markets, weakening consumer confidence, and a falling dollar will bring about any change of policy remains to be seen.

Many Europeans might secretly agree with the current British Foreign Secretary, who had described Trump in the past as 'a woman-hating Neo-Nazi-sympathising sociopath'. Only Viktor Orban of Hungary, who held the EU Presidency with the slogan of 'Make Europe Great Again', was happy. The initial reaction around the world was a mixture of bewilderment, nervousness, and trepidation.

Implications for Democracy

Immediately after Trump's election, it is difficult to see what America will look like in the future. Many people would agree with Kamala Harris' fear that the country is entering a 'Dark Period', rather than a 'New Golden Age', as promised by Trump. In particular, will he 'Make America Great Again'? Unfortunately, it is hard to predict the actions of a man who ignores advisors and acts impulsively. Certainly, it seems that he is aiming to demolish the US State. [21] One of the great admirers of liberal democracy accepts that it is now under attack, as never before. [22]

Democracy in America will certainly experience a profound change. Trump in America is as dominant as Putin is in Russia. Putin continues to make his influence felt by far-right parties, whose main spokesman in Europe is Viktor Orban. Struggling democracies in Europe and elsewhere can take no comfort in the result. How the loss of democracy in America will affect democracy in the wider world is unclear and will take longer to evaluate, as Trump, Putin's preferred candidate, has become President of the United States for a second term. It is a major setback in the number of countries aspiring to become democracies and encourages populists around the world.

Perhaps, as Stephen Hessel warned over Israeli treatment of Palestinians in 2011, so too in America, it could end badly during a Trump presidency.

If Trump orders Ukraine, a democracy, to cede vast territory to a hostile, invading autocracy, America's support for democracy will have ended. Putin has referred to discussions with "our American colleagues and partners". It will also vanish if Trump does not restrain Israel and unequivocally back a ceasefire. The uncertainties are enormous, ranging from foreign policy, peace, deportation of immigrants, to climate change, but it is difficult to be optimistic either for America or the world. It may well become a world of increasing disinformation, as Musk and Trump seek to deregulate social media. A right-wing UK newspaper claims that America under Donald Trump, with its patrician families and flirtation with cultural suicide, resembles Rome in decline. [23]

Unlike Brexit in the UK, the American political system was not robust enough to fend off a populist takeover by the Executive. The traditional separation of powers failed to defeat the challenge. It may be that he will be constrained by practical problems, as Russia attempts to cut communication cables and China hacks the US treasury system. Democracies can then decide if they wish to follow suit. If democracy in America devolves into libertarianism, it will diverge fundamentally from the European model, which is facing its own challenges.

The Emerging Picture

The evidence of his first day in office, when he issued a long list of Executive Orders, provides some clues. Trump's border tsar has promised a 'Shock and Awe' approach to deporting illegal immigrants, freeing prisoners guilty of attacking the Capitol in 2020, while deregulation will proceed at a pace to help the fossil fuels industry. Trump promised to embrace a libertarian policy on deregulation, ignoring any adverse consequences for its citizens.

Domestically, no opposition will be tolerated, and critics will be pursued with a vengeance. Some civic freedoms, such as freedom of speech, may suffer as the result that America ceases to be the 'Land of the Free'. He has started by cutting federal funding to 'Voice of America', America's largest and oldest international radio broadcaster, which he deemed to be hostile to him, a ban which was welcomed in Moscow and Beijing.

University independence may vanish if its students dissent with Trump's views on Israel and Gaza. Trump has started down this track by withholding funding from Columbia and Harvard universities, while also attempting to prevent Harvard from enrolling foreign students, an alarming attack on both university freedom and the right of students to protest. America has withdrawn from major international agreements, such as the WHO and the Paris Climate Change Agreement, reducing its influence and leadership in these fields.

Overseas, the first element of policy is territorial expansion, which is the first imperial move by America since President McKinley in 1897. Trump has stated that he wishes to take back Panama, an ally and a relatively prosperous functioning democracy, because it is strategically important, and claims that they have some unwelcome link with China. He wants to buy Greenland and does not rule out military intervention and draconian economic sanctions to achieve this goal. Whether his belligerent, imperialistic ambitions will be extended to further countries in his efforts to 'Make America Great Again' remains to be seen. He is willing to support other imperial powers, such as Israel, in their determination to expand their territories by force overseas.

But the most astonishing goal is to make Canada a State of the USA, an act which is eerily reminiscent of Hitler's Anschluss with Austria, merging the two countries in 1939. Canada has always been a friendly neighbouring State and takes seriously this hostile act to destroy its independence, possibly backed up by punitive tariffs. It has a very different culture and values from the USA. It has a generally better education system, medical services open to all its citizens, and a longer life expectancy. Its attitude to inequality is totally different, and its minimum wage is almost double that of America. It dislikes the US gun control policy and has no intention of abandoning its independence. [24] It has managed its two separate peoples, English and French, much more successfully than America has when it deals with black and brown people. It is difficult to accept Trump's assertion that Canada, which has run as a democracy, is not a 'viable entity'. Certainly, Canadians, under the leadership of Paul Carney and the Liberal Party, have quickly united to fend off the threat.

Some Trump proposals are extraordinary. No colonial power in the nineteenth century ever tried to obtain mineral rights without any existing presence in the country, as Trump has done in Ukraine. His claim that President Zelensky is an unelected dictator with only 4% public support is absurd, since Zelensky was elected democratically before the Russian invasion and, according to opinion polls, still enjoys 57% public support, though this would decline when voters became concerned about the impact of tariffs on the cost of living. His criticism of

Zelensky's dress was inconsistent with his own blatant disrespect shown at the funeral of Pope Francis. The demand that the people of Gaza be depopulated permanently in the interests of a real estate deal benefiting America is unprecedented. Both ideas are morally indefensible.

The second strand of its foreign policy is interference in the workings of functioning democracies by supporting far-right parties around the world. Trump and Musk have turned their attention to their allies in Western Europe, rather than their traditional adversaries, such as Russia and China. There are disturbing reports that Elon Musk may make a substantial donation to the UK Reform Party, which could spread the Trump right-wing political model into Europe, resulting in calls for the protection of the UK's political integrity. [25] He seems to exclude the Gulf States, a strange but pragmatic attitude. [26] Musk, the US spokesman on the issue, is unelected, and his main qualification is his enormous wealth.

In an extraordinary intervention, Musk has even called for the release of a far-right Islamophobic fascist from prison for contempt of court in the UK, attacked the British Prime Minister, and called for fresh elections. Initially, this evoked no official UK response, though it was criticised by some MPs and subsequently by Prime Minister Keir Starmer, who accused him of lies and disinformation when Musk described him as 'despicable' and advocated the jailing of the Home Secretary. Later, it was reported that Musk was seeking to find ways to get rid of Starmer ahead of the next election and decide who should or should not be the leader of the Reform Party.

The following day, Trump tweeted a criticism of the UK's green policy. The devastating January 2025 Los Angeles fires were conveniently ignored as evidence of the impact of global warming, caused by burning fossil fuels. It would seem to demonstrate very crudely a willingness of the USA to interfere with the domestic affairs of other countries. [27] Trump has even attempted to impose his policies opposed to diversity, equality, and inclusion on companies overseas, with which America has a significant trading relationship, even if they are not American-owned. The idea of any foreigner trying to interfere in the politics of another country is abhorrent, whether Russian or American. These unwelcome developments, if repeated, could prove damaging for democracies around the world.

Vice President Vance, in a visit to Europe, reiterated Trump's far-right anti-immigrant rhetoric, while downplaying the danger posed by Putin. The EU will face major challenges from a country whose vice-president does not respect EU democracy. Trump has always held the EU in contempt, claiming that it was formed to damage the USA. He prefers to deal with its members individually in an attempt to divide and rule, as was shown when the Italian President was the only EU Head of State to attend the Trump inauguration. [28]

There could be a currency crisis. If Trump persists with tax reductions for the rich and further fiscal irresponsibility, a steep decline in the dollar is probable. [29] The consequent reduction in its role as a reserve currency would damage America and the world. China could decide to sell off significant holdings in US bonds, which would exacerbate the problem, but there is a possible silver lining. Less dependence on the dollar as a reserve currency, as proposed by Brazil, would strengthen the EU's hand.

The problem is made more difficult by the fact that all EU States are experiencing economic difficulties, while some are favourably disposed to Russia. Trump supports AfD in

Germany, describing it as that country's 'last hope' to the delight of far-right European parties. The German Government has criticised the US for interfering with German elections. Any substantial imposition of tariffs is serious, but the EU should not allow itself to become a victim and may have to impose counter tariffs, while resisting attempts to impose deregulation of social media, if it wants to preserve its culture and values. [30]

One hundred eighty countries have been directly impacted by Trump's new tariffs. The EU should seek to provide a wider coordinated response to tariffs by linking up with Canada, Mexico, Australia, the Central Asian bloc of countries, and possibly China. Europe's worst nightmare has become a reality, as it was excluded from the Ukraine peace talks. [31] The old adage springs to mind, that if you are not at the table, you are probably on the menu.

Trump assumed the presidency on the same day as the opening of the World Economic Forum in Davos, which epitomises an elite-driven globalisation in existence for thirty years, but may become increasingly irrelevant during a second Trump presidency.

Trump is challenging the longstanding liberal international order, while European security is under threat, as Trump undermines NATO. The imposition of massive tariffs could precipitate a trade war, not only with China, but also with the traditional allies of the USA in Europe, North and South America, and Asia. His threat to use military intervention in

Greenland, which is a self-governing part of Denmark, a NATO ally, and Panama, are both unprecedented and extremely dangerous.

Trump has started out with an aggressive tariff policy towards China, but he has spoken of his respect for Xi. Some form of entente or rapprochement could happen. It is possible that Trump, Putin, and Xi will reach an accommodation between them, since they are all territorially aggressive and equally opposed to democratic values. They might mark out and agree on their spheres of influence around the globe, which would be off limits for the other Powers. For Putin, this constitutes the former USSR; for Xi, it is the Pacific and Taiwan, while for Trump, it is an update of the 1823 Monroe Doctrine, whereby an attack on any American country would be deemed to be an attack on the USA. The US sphere of influence would include the entire continent of America, North, South, and Central, with possibly some of Europe as well. Trump's very close ally, Israel, would mark out its sphere widely over the Middle East.

Trump has backed Russia in Ukraine peace talks, blaming Ukraine for starting the war and voting along with Russia at the United Nations. In view of his exclusion of President Zelensky and the EU, this may be fundamental, dependent only on receiving mineral rights. It has been suggested that China and the USA have a common interest in maintaining the renminbi exchange rate, [32] while a resolution of the TikTok investment might avoid a tariff war. If that were to happen, Taiwan would become a target, along with many Pacific islands, as would also most States of Eastern Europe, while America would focus on Panama, Canada, and Greenland. Israel may attack any of its neighbours. International cooperation in dealing with problems, such as climate change, will become a major issue in a new geopolitical order.

Domestically, it is not clear what the poor and those left behind can expect, but it is likely that the cuts in public expenditure will adversely impact their existing benefits. Currently, there is an absence of an equitable distribution of wealth, which is likely to deteriorate further in an era of massive deregulation. Business ethics will degenerate into a race to the bottom, as Trump legitimised bribery of foreign officials. This move is unsurprising, since Trump is himself a convicted felon. It should attract funds from the most corrupt regimes around the world and severely damage America's business reputation.

There are indications that he may encroach on the powers of individual States to do as they are told, particularly on matters such as immigration. [33] Some people may emigrate to avoid his wrath, while others may leave the country, rather than live in a Fascist State, where the traditional American values have come under attack. Democracy in America is truly under siege. Trump is prepared to support tyranny around the world, in particular, Putin and Russia, a traditional enemy of America.

Trump has ignored a unanimous Supreme Court ruling to repatriate an illegally deported man from El Salvador, a practice commonplace in Police States. [34] A more recent example has been Trump's threat to impose heavy tariffs on Brazil, unless they withdrew charges against Bolsonaro, the defeated presidential candidate and kindred spirit of Trump.[35] He wants to reopen Alcatraz, the notorious, harsh prison, to hold illegal immigrants without trial. The FBI has arrested a Wisconsin judge for allegedly breaching immigration rules. America is, in practice, also becoming a 'Rogue State', supporting another Rogue State, disseminating Russian misinformation and propaganda. The cessation of world aid will result in many deaths and widespread hardship. America's traditional benign role on the world stage has undergone a fundamental change. It can no longer claim to be the global upholder of freedom, democracy, international prosperity, and a just peace. It will also help Trump's threat to silence free media, a development welcomed by Putin and Xi. [36]

Astonishingly, after his first month in office, Trump enjoyed the broad support of the American people, even though he completely undermined democracy and destroyed the existing world order in an unpredictable way. This quickly changed as Trump received the lowest rating of any president after 100 days, according to a CNBC poll. [37] There will be several challenges to Trump's America at the outset. FBI members have already gone to court to protect the freedom of their members. [38]

An academic who revealed his adoption of authoritarianism in the first year of his previous presidency has reported how quickly the same pattern is being repeated in 2025. [39] Trump has indicated that he may seek to impeach judges who stand in his way and has already started to dissolve by decree many Government Institutions. He has appointed loyalists to key positions in the judiciary, intelligence services, and regulatory agencies, while the unelected Elon Musk exercises enormous power over the government. This is tantamount to 'competitive authoritarianism', under which the Constitution and the Institutions of State remain intact, but are powerless.

The willingness of Republican members of Congress will need to decide if their own personal career progress outweighs their duties as legislators, or result in a supine acceptance of

Trump's demands. It seems that they are being threatened by violence, both to themselves and their families, if they step out of line, while the Democrats have been stunned into silence. If the Executive can control both the Judiciary and the Legislature, democracy is well and truly dead.

The American media is not optimistic. *The Washington Post* fears that Trump may deliberately undo good reforms put in place by Joe Biden.[40] *The New York Times* emphasises that Trump rules by fear, as was evidenced by his first presidency. Republicans must stand up to him, particularly over poor cabinet appointments, which is not evident with his initial appointments, except for Mitch McConnell. [41] But the most worrying analysis comes from *The Economist.* [42]

Donald Trump will undo 80 years of American foreign policy. He has little time for alliances and multinational agreements, which have defined the post-war order. His proposal to occupy Gaza with American troops and forcibly relocate over 2,000,000 Palestinians in support of Israel's Zionist imperial expansion is unacceptable to all Muslims and others who support the need for a Palestinian State. The plan, which constitutes ethnic cleansing on a grand scale, quickly met strong, vehement resistance and condemnation not only from Palestinians but also throughout the Middle East and around the world.

Many people have recognised America's relative decline on the world scene with the rise of China, India, Brazil, and Russia, and the rising power of consumers around the world. [43] But Trump does not accept settled international borders, and he is entirely unpredictable, approaching every issue on a purely transactional basis, which will inevitably bring chaos on a grand scale. It subsequently described Trump's transactional style as a gangster's paradise, which ultimately would harm America. [44] It seems that the Irish poet William Butler Yeats was prescient when, a century ago, he wrote: "The centre cannot hold, mere anarchy is released on the world". "Might is Right" has replaced democracy. It sometimes seems that Trump is playing "World of Empires" on the real-world stage.

Democracy in America

The likelihood is that traditional democracy in America will disappear for at least the expected four years of the Trump presidency, driven by a policy of extreme greed and unrestrained national self-interest, unless the Democrats gain control of the House of Representatives in the Midterm elections, but it could last longer. Trump once stated that voters need not vote again, and there are rumours that he wants to create a dynasty [45] or at least to cement the Republican Party in power with the assistance of a friendly judiciary.

One account of the 2024 election does suggest that it could be the last election. The description portrayed was of Trump, ranting, abusive, incandescent, incoherent with rage in a world of sleaze and dishonesty, surrounded by grasping, obsequious, sycophants, charlatans, and lawbreakers, who wish to crush the status quo. Either Trump will destroy the Establishment, or the Establishment will destroy him. [46] But, even if an election is held in 2028, it may not be fair, swamped by a deluge of unchecked disinformation. Trump has stated that he will seek a third term in breach of the Constitution, although this threat was later withdrawn.

Joe Biden's farewell address to the nation set down a stark, chilling, ominous warning.[47] Confirming Bernie Sanders' view, he stated that an oligarchy of extreme wealth, power, and influence is taking shape in America, which threatens democracy by damaging civic rights and freedom. He is also concerned about the emerging technology industrial complex, which could yield abuses of power if it is left unchecked. The free press, where many editors have resigned, is under threat from a flood of misinformation on social media. If AI is to develop successfully, it should not be driven purely by power and profit without any fact-checking, but this appears to be what is happening.

Democracy has shifted from Lincoln's definition to 'Government of the People by the People and for the People'. The new description is 'Government of the People by the Rich for the Rich'. It should come as no surprise that Trump sees the solution to Gaza as a real estate proposition, based on the forcible deportation of over two million Palestinians, whose ancestors have lived there for thousands of years. It would probably constitute the greatest and most cruel ever cruellest act of ethnic cleansing in history for the furtherance of American business interests.[48]

America is now an imperial power, abandoning its traditional values and allies. Ignoring the universal religious basis of mutual respect, it is now acting as a 'Bad Samaritan', not just ignoring the troubles of its neighbours, who had been previously freely assisted, but actively taking advantage of them. The Rich should become much richer and the Poor much poorer with the cost borne by future generations, as $3.3 trillion is added to the already overstretched national budget. No country assisting America after the 9/11 Twin Towers atrocity regarded their help as a loan, which makes America's expectation unique.

I am glad that the Americans who explained to me the prevailing ethics in the USA over sixty years ago are no longer alive to see it. They would regard Trump's way of 'Making America Great Again' as grotesque and totally incompatible with their traditional, cherished values. The moral compass has profoundly shifted and is now based on force, threats, and intimidation. It seems increasingly to be 'One Man, One Vote, and One Time'. The implications of his presidency are not just the future of liberal democracy, but also affect world peace and the future of the planet. It seems that the world is destined to live under the old Chinese curse, 'May you live in interesting times'! If a further economic crisis were to arise, caused possibly by an insurance collapse due to climate change, America and the world are ill-prepared to deal with it.[49]

A populist demagogue has taken the wheel on board the ship, called 'Liberal Democracy', and is entering uncharted waters, which would have dismayed Plato. Nevertheless, liberal democracy remains the best form of government, as already outlined in Chapter 1. Unfortunately, it has already disappeared in America, and European liberal democracies increasingly regard America as an adversary, supporting Russia, which was regarded by previous presidents as 'the Evil Empire', rather than an ally. There now exists a new world order, which makes international agreement on important matters very problematic.[50]

Those remaining countries which value liberal democratic values, such as Britain, Canada, Australia, New Zealand, Japan, South Korea and most western European countries should cooperate with each other and prepare a plan of action, as outlined in chapter 23. For some years, it has been apparent that complacency is not the answer to Russian rage and Chinese ambition.[51] It is worth repeating that there can be no liberty without democracy.[52] Otherwise the number of real democracies will continue to fall to 1945 levels or even fewer and be replaced by corrupt autocracies.

Is Democracy at an End in America?

The enigma has been explained. What is less clear is whether a real effort will be made to save democracy and restore confidence in it as the best system of government. The alternative to inaction is frightening.

It seems that some courageous Republicans have recognised the damage that Trump is inflicting on the long-term interests of the Party when they refused to back his "big, beautiful" finance bill. It is time for others to follow suit and for Democrats to form a more effective Opposition. It was stated at the outset that the wake-up call had sounded. True supporters of democracy need to get out of bed and act without further delay.

REFERENCES

Preface

1. "It's ok to be Angry about Capitalism", Senator Bernie Sanders. Penguin, 2024.

Introduction

1. "Silent Spring", Rachel Carson, Penguin, 1962.
2. "Quinn", Trevor Birney, Merrion Press, 1922.
3. "What Just Happened", Marina Hyde, Guardian Faber, 2022.

Chapter 1: The Benefits and Attractions of Liberal Democracy

1. "The End of History and the Last Man", Professor Francis Fukuyama, Penguin, 2020.
2. Freedom House Annual Reports 2023, 2024.
3. "Freedom of Speech", Ngozi Adichie Reith Lecture, 2022.
4. "Freedom of Worship", Rowan Douglas Williams, Reith lecture 2022.
5. "Freedom from Want", Darren McGarvey, Reith lecture 2022.
6. "Freedom From Fear", Dr Fiona Hill, Reith lecture 2022.
7. "Development as Freedom", Amartya Sen, Oxford University Press, 1999.

8. "Putting the democratic crisis into perspective", Janan Ganesh, *Financial Times,* 3 January 2024.
9. Freedom House 2023 Annual Report.
10. "Our Democratic Future", Ben Ansell, Reith Lecture, BBC4, 29 November 2023.
11. India Alone", Aljazeera News, 28 February 2923.
12. "Democracy in Danger", *Economist leader,* 29 November 2023.
13. "Next year's greatest danger". *Economist,* 29 November 2023.

Chapter 2: Democracy from Early Days to the Present

1. "The Republic", Plato.
2. "What ancient Athens can teach about law and democracy", William Magnusson, *Financial Times, 2* February 2024.
3. "Democracy", Melvyn Bragg, BBC4, 18 October 2001.
4. "Rights of Man", Thomas Paine, 1791.
5. 'The Social Contract', Jean-Jacques Rousseau, 1782.
6. 'Lettres Philosophiques', Voltaire, 1734.

Chapter 3: Democracy and Fundamental Political Divides

1. "The Profession and Vocation of Politics", Max Weber, 1919.

2. "A Letter Concerning Toleration", John Locke, 1689.
3. "On Liberty", John Stuart Mill, 1859.
4. "A Vindication of Natural Society", Edmund Burke, 1756.
5. "The Conservative Case", Viscount Hailsham, Penguin, 1959.
6. "The Wealth of Nations", Adam Smith, 1776.
7. "The Communist Manifesto", Karl Marx and Friedrich Engels, 1848.
8. "The Concept of the Political", Professor Carl Schmitt, 1928/1932.
9. "The Road to Serfdom", Friedrich Hayek, Routledge, 1944.
10. "Capitalism, Socialism and Democracy", Joseph Schumpeter, Routledge, 2010.
11. "The Open Society and Its Enemies", Karl Popper, Routledge, 1945.
12. "The Future of Socialism", Anthony Crosland, 1963.
13. Libertarian National Conference, 24 May 2024.

Chapter 4: Different Models of Democracy

1. "In Search of Democracy, Larry Diamond, Routledge, 201.
2. "The Spirit of Democracy", Larry Diamond, Centre Books, 2008

3. "How Trump allies are sowing election results", Eva Xiao & Peter Adringa, *Financial Times,* 14 October 2024.
4. "Freedom on the Net 2024", Freedom House, 2024.
5. "How the Kremlin is trying to hijack Moldova's election with dirty money", *The Observer,* 13 October 2024.
6. "Moldova battles Russian cash for votes bid", Polina Ivanova, *Financial Times,* 20 October 2024.
7. Euroactiv, 29 March 2024, 2 April 2024.
8. Usually referred to as 'The Good Friday Agreement'.
9. Electoral Commission research, Irish Times, 6 May 2024.
10. Euronews, 27 December 2024.

Chapter 5: Liberal Democracy, Economic Growth, and the Role of Banks

1. "Extraordinary Popular Delusions and the Madness of Crowds", Charles Macay, Wiley, first published in 1841.
2. "Stabilising the Unstable Economy", Hyman Minsky, McGraw-Hill. 2008.
3. "Meltdown Iceland – How the Global Financial Crisis Bankrupted a Country", Roger Bayes, Bloomsbury. 2009.
4. *The Economist,* 8 April 2023.
5. "Banking Needs a Radical Change", Martin Wolff, *Financial Times*, 23 March 2023.

6. "An Irish Banking Manifesto, the Views of a Disenchanted Banker", Tim McCormick, The Liffey Press, 2015.
7. "How to End the Democratic Recession", Larry Diamond, *Foreign Affairs,* November/December 2024.

Chapter 6: Democracy Beyond National Boundaries

1. "The IMF faces a nightmarish identity crisis", *The Economist,* 4 April 2023.
2. "Can the IMF solve the poor world's debt crisis?", *The Economist,* 18 April 2024.
3. "Principles of Political Economy", David Ricardo, 1817.
4. "Time to Clean up the Act?" Euronews 18 May 2024.
5. "The future of European competitiveness – A competitiveness strategy for Europe", Mario Draghi, The European Commission, 2024.
6. "Europe in mortal danger", *The Economist,* 4 May 2024.
7. "The rise of the hard-right threatens Europe's political stability", *The Economist,* 1 June 2024.
8. Irish Times, 8 June 2024.
9. "Far-right using 'mask of protest claims Higgins', *Irish Times,* 17 June 2024.
10. BBC News 14 October 2021.
11. "Atlanticist Tories failed to understand US", Janan Ganesh, *Financial Times*, 28 May 2024.

12. "A Nightmare, the cost of doing business, eight years after Brexit", Jack Simpson, *The Observer,* 23 June 2024.
13. "Heroic Failure – Brexit and the Politics of Pain", Fintan O'Toole, Apollo Books, 2018.
14. "Three Years in Hell – The Brexit Chronicles", Fintan O'Toole, Apollo Books, 2020.
15. "All Out War": The Full Story of how Brexit sank Britain's Political Class, Tim Shipman, William Collins, 2016.
16. "What happened to conservatism?", Edmund Faucett, *Financial Times,* 8 June 2024.
17. Euronews, 26 March 2025.

Chapter 7: Influences on Voters

1. "It's ok to be Angry about Capitalism", Senator Bernie Sanders. Penguin, 2024.
2. "Citizens Union v Federal Election Commission, 2010.
3. "Democracy Rules", Jan-Werner Muller, Penguin, 2022.
4. "It's ok to be Angry about Capitalism", Senator Bernie Sanders. Penguin, 2024.
5. "Can Elon Musk rule the world?", Channel 4, 6 February 2025.
6. "Bunker Mentality; the billionaires prepping for doomsday", Adam Maguire, RTE, 11 May 2025.

7. "The kleptocrats aren't just stealing money. They're stealing democracy", Anne Applebaum, *Financial Times,* 31 August 2024.

Chapter 8: The Clash of Cultures: Autocracy and Liberal Democracy

1. "The Age of the Strongman – How the Cult of the Leader Threatens Democracy around the World", Gideon Rachman, Vintage, 2023.
2. *"1984",* George Orwell, Secker & Warburg, 1949.
3. *"Prophet Song",* Paul Lynch, One World, 2023.
4. *Leviathan,* Thomas Hobbes, 1651.
5. "Confronting Leviathan", David Runciman, Profile Books, 2022.
6. BBC News, 28 February 2020.
7. BBC News, 25 June 2020.
8. Irish Times, 2 May 2022.
9. "Red Notice", Bill Browder, Corgi, 2016.
10. "Freezing Order", Bill Browder, Schuster & Schuster, 2022.
11. "Patriot", Alexei Navalny, Penguin Random House, 2024.
12. Euronews, 17 January 2025.
13. "Eichmann in Jerusalem: A Report on the Banality of Evil", Hannah Arendt, Penguin 2006.
14. "The Origins of Totalitarianism", Hannah Arendt, 1951.
15. Financial Times, 15 April 2024.

16. "Bukele's authoritarianism in El Salvador may prove contagious", Michael Stott, *Financial Times,* 7 February 2024.
17. Electoral Committee Research, *Irish Times,* 6 May 2024.
18. "Why Democracy Matters", TED Talks, Houses of Parliament, Rory Stewart, 2012.
19. NHCR Report, 1 September 2022.

Chapter 9: Reducing Inequality

1. "The New Colossus", Emma Lazarus, sonnet, 1883.
2. *Irish Times,* June 2023.
3. "It's Ok to be Angry about Capitalism", Senator Bernie Sanders. Penguin, 2024.
4. *The Economist,* 21 October 2023.
5. Joe Brennan, *Irish Times,* 28 July 2023.
6. "Can Elon Musk derail Delaware?"Sujeet Indap & Myles McCormick, *Financial Times,* 5 February 2024.
7. "How long can the 'Texas miracle last?" Myles McCormick, *Financial Times,* 25 July 2024.
8. "Capital in the Twenty-First Century", Thomas Piketty, Harvard University Press, 2014.
9. "Oxfam Submission to Oireachtas Committee Budgetary Oversight, 2023.
10. *Irish Times* leader, 19 October 2024.
11. "Global Inequality Report", IMD, 2022.
12. "How the poor stopped catching up", *The Economist,* 21 September 2024.

Chapter 10: Satisfying Basic Human Needs

1. "A Theory of Human Motivation", Professor Abraham Maslow, Journal of Psychological Review, 1943.
2. "The Future of Security", Ben Ansell, Reith Lecture, BBC, 7 December 2023
3. National Competitiveness and Productivity Council.
4. IMD World Competitiveness Ranking 2023.
5. "Infrastructure Deficit: Productivity is the key", *Irish Times leader,* 31 October 2024.
6. "Private sector can help us to avoid public infrastructure mess", Conor Skehan, *Sunday Independent*, 3 November 2024.
7. "Ireland Gridlocked", Lorcan Allen, Daniel Murray, Killian Woods & Catharine Sanz, *Sunday Business Post,* 14 May 2023.
8. *Irish Times,* 12 February 2024.
9. Sunday Business Post, 12 May 2024.

Chapter 11: Achieving Transnational Cooperation

1. World Meteorological Service and Copernicus, 2024.
2. "How to Avoid a Climate Disaster", Bill Gates, Penguin, 2021.
3. Davy Stockbrokers, 2023.
4. "The Energy transition's shortage of returns", Myles McCormick, *Financial Times,* 23 May 2023.

5. Jon Ungoed-Thomas Maximillian Jenz, *The Observer,* 13 August 2023.
6. "Blue Machine", Helen Czerski, Penguin Random House, 2023.
7. "Rewilding the Sea -How to Save our Oceans", Charles Clover, Penguin, 2022.
8. "Fishing – How the Sea Fed Civilisation", Brian Fagan, Yale University Press, 2017.
9. "The Compleat Angler", Isaak Walton and Charles Cotton, 1653.
10. "The High Seas: Ambition, Power and Greed on the Unclaimed Ocean", Olive Heffernan, Greystone Books, 2024.
11. United Nations Environmental Programme.
12. "The New Fish", Simon Saetre & Kjetil Ostli, English Edition, Patagonia, 2023.
13. Salmon Watch Ireland website.
14. "Wading into the Fishing Debate", Scottish National Trust, 18 May 2018.
15. "Dead Loss", Just Economics, Executive Summary, 12 February 2021.
16. "A better way to farm fish?", Food Revolution, October 2023, *Financial Times video,* 18 March 2021.
17. "Are Open-pen Salmon Farms Really Sustainable?", Tim McCormick, Salmon Watch Ireland website, April 2023.
18. "Are Open-pen Salmon Farms Really Sustainable?", Tim McCormick, Salmon Watch Ireland website, April 2023.

19. “Salmon Wars, the soft underbelly of our favourite fish”, Douglas Frantz & Catherine Collins, 2022.
20. “Ocean”, David Attenborough, 2025
21. “Understanding knowledge as a commons from theory to practice”, Elinor Ostrom, Cambridge, Massachusetts Press, 2007.
22. Ben Turner, *Life Science,* 25 October 2024.
23. Euronews, 11 November 2024.
24. Eamon Ryan, RTE 1 news, 24 November 2024.
25. “No Miracles Needed: How Today’s Technology Can Save Our Climate and Clean Our Air”, Mark Z. Jacobson, Professor of Civil and Environmental Engineering, Stanford University, Cambridge University Press, 2023.
26. “Oceans Rise, Empires Fall”, Professor Gerald Toal, Oxford University Press, 2024.

Chapter 12: Achieving Peace

1. “Project for a Perpetual Peace”, Immanuel Kant, 1795.
2. “Hitler, A Study in Tyranny”, Alan Bullock, Penguin, 1990.
3. “What is a viable objective in Ukraine?”, Fintan O’Toole, *Irish Times,* 3 February 2023.
4. “Time for Outrage”, Stéphane Hessel, Essay, 2011.
5. “Holocaust should not prevent the world from seeing Israel as it is”, Hagai El-Ad, Opinion, *Irish Times,* 17 June 2024.

6. "Israel and Palestine", Professor Noam Chomsky, lecture at Clark University, 12 April 2011.
7. "Jerusalem: The Biography", Simon Sebag Montefiore, Weidenfeld and Nicholson, 2011.
8. "Night of Power: The Betrayal of the Middle East", Robert Fisk, Harper and Collins, 2024.
9. "Israel Democracy in Peril", *Financial Times View*, 25 July 2023.
10. Sky News, 7 September 2024.
11. "There is no safety there, say Irish volunteers working in harrowing West Bank conditions", Hannah McCarthy, *Irish Times,* 9 September 2024.
12. "How far-right minister Itamar Ben-Gvir weaponised Israel's police", Neri Zilber, *Financial Times,* 16 September 2024.
13. "Kill Zone inside Gaza – Despatches", Channel 4, 27 May 2024.
14. "Detention of writers opens new front", Hannah McCarthy, *Irish Times,* 22 June 2024.
15. "West Bank Palestinians live in fear of settler attacks", *Financial Times,* November 2023.
16. Sky News, 17 June 2024.
17. "The Long View from Lebanon", Ghassan Salame, *Financial Times*, 7 October 2024.
18. "Israel's Reinvasion is a Strategic Disaster", Ehud Barak, *Financial Times,* 23 May 2025.
19. "Life and Death in Gaza", BBC2, 16 October 2024.
20. Chuck Starmer, Senate Speech, 14 March 2024.

21. "Israel cannot remain a democracy without protecting journalists", Freedom House, 7 November 2024.
22. Euronews, 24 December 2024.
23. "Hong Kong: A Modern Tragedy", The Challenges of Democracy and the Rule of Law, Jonathan Sumption, Profile Books, 2005.
24. "The war in Gaza must end", *The Economist,* 10 May 2023.
25. "Reflections on Gaza and Israel's War Against the Palestinians", Ilan Pappe & Noam Chomsky, Penguin, 2007.
26. "On Palestine", Noam Chomsky & Ilan Pappe, Penguin, 2017.
27. Genesis Chapter 12, 10-20, Holy Bible, New International Edition, Hodder & Stoughton, 2011.
28. "The Clash of Civilisations", Samuel Harrington, Schuster & Schuster, 1996.
29. "Jammu and Kashmir: A neighbourhood nightmare", *The Economist,* 3 May 2025.
30. "The New Leviathans", John Gray, Professor of Philosophy, University of Oxford. Penguin, 2023.

Chapter 13: How and Why Democracies Fail

1. The Economist, 1 April 2023.
2. "Whose Constitution, Whose Democracy?", Joshua Leifer, *New York Review,* 13 April 2023.

3. "38 Londres Street", Philippe Sandys, Weidenfeld and Nicholson, 2025.
4. "How Democracy Ends", David Runciman, Profile Books, 2018.
5. Michael Portillo, BBC4, 23 May 2010.
6. Irish Times, 3 November 2023.
7. Opinion, *The Guardian,* Max Hastings, 24 June 2019.
8. *Irish Times,* 2 November 2023.
9. "Scandal after scandal: Timeline of Tory sleaze under Boris Johnson", *The Guardian,* John Halliday, 1 July 2022.
10. Antony Barber, Chancellor of the Exchequer, 1970 to 1974.
11. "Bring Back Boris", *The Economist,* 24 May 2025.
12. The Long Game – Inside Sinn Féin, Aoife Moore, Penguin, 2023.
13. "Mary Lou McDonald – A Republican Riddle", Shane Ross, Atlantic Books, 2022.

Chapter 14: A Classification of Autocracy Types: Ski Runs

1. 'The Spirit of the Law', Baron de la Brede et de Montesquieu, 1748.
2. "Saturday Profile", Farnaz Fassihi, *New York Times,* 2 June 2023.
3. "Bloodbath threat hangs over voters in Venezuela", Tom Hennigan, *Irish Times,* 27 July 2024.

4. "Democracy Inc: The Dictators Who Want to Run the World", Anne Applebaum, Allen Lane, 2024.
5. *The Prince,* Nicolo Machiavelli, Penguin,1975 (First published 1532).
6. "How El Salvador became a model for the global far right". *Financial Times,* 13 January 2025.
7. "Diplomatic Inertia", *The Economist,* 1 June 2024.
8. "Russia built a covert channel with India, leaks reveal", *Financial Times,* 4 September 2024.
9. "A triumph for Indian democracy", *The Economist,* 8 June 2024.
10. "The Fate of Young Democracies", Nathan Convers & Ethan B. Kapstein, Cambridge University Press, 2008.
11. "Deadly Violence", *The Economist,* 11 May 2024.
12. "The Age of the Strongman", Gideon Rachman, Vintage, 2023.
13. "Autocracies Inc: The Dictators who Want to Run the World", Anne Applebaum, Allen Lane, 2024.
14. "The Rest is Politics", Alastair Campbell & Professor Rory Stewart, 10 December 2024.
15. Armed Conflict Locations and Event Data, quoted in the *Irish Times,* 26 August 2024.

Chapter 15: Autocracy by Stealth: Breaking the Four-Legged Chair

1. "Twilight of Democracy, The Failure of Politics and Parting of Friends", Anne Applebaum, Penguin, 2021.
2. "Poland's Remarkable Rise", *The Economist,* 24 May 2025.
3. "The Age of the Strongman: How the Cult of the Leader Threatens Democracy around the World", Gideon Rachman, Vintage, 2023.
4. "Escaping capture", *Economist,* 10 February 2024.
5. "How Authoritarian Regimes go after Journalists beyond their Borders", Michael Abramowitz & Jessica White, Freedom House, 6 December 2023.

Chapter 16: The Allure of Populism

1. "Adolf Hitler – A Study in Tyranny", Alan Bullock, Penguin, 1990.
2. "Populism", Paul Taggart, Oxford University Press, 2000.
3. "How paranoid nationalism corrupts", *The Economist,* 2 September 2023.
4. "Populism and Liberal Democracy", Takis S. Pappas, Oxford University Press, 2019.
5. "Twilight of Democracy, The Failure of Politics and Parting of Friends", Anne Applebaum, Penguin, 2021.
6. "Chums – How a Tiny Caste of Oxford Tories Took Over the UK", Simon Kuper, Profile Books, 2022.

7. "Disordered Minds: How Dangerous Personalities are Destroying Democracy", Dr Ian Hughes, Zero Books, 2018.
8. "Hitler – a junkie", National Geographic Television Channel, 17 April 2024.
9. "The Age of the Strongman: How the Cult of the Leader Threatens Democracy around the World", Gideon Rachman, Vintage 2024.

Chapter 17: The Influence and Dangers of Social Media

1. "Why is almost three-quarters of internet traffic in Ireland of malicious intent?" Dr Chris Horn, Irish Times, 4 July 2024.
2. "Elon Musk", Walter Isaacson, Schuster & Schuster, 2023.
3. "Pro-Israel bot networks spread disinformation about Irish troops", Irish Times, 2 November 2024.
4. "Institute of Strategic Dialogue Report", reported in the Irish Times, 20 November 2023.
5. Sunday Business Post, 17 December 2023.
6. "Far-right posts mainly come from overseas", Irish Times, 5 December 2023.
7. Irish Times leader, 29 November 2023.
8. CNN News, 26 October 2024.
9. "Democracy Inc: The Dictators Who Want to Run the World", Anne Applebaum, Allen Lane, 2024.
10. "Understanding Media: The Extension of Man.", Marshall McLuhan, 1964.

11. "The Coming Storm: A Journey into the Heart of the Conspiracy Machine", Gabriel Gatehouse, Ebury Press, 2024.
12. "Populism in Times of Social Media", Hai-Thu Nguyen, Populism and Democracy, Eleven International Publishing, 2020.
13. Euronews, 19 June 2024.
14. "Why China wants Musk to save TikTok, Sonya Hutson, Joe Miller, and Sarah Dadoceck, Financial Times, 13 January 2025.
15. "France uncovers a vast Russian disinformation campaign in Europe", The Economist, 12 February 2024.
16. "Witness", Euronews, 18 June 2024.
17. "Darwin Among the Machines", Samuel Butler, The Press, Christchurch, 1863.
18. Irish Times, 23 October 2023.
19. "Will AI technology ever justify its investment?", Dr Chris Horn, Irish Times, 21 September 2024.
20. "Zucked: Waking up to the Facebook Catastrophe", Roger McNamee, Penguin, 2018.
21. "The Age of Surveillance Capitalism: The Fight for a Human Future at the Frontier of Power", Shoshana Zuboff, Profile Books, 2019.
22. "The steely Brazilian judge facing down Musk", Financial Times, 7 September 2024.
23. Prime Time, RTE television, 16 April 2024.
24. "Irish Times, 23 October 2023.
25. "Authoritarianism, Discourse and Social Media: Trump as the 'American Agitator'",

Panayota Gounari, in Critical Theory of Populism, Westminster University Press, 2018.
26. "How a real video became a fake news story", Irish Times, 1 June 2024.
27. "Election ads on TikTok breach company's rules and EU code", Irish Times, 1 June 2024.
28. "Lawyer leaves META to its own devices, Irish Times, 16 January 2025.
29. "The Handover", David Runciman, Profile Books, 2024.
30. University of California, Berkeley, Euronews, 13 February 2025.

Chapter 18: American Democracy During Trump's First Presidency

1. "The kleptocrats aren't just stealing money. They're stealing democracy", Anne Applebaum, *Financial Times,* 31 August 2024.
2. "The Holes in Trump's win story: Members of his club surprised–but not shocked.", Daily Mail, 23 January 2023.
3. "Commander in Cheat: How Golf Explains Trump", Rick Reilly, Hachette Books, 2019.
4. "Ship of Fools", Tucker Carlson, October 2018.
5. "Fear", Bob Woodward, Schuster & Schuster, 2018.
6. "Rage", Bob Woodward, Schuster & Schuster, 2020.
7. "Two Cheers for Democracy", Dan Hill, Sensory Logic Books, 2019.

8. “Peril”. Bob Woodward & Robert Costa, Simon & Schuster, 2021.
9. “How the Nazis lost the war”, Sky History Channel, 25 February 2024.
10. “The Dangerous Case of Donald Trump”, Bandy Lee, Thomas Dunne Books, 2017.
11. “Former president faces a criminal trial”, James Polito, *Financial Times,* 1 April 2023.
12. “Trump: Moscow’s Man in the White House?” Channel 4, 17 July 2025
13. “Fire and Fury”, Tom Wolff, Little Brown, 2018.
14. “Freedom: Memoirs 2054 - 2021”, Angela Merkel, with Beate Bauman, MacMillan, 2024.
15. “How Democracies Die”, Professor Steven Levitsky & Professor Daniel Ziblatt, Penguin, 2018.
16. Michael Crowley & Tyler Pager, *Politico,* 27 July 2016.
17. “Fire and Fury”, Tom Wolff, Little Brown. 2018.
18. “Siege, Trump under Pressure”, Tom Wolff. Little Brown, 2019.
19. “Landslide, the final days of the Trump Presidency”, Tom Wolff, The Bridge Press, 2021.
20. “America’s anything goes Supreme Court”, Edward Luce, *Financial Times,* 3 May 2023.
21. “Supreme Court justice’s activist wife caught up in payments furore”. *Financial Times,* 20 May 2023.

22. "Reform thyself", SCOTUS and ethics, *The Economist,* 9 September 2023.
23. "US Supreme Court is rotten and corrupt", Maureen Dowd, Opinion, The *New York Times,* 4 June 2024.
24. "Stop judge-mandering", *The Economist,* 11 May 2024.
25. "Confidence in US Democracy", Washington Post and University of Maryland joint survey, 2014.
26. "Trump's people could not care less about American values", Maureen Dowd, *New York Times, Irish Times,* 19 February 2024.
27. "The real RINO", Simon Schama, *Financial Times,* 3 September 2023.
28. "The tyranny of America's Supreme Court", Edward Luce, *Financial Times,* 6 March 2024.
29. "Trump more radical than average autocrat", Patrick Smyth, World View, *Irish Times,* 19 August 2023.
30. "Democracy Awakening – Notes on the State of America", Heather Cox Richardson, WH Allen, 2023.
31. "It's Ok to be Angry about Capitalism", Bernie Sanders, Penguin, 2024.
32. "The Return of Great Powers: Russia, China and the Next World War", Jim Sciutto, Penguin Random House, 2024.
33. "Make America Great Again? American Conservatism and Donald Trump", Justin Lange, Union College, 2019.

34. "Rebellion: How Anti-liberalism is Tearing America Apart Again". Robert Kagan, W.H. Allen 2024.
35. "Trump's bizarre claims no longer a shock factor", Edward Luce, *Financial Times,* 13 March 2024.
36. "Tired of Winning: Donald Trump and the End of the Grand Old Party". Jonathan Karl, Dutton, 2023.
37. *"The Apprentice",* director Ali Abbasi, film released in 2024.
38. "Trump on Russian Dispute: Ultimately I am Always Right", Caitlin Oprysko, *Politico*, 12 June 2019.
39. "The Fifth Risk: Undoing Democracy", Michael Lewis, Penguin, 2019.
40. "The Retreat of Western Democracy", Edward Luce, Little, Brown, 2017.

Chapter 19: The Scourge of Polarisation

1. "The Second Coming", William Butler Yeats, 2018.
2. "The Centre Cannot Hold", *The Economist,* 29 June 2024.
3. Ben Ansell, "The Future of Solidarity", Third Reith Lecture, December 2023.
4. "Wildland, A Journey Through a Divided Country", Evan Osnos, Bloomsbury, 2022.
5. "Cultural Backlash". Pippa Norris & Ronald Inglehart, Cambridge University Press, 2019.

6. "Rebellion: How Anti-liberalism is Tearing America Apart- Again". Robert Kagan, W.H. Allen, 2019.
7. "RTE Investigates: Inside the Protests", 19 September 2024.
8. *Irish Times* opinion poll, 10 February 2024.
9. *Irish Times,* 24 July 2024.
10. "The Cube Investigation", Euronews, 7 June 2024.
11. "The Irish right-wing extremists getting ready for violence", *Irish Times,* 20 July 2024.

Chapter 20: The Danger of Complacency

1. "The Challenge of Democracy and the Rule of Law", Johnathan Sumption, Profile Books, 2025.
2. "On Freedom", Timothy Snyder, Professor, Yale University, The Bodley Head, 2024.
3. "The Future of Freedom: Illiberal Democracy at Home and Abroad", Fareed Zakaria, 2005.
4. "Brave New World", Aldous Huxley, 1934. "Liberal Capitalist Democracy – the God That Failed", Krishnan Nayar, Hurst, 1988.
5. "Our democratic future", Ben Ansell, Reith Lecture, December 2023.
6. "Anarchy, State and Utopia", Robert Nozick, Basic Books, 1974.
7. "Why Politics Fail", Ben Ansell, Penguin, 2023.

8. “Politics on the Edge – a memoir from within”, Rory Stewart, Professor, Yale University, Penguin, 2024.
9. “The Prince of the Marshes and other occupational hazards of a year in Iraq”, Rory Stewart, Harvest Books, 2007.
10. “Our democratic future”, Reith Lecture. 23 December 2023.
11. “In the Long Run: The Future as a Political Idea”, Johnathan White, Profile Books, 2024.
12. “Our Own Worst Enemy – the Assault from Within our Modern Democracy”, Tom Nichols, Oxford University Press, 2021.
13. “The Crisis of Democratic Capitalism”, Martin Wolf, Penguin, 2023.
14. “Saving Democratic Capitalism: the Democratic Recession”, Martin Wolf & Larry Diamond, *Financial Times,* 3 June 2023.
15. “Saving Democratic Capitalism: Resisting Autocracy”, Martin Wolf & Anne Applebaum, *Financial Times,* 8 June 2023.
16. “Saving Democratic Capitalism”, Martin Wolf & Hillary Clinton, *Financial Times,* 17 June 2023.
17. “Vulture Capitalism, Corporate Crimes, Backdoor Bailouts and the Death of Freedom”, Grace Blackley, Bloomsbury Publishing, 2024.
18. “It’s ok to be Angry about Capitalism”, Senator Bernie Sanders. Penguin, 2024.
19. “Living Well at Others' Expense”, Stephen Lessenich, Polity, 2019.

20. "Caring Democracy: Markets, Equality, and Justice", Joan Tronto, NYU Press, 2013.
21. "Adventures in Democracy", Erica Benner, Penguin Random House, 2024.
22. "The Road to Serfdom", Friedrich Hayek, Routledge, 1944.
23. "In the Ruins of Neoliberalism - The Rise of Antidemocratic Politics in the West", Wendy Brown, Columbia University Press, 2009.
24. "Capitalism and Freedom", Professor Milton Friedman. University of Chicago, 1964.
25. "Disaster Nationalism: The Downfall of Liberal Civilization". Richard Seymour, Penguin Random House, 2024.
26. "Thus Spake Zarathustra", Friedrich Nietzsche, Penguin Modern Classics, 2003, (first published 1888).
27. "The History of Ideas: Equality, Justice and Revolution.", David Runciman, Profile Books, 2024.
28. "Undercover: Exposing the Secrets of the Far-right", Hope not Hatred anti-fascist group. Channel 4, 21 October 2024.
29. "Burn Them out: A History of Fascism and the Far-Right in Ireland", Padraig Og O Ruairc, Apollo, 2025.
30. "Trump's European allies think history is turning in their direction", Gideon Rachman, *Financial Times,* 11 November 2024.
31. "The Putinisation of central Europe", *The Economist,* 11 January 2025.

32. "The Demise of the Liberal Elite", Derek Scally, *Irish Times,* 11 January 2025.
33. "Stealth Democracy: Americans' Belief about how Government Should Work".
34. Elizabeth Terese-Morse and John R. Hibbing, Cambridge University Press, 2002

Chapter 21: Conclusions

1. "How Anti-liberalism is Tearing America Apart – Again, Robert Kagan, W.H. Allen, 2024.
2. "The Road to Unfreedom". Snyder Timothy, Vintage Books, 2019.
3. "On Liberty and Other Essays". John Stuart Mill, 1869.
4. "Democracy Rules", Jan-Werner Muller, Penguin, 2022.
5. Speech to the House of Commons, Winston Churchill, November 1947.
6. "The Carnation Revolution: The Day that Portugal's Dictatorship Fell", Alex Fernandes, *Oneworld,* 2024,
7. "Axis of upheaval led by Russia and China will not stop at Ukraine war", Lucinda Creighton, *Sunday Business Post,* 9 June 2024.
8. "Over a billion people have voted in 2024. Has democracy won?", *The Economist,* 12 October 2024.
9. "Progress", Johan Norberg, One World, 2016.

10. "Allotted Chambers as defenders of democracy", Peter Stone, Wiley Publications, 2 July 2021.
11. "Mexico's first female president takes power with a pledge of continuity", Christine Murray, *Financial Times,* 2 October 2024.
12. "Democracy Awakening – Notes on the State of America", Heather Cox Richardson, WH Allen, 2022.
13. "A Theory of Justice", John Rawls, Harvard Paperbacks, 1971.
14. "An Introduction to the Principles of Morals and Legislation", Jeremy Bentham, 1762.
15. Speech to the Conservative Political Action Conference, 4 March 2023.
16. "When the Clock Broke: Conmen, Conspiracists, and How America Cracked in the Early 1990s", John Gantz, Ebury Press, 2024.

Chapter 22: A Wish List to Avoid the Abyss

1. "The Second Sex", Simone de Beauvoir, France, 1949.
2. "Light that Cannot Be Extinguished: Exiled Journalism and Transnational Repression". Freedom House, 6 December 2023.

3. "Platonism and the World Crisis, for the Study of the Platonic Tradition", Professor John M. Dillon, Dublin Centre 2007.
4. Gettysburg Address, Abraham Lincoln, 19 November 1863.

Chapter 23: A Plan and a Plea for Action

1. Freedom House Annual Report 2021.
2. "Negative Partisanship: The anti-politics eating the West", *The Economist,* 2 November 2024.
3. "Russia's Intelligence Goes Viral", *The Economist,* 19 October 2024.
4. "What Put wants", *The Economist,* 10 May 2025.
5. *The Economist*, 7 July 2024.
6. "Trump versus Harris: The American Election", Channel 4, 10 October 2024.
7. "An unheroic but understandable failure: German Social Democrats and the collapse of the Weimar Republic", Weimar's Long Shadow, Cambridge University Press, 2024.
8. "Society at a Glance". OECD Social Indicators, 2019.
9. "Freedom in the World: Democracy under Threat", Sarah Vespucci & Amy Slipowitz, Freedom House, 29 January 2020.
10. John Burn-Murdoch, *Financial Times,* 30 December 2024.
11. "Freedom in the Net", Freedom House, 2024.

Chapter 24: The Future of Democracy after the 2024 American Presidential Election.

1. "Shades of McCarthyism around Trump's amorality' Maureen Dowd, *New York Times,* published in *The Irish Times,* 21 October 2024.
2. Detroit Campaign Rally, 19 October 2024.
3. Lauren Fedor, *Financial Times,* 28 October 2024.
4. CNN News, 28 October 2024.
5. "Trump versus Harris: The American Election", Channel 4, 10 October 2024.
6. CNN, 23 October 2024.
7. "M: Son of the Century", Antonio Scurati, Fourth Estate, 2025.
8. An unheroic but understandable failure: German Social Democrats and the collapse of the Weimar Republic, Professor Douglas Webber, Weimar's Long Shadow, Cambridge University Press, 2024.
9. "The Envy of the World", *The Economist,* 19 October 2024.
10. "The Trump shift was there for all to see", Jemima Kelly, *Financial Times,* 24 November 2024.
11. "America isn't too worried about fascism", Edward Luce, *Financial Times,* 29 October 2024.
12. "Saving trade from Trump", *Washington Post,* 8 November 2024.
13. "Comeback King", *Economist briefing,* 9 November 2024.
14. "Donald Trump Returns to Power, Ushering in a New Era of Uncertainty", Shane Goldmacher & Lisa Lerer, *New York Times,* 8 November 2024.

15. "Split-screen America: disbelief and delight after Donald Trump's triumph, Christopher Grimes & Myles McCormick, *Financial Times*, 7 November 2024.
16. "Politics", Anita Chabria, *Los Angeles Times,* 21 November 2024.
17. "Brave New World: Donald Trump's victory signals end of US-led postwar order". Henry Foy, Alec Russell & Michael Stott, *Financial Times,* 7 November 2024.
18. Henry Foy, Alec Russell, Michael Stott, *Financial Times,* 9 November 2024.
19. Euronews, 12 November 2024.
20. "America v the world", *The Economist,* 16 November 2024.
21. "Trump's demolition of the US State", Edward Luce, *Financial Times,* 19 November 2024.
22. "What Trump unleashed means for America", Francis Fukuyama. *Financial Times,*
23. November 2024.
24. "Trump's America reminds us of Rome in decline", Tim Stanley, *The Telegraph,* November 2024.
25. "Canada, Trump and the new world order", Michael Ignatieff, *Financial Times,* 18 January 2025.
26. "Elon Musk Meeting renews reports he could fund UK Reform Party", *The Guardian*, 17 December 2024.
27. Fareed Zakaria, CNN, 16 May 2025.
28. "Donald Trump attacks UK's North Sea policy as 'very big mistake', Rachel Millard, Jim Pickard & Lucy Fisher, *Financial Times,* 3 January 2025.

29. “Vance’s real warning to Europe”, Gideon Rachman, *Financial Times,* 18 February 2025.
30. “How a Dollar Crisis Could Unfold”, *The Economist*, 19 April 2025.
31. Ivan Krastev, *Financial Times,* 16 January 2025.
32. “Europe’s Worst Nightmare”, *The Economist,* 22 February 2025.
33. “An out-of-the-box idea for China and Trump, Mark Sobel, *Financial Times,* 13 January 2025.
34. “Federalist Capers”, *The Economist,* 15 February 2025.
35. “Trump is halfway to making America a police state”, Edward Luce, *Financial Times,* 15 April 2025.
36. “Strongmen celebrate as Trump aide freezes, threatens to silence free media”. Courtney Weaver & Morton Dunai, *Financial Times,* 8 February 2025.
37. “How Donald Trump’s honeymoon turned sour so quickly”, James Politi & Myles McCormick, *Financial Times,* 26 April 2025.
38. “FBI agents sue Trump administration to block naming of investigators”, Myes McCormick, *Financial Times,* 4 February 2025.
39. “Right Now the U.S is Ceasing to be a Democracy”, Steven Stiglitz, interviewed by Claus Hessing, *Der Spiegel*, 24 March 2025.
40. “Biden’s presidency is unpopular now. History may be kinder. Opinion: The Editorial Board, *The Washington Post,* 18 January 2025.

41. "Standing Up to Donald Trump's Fear Tactics", the Editorial Board, *The New York Times,* 17 January 2025.
42. "The Trump Doctrine: America's new foreign policy". *The Economist,* 16 January 2025.
43. "The Post-American World and the Rise of the Rest", Fareed Zakaria, W & W. Norton, 2008.
44. "Briefing Geopolitics, Trump-style", *The Economist,* 1 March 2025.
45. "What is next for the 21st century's most intriguing political dynasty? Ed Cumming, *The Telegraph,* 4 November 2024.
46. "All or Nothing: How Trump Recaptured America", Martin Wolf, Bridge Street Press, 2025.
47. Presidential Address, the White House, 15 January 2025.
48. "Trump's anti-war pledge tested as Israel's attack on Iran splits MAGA base". *Financial Times,* 16 June 2025.
49. "How the next financial crisis starts" Pilita Clark, *Financial Times,* 29 June 2025.
50. "The Birth of a New World Order", Gideon Rachman, *Financial Times,* 29 December 2024.
51. Ill Winds: Saving Democracy from Russian Rage, Chinese Ambition and American Complacency", Penguin Press, 2019.
52. "Liberty as Independence: The Making and Unmaking of a Political Ideal", Quentin Skinner, Cambridge University Press, 2025.

BIBLIOGRAPHY

Adichie, Ngozi. "Reith Lecture". BBC4, 2022.

Ansell, Ben. *Why Politics Fails*. Penguin, 2023.

Ansell, Ben. "Our Democratic Future". Reith Lecture No. 2, BBC4, November–December 2023.

Ansell, Ben. "The Future of Democracy". Reith Lecture No. 1, BBC4, November–December 2023.

Ansell, Ben. "The Future of Prosperity". Reith Lecture No. 4, BBC4, November–December 2023.

Ansell, Ben. "The Future of Security". Reith Lecture No. 4, BBC4, November–December 2023.

Ansell, Ben. "The Future of Solidarity". Reith Lecture No. 3, BBC4, November–December 2023.

Applebaum, Anne. *Twilight of Democracy: The Failure of Politics and the Parting of Friends*. Penguin, 2021.

Applebaum, Anne. *Democracy Inc: The Dictators Who Want to Run the World*. Allen Lane, 2024.

Arendt, Hannah. *The Origins of Totalitarianism*. Penguin Modern Classics, 2017. (Original work published 1951.)

Arendt, Hannah. *Eichmann in Jerusalem: A Report on the Banality of Evil*. Penguin, 2006.

Baron de la Brède et de Montesquieu. *The Spirit of the Laws*. 1748.

Benner, Erica. *Adventures in Democracy*. Blackwell, 2024.

Bentham, Jeremy. *An Introduction to the Principles of Morals and Legislation*. 1762.

Boyes, Robert. *Meltdown Iceland: How the Global Financial Crisis Bankrupted an Entire Country*. Bloomsbury, 2009.

Browder, Bill. *Red Notice*. Corgi, 2016.

Browder, Bill. *Freezing Order*. Simon & Schuster, 2022.

Brown, Wendy. *In the Ruins of Neoliberalism: The Rise of Antidemocratic Politics in the West*. Columbia University Press, 2019.

Bullock, Alan. *Adolf Hitler: A Study in Tyranny*. Penguin, 1990.

Burke, Edmund. *A Vindication of Natural Society*. 1756.

Butler, Samuel. "Darwin Among the Machines". *The Press*, Christchurch, 1863.

Campbell, Alastair, and Rory Stewart. *The Rest Is Politics*. Podcasts, 2022–2025.

Carson, Rachel. *Silent Spring*. Penguin, 1962.

Carson, Tucker. *Ship of Fools*. October 2018.

Chomsky, Noam, and Ilan Pappé. *Gaza in Crisis: Reflections on Israel's War Against the Palestinians*. Penguin, 2011.

Clover, Charles. *Rewilding the Sea: How to Save Our Oceans*. Penguin, 2022.

Convers, Nathan, and Ethan B. Kapstein. *The Fate of Young Democracies*. Cambridge University Press, 2008.

COP 29: Conference of the Parties. Meeting annually to review targets on climate change by 2029.

Czerski, Helen. *Blue Machine*. Penguin Random House, 2023.

De Beauvoir, Simone. *The Second Sex*. France, 1949.

Diamond, Larry. *The Spirit of Democracy*. Times Books, 2008.

Draghi, Mario. "The future of European competitiveness – A competitiveness strategy for Europe". The European Commission, 2024.

Eatwell, Roger, and Matthew Goodwin. *National Populism. The Revolt against Liberal Democracy*. Pelican, 2019.

European Green Deal, 2020: A set of EU policy initiatives to make the EU climate neutral in 2050.

Fernandes, Alex. *The Carnation Revolution: The Day that Portugal's Dictatorship fell*. Oneworld, 2024.

Fisk, Robert. *Night of Power: The Betrayal of the Middle East*. Harper and Collins, 2024.

Food Revolution. "A better way to farm fish?" *Financial Times* video, October 2023.

Frantz, Douglas, and Catherine Collins. *Salmon Wars, the soft underbelly of our favourite fish*. Holt, 2022.

Freedom House. Annual Report, 2023, 2024.

Freedom on the Net 2024. Freedom House, 2024.

Friedman, Milton. *Capitalism and Freedom*. University of Chicago Press, 1964.

Fukuyama, Francis. *The End of History and the Last Man*. Penguin, 2020.

Gantz, John. *When the Clock Broke: Conmen, Conspiracists, and How America Cracked in the early 1990s*. Ebury Press, 2024.

Gates, Bill. *How to Avoid a Climate Disaster*. Penguin, 2021.

Gray, John. *The New Leviathans*. Penguin, 2023.

Greene, Richard. "Is Donald Trump Mentally Ill? Three Professors of Psychiatry ask President Obama to conduct a Full Medical and Neuropsychiatric Evaluation". *Huffington Post*, 17 December 2016.

Hayek, Friedrich. *The Road to Serfdom*. Routledge, 1944.

Heffernan, Olive. *The High Seas: Ambition, Power and Greed on the Unclaimed Ocean*. Profile Books, 2024.

Hessel, Stephane. "Time for Outrage". Essay, 2011.

Hill, Dan. *2 Cheers for Democracy*. Sensory Logic Books, 2019.

Hill, Dr Fiona. Reith lecture. BBC4, 2022.

Hobbes, Thomas. *Leviathan*. 1651.

Holy Bible, New International Edition. Hodder & Stoughton, 2011.

Hughes, Dr Ian. *Disordered Minds: How Dangerous Personalities are Destroying Democracy*. Zero Books, 2017.

Huntington, Samuel. *The Clash of Civilisations*. Simon & Schuster UK, London, 1996.

Huxley, Aldous. *Brave New World*. 1934.

Hyde, Martina. *What Just Happened*. Guardian Faber, 2022.

IMD. Global Inequality Report, 2022.

IMD. World Competitiveness Ranking 2023.

Isaacson, Walter. *Elon Musk*. Schuster & Schuster, 2023.

Jacobson, Mark Z. *No Miracles Needed: How Today's Technology Can Save Our Climate and Clean Our Air*. Cambridge University Press, 2023.

Kagan, Robert. *How Anti-liberalism is Tearing America Apart – Again*. W.H. Allen, 2024.

Karl, Jonathan. *Tired of Winning: Donald Trump and the End of the Grand Old Party*. Dutton, 2023.

Kupper, Simon. *Chums – How a Tiny Caste of Oxford Tories Took Over the UK*. Profile Books, 2022.

Lange, Justin. *Make America Great Again? American Conservatism and Donald Trump*. Union College, 2019.

Lazaras, Emma. "The New Colossus". Sonnet, 1883.

Lebow, Richard Ned, and Norman Ludvig, eds. *Weimar's Long Shadow*. Cambridge University Press, 2024.

Lee, Bandy. *The Dangerous Case of Donald Trump*. Thomas Dunne Books, 2017.

Lessenich, Stephen. *Living Well at Others' Expense*. Polity, 2019.

Levitsky, Steven, and David Zitblatt. *How Democracies Die*. Penguin, 2018.

Lewis, Michael. *The Fifth Risk: Undoing Democracy*. Penguin, 2019.

Lincoln, Abraham. Gettysburg Address. 19 November 1863.

Locke, John. *A Letter Concerning Toleration*. 1689.

Luce, Edward. *The Retreat of Western Liberalism*. Little Brown, 2017.

Machiavelli, Niccolo. *The Prince*. Penguin, 1975 (first published in 1532).

Mackay, Charles. *Extraordinary Popular Delusions and the Madness of Crowds*. Wiley, 1996. (First published in 1841).

Marx, Karl, and Friedrich Engels. *The Communist Manifesto*. 1848.

Maslow, Abraham. *A Theory of Human Motivation*. BN Publishing, 2017.

McCormick, Tim, and Dermot Duff. *Strategic Cost Reduction - Cutting Costs without Killing Your Business*. 2nd Irish Edition. Chartered Accountants Ireland, 2012.

McCormick, Tim. *An Irish Banking Manifesto - The Views of a Disenchanted Former Banker*. Liffey Press, 2015.

McGarvey, Darren. Reith lecture, 2022.

McLuhan, Marshall. *Understanding Media: The Extension of Man*. 1964.

McNamee, Roger. *Zucked: Waking up to the Facebook Catastrophe*. Penguin, 2019.

Merkel, Angela, with Beate Bauman. *Freedom: Memoirs 2054 - 2021*. MacMillan, 2024.

Mill, John Stuart. *On Liberty and Other Essays*. 1869.

Minsky, Hyman. *Stabilising an Unstable Economy*. McGraw-Hill, 2008.

Montefiore, Simon Sebag. *Jerusalem: The Biography*. Weidenfeld and Nicholson, 2011.

Montesquieu, Baron de la Brede et de. *The Spirit of The Law*. 1748.

Moore, Aoife. *The Long Game – Inside Sinn Féin*. Penguin, 2023.

Moreland, Jeremy, editor. *Critical Theory of Populism*. Westminster University Press, 2018.

Muller, Jan-Werner. *Democracy Rules*. Penguin, 2022.

Navalny, Alexei. *Patriot*. Penguin Random House, 2024.

Nayar, Krishna. *Liberal Capitalist Democracy – the God That Failed*. Hurst, 1988.

Nichols, Tom. *Our Own Worst Enemy – the Assault from Within on Modern Democracy*. Oxford University Press, 2023.

Nietzsche, Friedrich. *Thus Spake Zarathustra*. Penguin Modern Classics, 2003 (Original 1888).

Norberg, Johan. *Progress: 10 Reasons to Look Forward to the Future*. One World, 2016.

Norris, Pippa, and Ronald Inglehart. Cambridge University Press, 2019.

Nozick, Robert. *Anarchy, State and Utopia*. Basic Books, 1974.

Nygun, Hai-Thu. "Populism in Times of Social Media". *Populism and Democracy*. Eleven International Publishing, 2020.

O Ruairc, Padraig Og. *Burn Them out: A History of Fascism and the Far-Right in Ireland*. Apollo, 2025.

O'Toole, Fintan. *Heroic Failure – Brexit and the Politics of Pain*. Apollo Books, 2018.

O'Toole, Fintan. *Three Years in Hell – The Brexit Chronicles*. Apollo Books, 2022.

Orwell, George. *1984*. Secker & Warburg, 1949.

Osnos, Evan. *Wildland, A Journey through a Divided Country*. Bloomsbury, 2021.

Ostrom, Elinor. *Understanding Knowledge as a Commons from Theory to Practice*. Cambridge, Massachusetts Press, 2007.

Paine, Thomas. *Rights of Man*. 1791.

Pappas, Takis. *Populism and Liberal Democracy*. OUP, 2019.

Pappe, Ilan. *Reflections on Gaza and Israel's War Against the Palestinians*. Penguin, 2007.

Piketty, Thomas. *Capital in the Twenty-First Century*. Harvard University Press, 2014.

Plato. *The Republic*. Penguin Modern Classics, 2007. (First published in Greek c375BC).

Popper, Karl. *The Open Society and Its Enemies*. Routledge, first published in 1945.

Rachman, Gideon. *The Age of the Strongman: How the Cult of the Leader Threatens Democracy around the World*. Vintage, 2024; previously Bodley Head, 2021.

Rashid, Khali. *The Hundred Years' War on Gaza: A History of Settler Colonial Conquest and Resistance*. Khalii Rashid; Profile Books, 2020.

Rawls, John. *A Theory of Justice*. Harvard Paperbacks, 1971.

Reilly, Rick. *Commander in Cheat: How Golf Explains Trump*. Hachette Books, 2019.

Ricardo, David. *Principles of Political Economy*. 1817.

Richardson, Heather Cox. *Democracy Awakening – Notes on the State of America*. WH Allen, 2022.

Ross, Shane. *Mary Lou McDonald – A Republican Riddle*. Atlantic Books, 2022.

Rousseau, Jean-Jacques. *The Social Contract*. 1782.

Runciman, David. *Confronting Leviathan*. Profile Books, 2022.

Runciman, David. *How Democracy Ends*. Profile Books, 2018.

Runciman, David. *The Handover*. Profile Books, 2024.

Runciman, David. *The History of Ideas: Equality, Justice and Revolution*. Profile Books, 2024.

SAC: Special Areas of Conservation under the EU's Habitats Directives.

Saetre, Simon, and Kytel Ostil. *The New Fish*. English Edition, Patagonia, 2023.

Sanders, Senator Bernie. *It's Ok to be Angry About American Capitalism*. Penguin, 2024.

Sandys, Philippe. *38 Londres Street*. Weidenfeld and Nicholson, 2025.

Schmitt, Carl. *The Concept of the Political*. Alibris Books, 2007. (Original 1932).

Schumpeter, Joseph. *Capitalism, Socialism, and Democracy*. Routledge, 2010.

Sciutto, Jim. *The Return of Great Powers: Russia, China, and the Next World War*. Penguin Random House, 2024.

Scottish National Trust. "Wading into the Fishing Debate", 18 May 2018.

Scurati, Antonio. *M: Son of the Century*. Fourth Estate, 2025.

Sen, Amaryta. *Development as Freedom*. Oxford University Press, 1999.

Seymour, Richard. *Disaster Nationalism: The Downfall of Liberal Civilization*. Penguin Random House, 2024.

Shipman, Tim. *How Brexit Sank Britain's Political Class*. William Collins, 2016.

Skinner, Quentin. *Liberty as Independence: The Making and Unmaking of a Political Ideal*. Cambridge University Press, 2025.

Smith, Adam. *The Wealth of Nations*. Adam Smith, 1776.

Snyder, Timothy. *On Freedom.* The Bodley Head, London, 2024.

Snyder, Timothy. *The Road to Unfreedom*. Vintage Books, 2019.

Stewart, Rory. *Politics on the Edge – a memoir from within*. Penguin, 2024.

Stewart, Rory. *The Prince of the Marshes and other occupational hazards of a year in Iraq*. Harvest Book, 2007.

Sumption, Jonathan. *The Challenge of Democracy and the Rule of Law*. Profile Books, 2025.

Taggart, Paul. *Populism*. Oxford University Press, 2000.

Toal, Gerald. *Oceans Rise, Empires Fall*. Oxford University Press, 2024.

Tronto, Joan. *Caring Democracy: Markets, Equality, and Justice*. NYU Press, 2013.

UN Convention on the Laws of the Seas, 1962. (100+ signatories).

UN Fish Stocks Agreement, 1995.

UN Species' Habitat directives.

UN Treaty on the High Seas, 2023.

United Nations Environmental Programme.

Voltaire. *Lettres Philosophiques*. 1734.

Walton, Isaac, and Charles Cotton. *The Compleat Angler*. 1653.

Washington Post and University of Maryland joint survey. "Confidence in US Democracy", 2014.

Weber, Max. "The Profession and Vocation of Politics". 1919.

White, Johnathan. *In the Long Run: The Future as a Political Idea*. Profile Books, 2024.

Williams, Lord Rowan. Reith lecture, BBC4, 2022.

Wolf, Martin, and Anne Applebaum. "Saving Democratic Capitalism: Resisting Autocracy". *Financial Times*, 8 June 2024.

Wolf, Martin, and Hillary Clinton. "Saving Democratic Capitalism". *Financial Times*, 17 June 2023.

Wolf, Martin, and Larry Diamond. "Saving Democratic Capitalism: The Democratic Recession". *Financial Times*, 3 June 2023.

Wolf, Martin. *All or Nothing: How Trump Recaptured America*. Bridge Street Press, 2025.

Wolf, Martin. "Banking needs a radical change". *Financial Times*, 23 March 2023.

Wolf, Martin. *Saving Democratic Capitalism*. Penguin, 2023.

Wolff, Tom. *Fire and Fury*. Little Brown, 2018.

Wolff, Tom. *Landslide, the final days of the Trump Presidency.* The Bridge Press, 2021.

Wolff, Tom. *Siege, Trump under Pressure*. Little Brown, 2019.

Woodward, Bob, and Rowan Costa. *Peril.* Simon & Schuster, 2021.

Woodward, Bob. *Fear*. Schuster & Schuster, 2018.

Woodward, Bob. *Rage.* Schuster & Schuster, 2020.

Woodward, Bob. *War*. Schuster & Schuster, 2024.

Yeats, William Butler. "The Second Coming". 1920.

Zakaria, Fareed. *The Future of Freedom: Illiberal Democracy at Home and Abroad*. W.W. Norton & Co., Inc., 2003.

Zakaria, Fareed. *The Post-American World and the Rise of the Rest*. W.W. Norton & Co., Inc., 2008.

Zuboff, Shoshana. *The Age of Surveillance Capitalism: The Fight for a Human Future at the Frontier of Power.* Profile Books, 2019.

A large number of the references, which total over 400, have been made to national newspapers and periodicals to illustrate topical points in the text. In the US, the main sources were the New York Times, New York Review, and Washington Post; in the UK, The Economist, Financial Times, Guardian, and Observer. Der Spiegel in Germany; in Ireland, the Irish Times, which provides ready access to world events, and The Sunday Business Post. Additionally, sources include nine television channels in Ireland, the UK, Europe, and America. These are not included in the bibliography.

INDEX

D

E

F

G

ACKNOWLEDGEMENTS

This could not have been undertaken without the support and assistance of my family, who provided relevant expertise. My son Myles, US Economic Correspondent to the Financial Times, has advised me continuously and in great detail through each draft. He has also kept me abreast of developments and the latest thinking in both economics and political science. My son Conor, who is a marine biologist with an interest in ecology, advised on the protection of the oceans and, as the only Dublin family resident, has managed to provide me with general practical assistance. My son Patrick, who has qualifications in psychology and media, advised especially on social media. My daughter Tara, who has a classics degree, kept me straight on Athenian democracy. My brother Simon, a retired libel lawyer, and my partner, Mary Warren-Darley, checked out successive drafts despite suffering long periods of neglect. My cousin Anne Strahan proofread the script and provided many invaluable early corrections.

Although they did not assist directly in this book, I would also like to thank the school of political science at Trinity College Dublin, especially the late Professor David Thornley, TCD academic, television presenter and Irish politician who, after I had first encountered the subject at school, introduced me as an undergraduate to the history and fundamentals of democracy, thereby kindling a lifelong interest in the subject. This was subsequently developed at the master's level at INSEAD in France, where I became a strong supporter of European integration as Ireland joined the EU.

Considerable advice also came from Douglas Webber, Emeritus Professor of Political Science at INSEAD, who provided invaluable assistance and guidance, especially when he introduced me to contemporary literature on the subject. Professor Rory Stewart, an academic at Yale and a former politician, provided important insights of both a theoretical and practical nature. Dermot McAleese, Emeritus Whately Professor of Political Economy at TCD, reviewed my economic writing. Dr Ian Hughes, an authority and writer on democracy, provided important advice on autocrats with deranged minds.

I am also indebted to the faculty of INSEAD, the prominent international business school, which, in 1971-72, broadened the scope of my general business knowledge by introducing me to communications, informational technology, organisational behaviour, psychology, and strategy as part of their MBA programme. This enabled me to adopt a wider perspective in understanding the challenges facing liberal democracy from many different disciplines and a range of nationalities. From 1990 onwards, my colleagues at the Irish Management Institute, together with visiting professors, showed me how to integrate different disciplines for practising managers and abandon silo thinking, often in a multinational, cosmopolitan environment. I was for over forty years a member of the governing body of the Church of Ireland, which strongly influenced my ethical perspective.

I am also grateful for the help provided by Mary Robinson, former President of Ireland and UN Commissioner for Human Rights, founder of the Mary Robinson Foundation for Climate Change, and an undergraduate contemporary.

Others who have contributed to the book include Ninian Falkiner, former history teacher; Tony Kirwan, solicitor, school friend and undergraduate roommate; Charles Lysaght, a lunch companion; Robert Neill, former chairman of the

Representative Church Body Executive in Ireland; Sheena McCambley, Stephen Barcroft, former history teacher, Hugh O'Donnell, solicitor, Alan Wolf, former banker, Vincent Browne, journalist, Shane Ross, journalist and former politician, Donal Byrne, journalist and broadcaster at RTE, Jonathan Williams, literary agent and Bill Browder, financier and co-founder of the Hermitage Fund.

Also, in a period of ill health throughout the last few years, I started and finished the book during spells in the hospital. I am indebted to the medical consultants, nurses, aides, and orderlies in both St James Hospital and the Blackrock Clinic, totalling well over 100 people, as well as my home carers, without whom the book would not have been completed.

Finally, I am grateful to the publisher, Woodbridge, whose sound advice, encouragement, and speed of response have allowed the book to be published at an early date.

I am solely responsible for the views expressed in this book and also for any errors.

TIM MCCORMICK'S BIOGRAPHICAL NOTE

After a time, teaching as a volunteer in the then little-known city of Bangalore in India, he read Economics and Political Science as an undergraduate at Trinity College Dublin. On graduating, he went on to qualify as a chartered accountant in London, with what is now KPMG, followed by an MBA at INSEAD in France, which renewed his interest in political science and made him a keen supporter of the EU. He then returned to Dublin, where he spent eighteen years in investment banking, followed by a similar spell running financial programmes for the Irish Management Institute, which provided its services to both domestic and multinational businesses, and where he subsequently acted as a consultant for many years.

His previous books were Strategic Cost Reduction, published by the Institute of Chartered Accountants in Ireland in 2009, and An Irish Banking Manifesto – The Views of a Disenchanted Former Banker in 2020. He has regularly published many articles in professional journals over the recent years, before he started to research materials for this book.

He first became interested in democracy at secondary school. Subsequently, both at undergraduate and master's levels, he became fascinated by the subject and undertook extensive research on the topic over many years, particularly with recent developments in populism, increasing polarisation, the spread of autocracy, and the impact of social media. His wide-ranging research over different related disciplines has covered reading 160 books, reports, and papers on the subject of democracy, the majority of which were published in the last three years. Further details can be found on his website timmccormickauthor.com.

Printed in Dunstable, United Kingdom

73274241R00239